PREFACE

Because of the frequency with which I was ar
uninformed opinion, I was motivated to write t
educating a wider audience. Not a single person
the subject was remotely aware of the extent, dep
of Government interference in the running of the
and other inland transport were nationalised in l.
option to control it directly as a Ministerial Department in a similar way
to the Post Office. They did not do so, but set up an apparently autonomous
corporation - the British Transport Commission. This gave Government the
best of both worlds, allowing them to dissociate themselves from unpopular
decisions by the BTC, which they were prepared to accept, whilst directing
railways (but not other nationalised transport or other nationalised
industries) in the most precise detail.

Most of those to whom I addressed my remarks were astounded by my
information and acknowledged that BR had not had a 'Square Deal'. Very few
seemed to be of the "Don't confuse me with the facts, my mind is made up"
brigade. My initial work in preparing this book was based on personal
knowledge or experience, both of BR and other industry and businesses.
Comparing my substantial catalogue of misfortunes at the hands of those in
almost every other walk of life with criticisms of BR, I intended to entitle
my book "Which perfect bloody industry do you work for?" As I researched
further information on the role of Government and its Appointees (some
classified under the 30 year rule), I found there was so much that ought to
be publicly ventilated, that I put the bulk of my personal condemnations of
Private Sector incompetence and indifference on the back burner, making
reference to only a few cases in this book for purposes of illustration.

I worked for the LMSR and BR for 40½ years until I took early retirement,
having been made redundant. In my final year I decided to conduct BR's
first critical analysis of complaints and discovered that misleading
conclusions were being drawn from our statistics. The book is not an
autobiography. A few personal anecdotes and experiences are included to
illustrate or prove a particular point. Had time permitted, I could have
obtained details of similar illustrative experiences from many former
colleagues, but wished to bring my task to an early conclusion in view of
current debate surrounding the future of BR.

It is not my intention to suggest that there is no room for improvement on
BR in service or safety, or for reducing costs. That stage will never be
achieved in any company, whether in the public or private sector. Any
company which believes otherwise is not one for the wise investor. Those
who work in what they think is the Perfect Sector are also fallible. It is
my hope that my book will lead to fair comparisons being made for the first
time, with reason replacing uninformed sarcasm, and BR's failings presented
in a comparative light.

Ted Gibbins

CONTENTS

INTRODUCTION

BR has been unjustly criticised by Government, media, public and others for a state of affairs which is primarily the fault of Governments, who created the 'Blueprints for Bankruptcy', before, during and since the 1939-45 War. Others outside the industry adversely affected BR's performance and results. Some management and staff actions impaired BR finances, but even with these, given a level playing field and freedom to apply standard business principles, BR would have avoided deficits had Government not interfered. Moreover, any industry subject to the volume of uninformed folklore which has been built up around BR, would have seen its business decimated.

BR insolvency stems from Government's decision to bury BR for fourteen years in the monolithic BTC, headed first by a retired Civil Servant and then a General. (The Civil Servant, Sir Cyril Hurcomb, led talks with Wartime Railways which forced through a reduction in the "Rental"). Government gave commercial freedom to road haulage, in 1953, nine years before conceding freedom to BR. Unique statutory control of BR fares remained until 1968. Government ineffectively and irrelevantly used BR prices to try to control UK inflation. Having given the BTC a financial structure, which no Private Sector company would have accepted, it is not surprising that problems arose. BTC capitalisation was based on Fixed Interest Loans - a recipe for ruin, and its objective was to pay its way "taking one year with another" (An objective, Halsbury's Statutes could not define), including interest payments and capital redemption. BR could have succeeded as a separate entity from 1948, given a fair allocation of Government controlled resources and the commercial freedom enjoyed by all other industries. In that event, BR would have owned itself, since BR, not the Government was to redeem the loans. Alternatively, had Government acquired BR in 1948 using funds gained from wartime control of railways, BR would have been paying dividends to the shareholder (Government) - instead of paying "Central Charges" to the BTC. Although, the private sector has occasionally been subject to price restraint, BR lived with controls for most of its life. Government control of BR prices was clumsy and misguided - contemporary evidence showed that inflation was industry, not transport led. Occasionally, debt was written off, but it arose from Government actions. Improvements in services were held back by Government policies and adversely affected by users and others.

Had you been advised in 1948, to invest in a company, with no share capital, which could not close loss making "plant", whose prices would be decided by a Court of Law, (delaying essential increases by a year or more, whilst your suppliers were uninhibited in increasing prices), whose wages (around 66% of costs) would be increased, at your expense by Government interference, you would have concluded that your advisor had lost his touch. If you did invest and the company attempted to fulfill its impractical remit, you would be amazed to learn that customers expected you to fund new assets without profits or reserves. You would find that Government enforced loans on the company as "recompense" for enforced decreases in real prices.

No industry could have succeeded against a backdrop of the unconstructive and unbalanced criticism which has continually faced BR. For some totally inexplicable reason, BR are expected to become UK's first perfect industry - having no defects, no delays, no complaints and at prices below the rate of inflation. I confidently predict BR will be the second, because there will never be a first, all those in the front line of criticising BR, not excepted. Any company trying to claim first place, must prove it remained as far below the inflation rate as BR since 1948, and open its books on complaints, including records of returned goods. Were any other company subjected to so many watchdogs, they would take full page advertisements to boast of the minute ratio of complaints to customers which BR experiences.

1

The avarice of users closed their minds to the fact that you cannot make bricks without straw. Their perennial objections which held BR fares below the rate of inflation, which other companies were obviously exceeding, coupled with Government policies and practices have kept BR standards at prevailing levels. When other industry tells customers that 'you get what you pay for', they will, without complaint, pay over the inflation rate. BR customers steadfastly objected even to matching the inflation rate. Those companies which are "self regulated" would receive many more complaints if they had independent "watchdogs".

BR managers or staff have made mistakes - perfection in humans has yet to be achieved in any business. Some companies believe they are perfect, I have yet to find one. Some radio personalities, who are critical of BR errors, make 'deliberate mistakes' - for which no apologies are offered. I cannot understand why anyone makes a deliberate mistake - it is pointless, unless a large prize is offered for detecting it. Most who make a mistake, stating it was deliberate, are afraid to admit to human error. When I complained to a salesman that the Answerphone he had sold me had an instruction leaflet for a similar model, but with critical variations causing me to waste an hour trying to get it to work, he thought my complaint unreasonable, saying "Its only human error". I added - "Yes - in the Private Sector - but in the Public Sector it is 'incompetence'". Enclosing the wrong leaflet was careless. Printing two leaflets, each identifying the same controls as performing different purposes on the two models, instead of a supplementary page applicable to the remote access facility on one model, defied belief.

An illusion, worthy of the Magic Circle has been created that the Private Sector is perfect, whilst the Public Sector alone is not. My impression of the Private Sector is summed up by "out of stock", late deliveries, promises, promises. The media and public have a schizophrenic attitude towards analogous Public and Private Sector failings. I have complained to many Private Sector companies who were very defensive. A few eventually made refunds - most offer cheaper "sincere apologies". My files bulge with complaints to stockbrokers, banks, building societies, insurance companies, hotels, restaurants, credit card companies, newspapers, supermarkets and other suppliers. When THEY tell you that you are wrong, that is virtually "end of story"; with the Public Sector, one has many avenues to follow. The Private Sector "Guarantees" to replace an item within twelve months - the "Big Deal". When you buy a car, camera or TV, you are certainly hoping it will give you far more than one year's service. Such documents guarantee their product for one tenth of a reasonable life expectancy. Five minutes after 12 months your "piece of paper" is worthless. It is analogous to BR guaranteeing that a train will be on time for the first 10% of its journey.

Government intends to sell parts of BR. For a fair comparison, Privatised Rail should have the same capital structure, social burdens, and external interference BR suffered from 1948. That will not happen. Should Inter City be sold, it will improve performance by breaking connections with trains owned by other companies, and will avoid passengers standing, by higher fares and compulsory reservations, the cost being built into fares. Those who would have been willing to stand will have to travel by the next train or by other means - options currently available, but invariably dismissed with an abusive remark. Privatised Inter City will off-charge substantial costs for assets shared by other operators, who will need larger "subsidies" than BR have. I look forward to them tackling snow, but doubt that they will invest in costly machines to stand idle for 360 days out of 365; and of overcoming leaves on the line by 'praying or spraying' and destroying trees, including those which have been growing in residential lineside gardens in the past 20 years or so. It will be interesting to see how they respond to critics whose expertise stems from the playroom floor.

ABBREVIATIONS

ABCC	Association of British Chambers of Commerce
APT	Advanced Passenger Train
ARP	Air Raid Precautions
ASLEF	Associated Society of Locomotive Engineers & Firemen.
ATI	Advanced Traffic Information
BBC	British Broadcasting Corporation
BISF	British Iron & Steel Federation
BRB	British Railways Board
BRHQ	British Rail HQ
BRS	British Road Services
BSC	British Steel Corporation
BT	British Telecom
BTC	British Transport Commission
BWB	British Waterways Board
CBI	Confederation of British Industry
CC	County Council
CCLAG	Cambrian Coast Line Action Group
CEGB	Central Electricity Generating Board
cms	centimetres
CSO	Central Statistical Office
CTCC	Central Transport Consultative Committee
d	pence (pre 1971 coinage; 1d = less than ½p)
DB	Docks Board
DHSS	Department of Health & Social Security
DMU	Diesel Multiple Unit
DoT	Department of Transport
EEC	European Economic Community
EMR	Early Morning Return ticket
FBI	Federation of British Industries
ft	feet (one foot = approximately 30.5 centimetres)
GCM	General Classification of Merchandise
GWR	Great Western Railway
HGV	Heavy Goods Vehicle
HQ	Headquarters of LM Region
HST	High Speed Train
ID	Train Identification Number
ICI	Imperial Chemical Industries
Jcn	Junction
KC	King's Counsel
LCC	London County Council
LM	London Midland
LMR	London Midland Region
LMSR	London Midland & Scottish Railway
LNER	London & North Eastern Railway
LPTB	London Passenger Transport Board
LB	London Board (London Transport)
LT	London Transport
LTB	London Transport Board
LTE	London Transport Executive
LT&S	London, Tilbury & Southend line
m	millions
MoT	Minister of Transport (includes Secretary of State)
MoWT	Minister of War Transport
M&GN	Midland & Great Northern Railway
MP	Member of Parliament
NASA	National Aeronautics & Space Administration
NALGO	National & Local Government Officers' Association
NBPI	National Board for Prices & Incomes

NCB	National Coal Board
NEDO	National Economic Development Office
NFC	National Freight Corporation
NFU	National Farmer's Union
NIMBY	"Not in my back yard"
NHS	National Health Service
NUR	National Union of Railwaymen
P&E	Pay & Efficiency Wage Deals.
PEP	Political & Economic Planning (an independent research group)
Picc/Vic	Proposed Manchester Underground
PLA	Passengers Luggage in Advance
PM	Prime Minister
PSO	Public Service Obligation Grant, (paid to BR, to cover losses on lines the Government require to be kept open)
PSV	Passenger Service Vehicle
P&TA	Parents & Teachers Association
PTA	Passenger Transport Authority
PTE	Passenger Transport Executive
QC	Queens Counsel
RCA	Railway Companies Association
RPI	Retail Price Index
RRT	Railway Rates Tribunal
RSNT	Railway Staff National Tribunal (Independent Arbitration)
s	shilling; (pre 1971 coinage; one shilling shown as 1/- = 5p)
SAG	Special Advisory Group (Stedeford Committee)
Sec.	Section (of an Act of Parliament)
SMMT	Society of Motor Manufacturers & Traders
SNCF	French State Railways
SR	Southern Region (or Prewar – Southern Railway)
TAC	Transport Advisory Council
TAJC	Travellers Associations Joint Committee
TEB	Telephone Enquiry Bureau
TGV	French High Speed Train
THC	Transport Holding Company.
TOPS	BR's Real time computer (Total Operations Processing System)
TSSA	Transport Salaried Staffs Association
TUC	Trades Union Congress
TUCC	Area Transport Users Consultative Committee
USA	United States of America
VoRR	Vale of Rheidol Railway

SOURCES

Most sources are shown within the text e.g. BTC, BRB, CTCC etc Reports
Transport Tribunal – Dorset Police case Proceedings: Public Record Office
                     – Other Proceedings: Central Library, Manchester.
                     – Annual Reports: House of Lords Record Office
Cabinet Papers – Public Record Office
Parliamentary Debates and Ministerial Answers – Hansard
Prewar Reports, Wartime Control & Revenue – Keesings Contemporary Archives
Special Advisory Group (Stedeford Committee) – Public Record Office
BTC Minutes and Railway Executive papers – Public Record Office
Minutes & Papers of LMSR, LNER and RCA – Public Record Office
Legal view on "Paying their way..." – Halsburys Statutes, (Butterworth).
Industrial earnings, RPI, Wholesale Price Index – CSO Abstract of Statistics

[ ] – these are used when the enclosed text was in the document, publication or statement concerned, or a related document.
( ) – These are used to enclose text from other sources. Any text not attributed to a particular source are the author's views.

4

Government's actions lie at the root of BR's service and image. Having set the objective in the Transport Act 1947 "to pay their way taking one year with another", their policies prevented that objective being achieved. Had railways been returned to their owners at the end of the war, they would have demanded the equality on rates which they had been denied since 1932, and almost obtained in 1939. By 1946 that should have been in place, and transport history would have been different. Government could have prepared legislation to implement this overdue moral change - they found time to plan post war housing, health, welfare and pass the Restoration of Pre War Trade Practices Act, 1940, to restore restrictive practices in industry - a price they were willing to pay to persuade "craft" unions to accept "unskilled" labour on some wartime work. BR should have had commercial freedom at once. Government interference was based on what seemed best in the short term for users, rather than what was best in the long term.

Wartime Control of Railways

The Prices of Goods Act 1939 (repealed 1953), permitted businesses to increase prices to reflect wartime increases in costs. The "Permitted Price" was the "Basic Price" [that on 21st August 1939], plus the "Permitted Increase". The "Permitted Increase" consisted of the cost of materials, expenses of manufacturing and processing operations, transport charges, wages, salaries, cost of premises, administrative & establishment expenses, pensions, benevolent and welfare schemes, customs duty, interest on money borrowed, advertising expenses and bad debts. There was independent arbitration to hear appeals. Between 1937 and 1946, the only Railway price increases took place in 1940 and were subject to two Public Inquiries - in the middle of a war! In the second increase, a Consultative Committee recommended to the MoT that fares should be increased to 16.66% above prewar - the first increase had lifted them to 10% above prewar - but that Season and Workmen's rates and all LT fares should not be increased. Railways were not given an opportunity to gain from increased activity, as Industry did. Rail profits for war years should have been not less than the Standard Net Revenue prescribed in the 1921 Act [£51m in aggregate for the four main line companies - see Page 58]. No doubt, 1921 law makers feared railways earning too much with their alleged 'monopoly' position, but the law called for net revenue to be maintained at that level. On 1st September 1939 the MoT took control of Main Line, LPTB and other railways under the Emergency Powers [Defence] Act 1939, to remain in force for a minimum of one year after the end of the war, (There was no explanation for an extra year). On 7th February 1940, finance arrangements of the sequestration were published - "Appropriate charges" being made for Government Traffic - implying on the low rather than the high side, soon confirmed when Government announced it had "negotiated" reductions of 10-33% for freight traffic, whilst it enjoyed up to 50% reductions for military and other Government travel. Receipts [excluding railway's road transport and Irish interests] were to be pooled:
1. Railways to be paid an average of the net revenue for 1935-6-7 [LPTB on year ending 30th June 1939] shared: LMS: 34%, LNER: 23%, GWR: 16%, SR: 16%, LT: 11%; - Total £40m.
2. Of the balance, £3.5m will be paid to them on the same basis.
3. If the Pool exceeds £43.5m the balance will be equally divided between Government and railways until £68.5m is reached. Shares of individual main line railway companies will not exceed the 1921 Standard Revenue; (This was taken into account at the end of calculations. Had net revenue crept above £51m at the beginning, Government would have taken account of it then).
4. Net revenue above £68.5m to go to the Government. At this level, the five undertakings will receive £56m guaranteeing a minimum return on capital of 3.3% and may envisage up to 4.7%". (£49.8m for the main line railways instead of £51.4m under the 1921 Act, and they would be moving increased war

traffic and traffic diverted to rail from sea and road transport by the MoWT
5. Rates, fares and charges would be adjusted to meet working costs.
6. Cost of restoring war damage, up to £10m pa were to be charged to
expenditure [before the net revenue was calculated].
On 30th August 1941, the MoWT implemented drastic changes – from 1st January
1941, eight months backdated, there would be a fixed rental of £43m which
included £4.83m to the LPTB leaving only £38.17m for main line railways –
£12.83m less than the 1921 Act prescribed. Government stated on 25th
October "it had assumed the risk of profit and loss in exchange for £43m pa
Rental", (There was no risk of loss). The Railways share of war damage was
to be 50%, [estimated at £2.5m pa], to be met from the rental, giving them
£40.5m, instead of £43.5m plus a share over £43.5m. Net revenue for 1941
was £65.1m – against £42.8m for 1940. By August, revenue would have reached
£43m leaving the remaining four months revenue to be picked up by the
Government. What prompted replacement of the original ungenerous payments
by this new arrangement? **Cabinet Minutes**, 24th July 1941: MoWT said that
future revenue may not be adequate to pay the current minimum Rental of £40m
[due to a Government decision not to increase rail prices, despite the terms
of the First Agreement]. The Cabinet wished to persuade Railways to agree,
rather than impose a new Rental. The MoWT Paper to the Cabinet admitted
that Government failure to act on the Agreement to raise charges had cost
the Railways about £13m and he estimated that, in 1941, Railways could earn
under the existing Agreement as much as £57.2m. The MoWT told the Railway
Companies that the Government proposed to substitute a fixed rental for the
existing Agreement, on the grounds that there were "major changes" affecting
the Agreement. Railways did not agree that there were grounds and wished to
keep the existing Agreement as Minutes of LMSR, LNER and RCA together with
correspondence and records of meetings with Government reveal. Railways
were confident that revenue would rise, as it did. Government made it clear
that the Agreement would be changed and pressured the Railways with talk of
the National Emergency. Railways gave way, but asked for £55m [Standard
Revenue plus about £4m for LPTB]. "The Treasury would not go above £41.7m".
This was eventually raised to £43m, the amount which the MoWT had told the
Cabinet he was prepared to offer. Railways wrote that this sum "in no way
represented the existing or potential earning capacity of the undertakings,
they regarded it as an accommodation to meet the Government in time of a
National Emergency". Railway papers show that they did not hold out for
£55m to which they felt entitled, because of fears of a bad Press. Receipts
and expenditure of the sequestrated railways from 1941, with the £43m
deducted from Net Revenue to produce the Government 'profit' were :– ,

Year	Receipts £m	Expenditure £m	Other debits £m	Net revenue £m	Govt "profit" £m
1941	293.8	(226.6)	(2.1)	65.1	22.1
1942	343.4	(251.7)	(2.6)	89.1	46.1
1943	381.7	(272.2)	(3.9)	105.6	62.6
1944	394.4	(301.2)	(2.9)	90.3	47.3
1945	383.9	(317.0)	(4.4)	62.5	19.5
1946	360.7	(325.2)	(3.3)	32.2	(10.8)
1947	355.6	(367.2)	(4.7)	(16.3)	(59.3)
	£2,513.5	(£2,061.1)	(£23.9)	£428.5	£127.5
	=====	=====	=====	=====	=====

In November 1943, the MoWT admitted "railways were carrying 50% more traffic than pre war, and still rising, without additional rolling stock and with staff depleted by the claims of the armed forces, (110,000 experienced men had been called up). In addition to normal traffic there are 2000 Government specials per week carrying troops and war stores, 6000 extra trains for workers in Government factories and 1100 extra block trains of coal direct from collieries to consuming areas. In the last six months the number of such trains has been steadily increasing". (There was also extra freight from industry). He warned of "the part to be played in the gigantic military operations planned next year" [D Day] and said "Railways have earned the gratitude of the country. No other transport agency could have moved the masses of men and materials required by modern warfare". The Prime Minister expressed "gratitude to every railwayman who has participated in this great transport effort which is contributing towards final victory". (That gratitude was never repaid, and the industry was taken away from the owners who were then criticised by Government for the poor state of many of the assets, which had been put into such condition by Government policy and the heavy war workload for which Railways had been grossly underpaid).

In 1946, the MoT said that net revenue was insufficient to pay the rental due to an increase of 70% in costs above prewar whilst rail charges were only 16.66% higher, (evidence of the lack of control over other industries' prices). The sole reason was that, on 25th October 1941, the Government had stated that "it would determine rates, fares and charges without obligation to adjust them to working costs". No increase was made after August 1940, until July 1946. In 1947 Government again drew attention to the gap between net revenue and the rental due to increasing costs. Had the 1939 Prices of Goods Act been applied to Railways, their prices would have been increased to reflect higher costs. Total costs for the period of Government control were £2,266.3m (£2061.1m for 1941-47, see above, plus £205.2m for 1940). The Permitted Increase is calculated by deducting £1268m (average cost of £158.5m pa for eight years), giving a balance of £998m by which rail charges should have been raised. Of this 11% was for LPTB, leaving £888m for main line railways. This, plus £113.5m (89% of £127.5m) taken overtly from main line railways was a discount of £1 billion used to finance the war effort by holding down the prices Government paid to industry through controlled rail charges. If 1939 costs were used, the Permitted Increase would be greater since 1939 costs were approximately £16m below average. Receipts would have been even higher had Government traffic been charged at rates reflecting the excessive wear and tear which it caused. Government's discriminatory price policy left BR behind the start line as the post war inflationary spiral took off. The Government did exceptionally well from railways, by having its traffic carried at up to 50% below Government controlled sub standard public charges, and then creamed off £127.5m. Railways received £301m [£43m pa for 1941-47 inclusive], plus £42.8m for 1940, = £344m. Of this, 11% went to the LPTB and £½m pa to minor railways, leaving the four main line railways with £303m for eight years sequestration compared to a minimum of £424m (Standard Revenue of £51.4m pa for 8.25 years), they should have gained. Running railway assets literally into the ground, Government gained enough to buy railways outright in 1948, leaving the BTC to operate the system free of debt. Then the State would have been able to claim that it owned BR, instead, they decreed that BR should buy itself.

Due to lack of materials and war damage, railways had to reduce train speeds and reduce the service. Passenger services were then further curtailed by MoWT to give preference to military traffic. From 1944 public passenger services were again reduced due to the demands arising in advance of D Day and for long thereafter due to the constant flow of war traffic to Europe. Given the vastly increased workload which railways handled during the war, without additional rolling stock and with fewer staff, the railway companies should have emerged from the war in a wealthy condition, instead they were penniless - entirely due to Government policy and practice.

The sequestration of railways in 1939 was not justified on either moral or practical grounds. In 1914, when there were over 120 railways to integrate, and the only alternative was the horse and cart, there were practical, but no moral grounds since Governments had not put a penny piece into railways. By 1939, with only four companies to integrate, it was unwarranted, needing only a Ministerial Directive to give priority to military traffic. The running of railways remained in railway hands in every single respect from top to bottom. Government had no grounds to seize the lions share of the silver lining which was emerging from behind the dark cloud which had overshadowed railways since 1928, and which Governments had obstinately refused to remove. Their meanness, in the 1940's, scaled new peaks. Having advised railways of the importance of ARP, the Government whittled down its contribution for railway ARP from 100%, through 50% to 25%. On War Damage, in 1939, the Government "promised to pay compensation at the highest possible scale at the end of hostilities", later reduced it to 50%, and then told railways they must pay their share from the "Rental" - not from the costs of running the railways, whilst Government covered its share from the fat sums they gained. In contrast, compensation for other industries was to be decided by independent Tribunals. By Treasury Order in June 1949, the Government paid £24.8m, ostensibly 72% of the Railways claim for the cost of damage sustained during the war. This was based on an inflationary uplift to reflect the decline in money values. Government papers show that, as at 1948, the claim was to be uplifted by 118% but this was amended in 1949 [when the claim was paid] to a factor of 100% - as prices were still rising the factor should have increased, not decreased. (BTC 1949 Report shows that the cost of commodities in general use had risen 145% over 1939 - applying this inflation rate brings the payment close to 50%). During the war, the railway companies appealed in vain to the Government to review the "Agreement" in the light of very much heavier traffic levels, and to introduce charges based on fair competition.

Governments learn little from history. Throughout the First World War, they kept railway charges unchanged and then in 1921 had to accept that rates would have to increase by 100-200% over 1913 rates to avoid railways becoming bankrupt. Pursuing a similar policy in the Second War, but not taking similar corrective postwar action, they expressed surprise when railways began to lose money.

Nationalisation
The **Transport Act, 1947** contained blunders which have cost customers and taxpayers dearly, namely :-
* burying BR inside the monolithic BTC, rather than retain it as a separate enterprise.
* enacting that the whole of the BTC "shall form one undertaking" which compelled offsetting profits of one business against losses of another - precluding the BTC from putting BR onto an independent financial footing when price rises were humbly requested.
* directing the BTC to "pay their way taking one year with another" instead of simply being run at a profit, prolonged Tribunal hearings - fully exploited by those who objected to increases in BR charges, whilst increasing their own prices, (Halsbury's Statutes criticise the lack of clarity of the objective).
* having a capital structure of Fixed Interest loans. BR was to buy itself out of revenue - redeeming the capital and paying interest. The State should have paid for BR from wartime gains and taken dividends in return. It would then have taken a different stance on prices, investment and closures. Denying BR start up capital or reserves, one didn't need a

crystal ball to forecast the outcome.

* retaining archaic statutory freight rates, allowing road transport to continue to abstract traffic from BR, lumbered with 40 year old wagons to compete with the inevitable post war built lorries, (see Pages 58-62). Nor could it be claimed that the BTC would have a monopoly of freight, since the prewar growth of 'C' Licence vehicles - carrying goods only for the owning company - was set to accelerate after the war, as was soon confirmed.

* compelling BR to apply to the Transport Tribunal to increase prices whilst not enforcing that policy on BR's suppliers, could have but one consequence. Depressed income held down wages, causing high staff turnover, which by 1951 reached 20% pa, increasing costs due to repetitive training costs for new staff. No other Nationalised Industry prices were controlled in this way.

* directing integration of inland transport without regard to the problem areas. Prewar railways sought equality of statutory treatment, not integration, (see Page 60). In 1939, the Conservative MoT said there was a case for relaxing existing statutory control of rail charges, provided that regard was paid to the ultimate - Government - objective of the co-ordination of all forms of transport.

* nationalising 544,000 privately owned life expired wagons of 19th century technology, whose paper 'value' was included in the balance sheet as 'assets' when they were really liabilities. They should have been left in private hands, until BR built modern wagons to replace them. Instead the BTC was directed to buy them for £43m, repair and maintain them until they had to be scrapped - some in the first year. Around 27% were still in use, causing train delays, ten years later. It has been claimed that the BTC decided to take over these wagons; in fact the Government announced their compulsory acquisition in January 1947, 8 months before the Act was passed which created the BTC, and long before its Members were appointed.

* setting up Consultative Committees with loosely defined duties which led to protracted closure procedures.

SUBSEQUENT LEGISLATION

Transport Act 1953

The Government Paper, "Transport Policy" [Cmnd 8538]: "the BTC will be given greater latitude to vary their Charges Schemes so as to improve the ability of the railways to compete with other forms of transport. Within prescribed limits they will be free to raise or lower their charges with subsequent approval by the Transport Tribunal and subject to the overriding power of the MoT. (Competitors had no 'prescribed limits' and no Minister with 'overriding powers'). The Draft of this Paper had envisaged total freedom, but when it was discussed in Cabinet in April 1952, the Prime Minister "would not accept that the BTC should be "free" - even with the approval of the Tribunal - to adjust railway rates without any intervention by Government or Parliament". This was not surprising, as Government had only a few days earlier blocked a legal judgement by the Transport Tribunal.

The Act perpetuated ineffective concepts - "operating as one undertaking" - "paying their way taking one year with another", "Charges Schemes" and the ritual of appearing in a Court of Law to beg permission to increase its prices to avoid losses, create reserves and compensate for unfettered increases made by suppliers. The Act made changes in charging powers, allowing the BTC to apply to the Tribunal for an Order amending a scheme or schemes, to match increases in costs up to 10% provided that proposed price increases were not more than 10%, for which the Tribunal may give temporary authority. This meant that they could not recover past losses, that fares would fall further below the RPI, losses would increase and could only ensure a worsening of BTC finances. The BTC must thereafter apply to the Tribunal for alteration of all or any Charges Schemes in force. Maximum charges were still controlled "in the Public interest". The Act perpetuated and even expanded the provisions of the 1921 Act which gave protection to coastal shipping and canals against "unfair competition" by BR. No provision was made to protect BR against unfair competition by any form of transport. It enacted protection for traders against unreasonable charges - there was no corresponding protection for BR against unreasonable charges by suppliers. 'Heads BR lose, tails they don't win'. Until 1953, BR was run by the same management which had run railways before and during the war, and with no extra rewards had produced a quart of wartime movement from a pint pot. If freed from the suffocating influence of the monolithic BTC and the Government, BR would have achieved no less than in wartime. The Act denationalised road haulage and abolished all Executives except LTE leaving the BTC to run its other erstwhile subsidiaries instead of abolishing the BTC and retaining BR, and the other Executives, as independent bodies. Before denationalisation, BTC road and rail businesses were required to submit Charges Schemes to the Transport Tribunal for approval, thereafter, road haulage didn't, reverting BR to their disadvantageous prewar situation. It is a common belief that BR took seven years to prepare a Freight Charges Scheme. The first Scheme, based on integration, was well advanced in 1951, had been discussed with interested parties, and was about to be submitted to the Transport Tribunal, when the Government asked the BTC to consult with Coastal Shipping who were apprehensive of losing statutory protection against lower rail rates. Soon thereafter, the BTC was told to shelve this Scheme, pending new legislation. The 1953 Act required the BTC to start a new Scheme from scratch based on new principles. To compete fairly with privatised road haulage, Government should have enacted the status of an autonomous State Corporation. Sec.20 para [4] of the Act rated a high fog index: "For the avoidance of doubt it is hereby declared that the power of the Transport Tribunal to alter a charges scheme ..... includes power so to alter a scheme that it extends to charges to which it would not otherwise extend or does not extend to charges to which it would otherwise extend".

Being buried in the monolithic BTC, BR was burdened with "Central Charges" averaging £50m pa from 1948 to 1953 inclusive, about 70% of the total of all "Central Charges", the rest being shared by LT, Inland Waterways, Road Transport, Docks and Hotels Executives. Despite price restraint, and before those Charges, BR's net working surplus averaged £28m pa. Had Government used its £1 billion wartime gain to buy BR and establish it as a separate corporation that surplus would have paid them a dividend. With commercial freedom from 1948, greater profits would have financed more investment.

Transport Act 1962
Reorganised the BTC into independent bodies - including BRB and LTB and repealed the concept of "Charges Schemes", but perpetuated the requirement for BRB and LTB to appear in a Court of Law to request authority to increase fares to meet increased costs in the "London Passenger Transport Area". (The 1950 Fares submission to the Tribunal stated total London area fares were £74.5m, of which the BTC 1950 Report shows £56m was LT rail & road. Total BR fares being £106.6m, £18.6m was 17.4%. London area fares were increased faster than average to narrow the gap to higher Provincial fares, so BR London fares would probably be about 20% of total BR fares by 1962). These then continued to lag behind provincial fares (see Pages 80, 81). The Act repealed the "reasonable charges" protection which traders had enjoyed against BR, (BR had never had similar protection against their suppliers). Sec.48 permitted BRB and LTB to announce an increase of up to 10%, to meet increased charges, but would then have to apply to the Tribunal for a confirming Order. The modest changes should have made in 1953. It continued the unsound concept of each of these new bodies "paying its way taking one year with another". (No other industry required to pay its way, was constrained from deciding its own prices). Coastwise Shipping continued to enjoy protection, exercised by the MoT, against "unfair" rail freight

10

rates. They could object to lower prices by BR but BR could not object to their rates. The protective clauses were not dropped until 1968.

Transport Act 1968
Introduced the long overdue concept that losses caused by enforced retention of loss making lines and services should be accepted as a social cost, not a BR deficit and paid for by the State which had decided to keep those services. The Act established Passenger Transport Authorities [PTA's] for some large conurbations, with responsibility for passenger services within their area by rail, road and waterway. Took away from BR its own collection and delivery road fleet requiring BR to hire back immediately, and at higher costs, the self same vehicles from the new NFC to continue to handle BR traffic. Transferred to the NFC, Freightliner - which BR had created to compete with door-to-door road haulage, at the moment when BR had increased carryings threefold. The relationship between BR and the NFC was described as a complex mixture of customer, supplier, competitor and partner. The Act retained the objective of "paying its way taking one year with another".

Transport [London] Act 1969
Abolished Transport Tribunal power over fares, leaving BR fares and charges subject only to political interference.

Railways Act 1974
Provided for grants to companies to encourage transfer of freight from road to rail for environmental or other reasons. Schemes were subject to Local Authority Planning controls, which, as most involved private sidings backing onto the railway, it was difficult to perceive justification for their role.

OTHER FACTORS IN THE ESCALATION OF BR INSOLVENCY
* Governments failed to control prices of goods which BR had to buy from the Private Sector. Records show that capital intensive (industrial) prices increased faster than labour intensive (rail) charges - unheard of in a modern economy, (see Pages 17-34, and Chapter 2).

* The MoT prevented closure of branch lines competing with cars instead of horses. If closures were approved there may be a condition that BR must subsidise bus services, (costing £1m pa by 1968, see Page 48) - proving that there was not enough profitable traffic for a bus. Consideration of schemes by TUCC, CTCC and MoT took up to three years. By 1963, approval for closure was awaited on 164 routes whose losses were carried by BR, which were in addition to losses incurred whilst proposals crawled through protracted procedures. With closures taking years, losses were horrendous. The Government should have repaid losses for these services from the day they were submitted for closure, which would have accelerated MoT action.

* In 1955, to secure the same commercial freedom which road haulage had had for 35 years, BR submitted a Freight Charges Scheme to the Transport Tribunal, who, 18 months later, watered it down, reduced some existing rates, when the object was to create headroom, and continued protection for coastwise shipping to object to any "unfair" rate!

* Whilst road haulage, including 'C' licence vehicles, were legally enabled to "cream off" BR's best traffic - leaving below cost business untouched, BR had to pay to resurface bridges and crossings, whose wear was accelerated by heavier traffic. Increased road traffic on level crossings, hitherto manned by resident keepers, required more staff working shifts to meet MoT safety standards. In 1958 the MoT contributed a miserly £2m pa towards these costs, but in 1961, it was withdrawn, reinflating BR operating losses.

* A "hidden" statutory cost BR has, unlike road, is to fence off its

"highway" from adjoining land, involving 22,000 miles of fence, (twice that mileage in the 1940's), which is often vandalised. Fences on land adjoining roads are provided by landowners, to prevent trespass or prevent livestock from straying onto the highway. When new roads are constructed which involve compulsory purchase of land, the Highway Authority erect fences or hedges at the new boundary, but after a year the fence becomes the responsibility of the adjoining landowner. A farmer will be compensated for an animal killed on the line after breaking through BR's fence whereas, on the road, he will be sued for damage to a road vehicle.

* BR has to maintain about 1,000 Historic structures including some which were never used for railway purposes, e.g. a stone pulpit used by ancient clergy at Shrewsbury! The hysteria which follows any failure to maintain them in their original condition, without any regard for costs or the non availability of matching materials, is quite remarkable. One thing is certain, if BR is privatised, these will become a direct charge on the Exchequer, instead of inflating BR's "losses".

* Tory and Labour Governments hived off railway businesses - buses, air services, road haulage, freightliner, hotels, shipping and the world's biggest hovercraft service. Hiving off BR ships lost priority for rail wagons on railway ferries to Europe.

* Governments are obsessed that BR - alone among transport - should be 100% safe. Road carnage is 500 times as great, but the spotlight rarely wavers from BR, an Everest among anthills in the realms of safety, which is pressed to spend more to produce very marginal improvements. Many, who advocate spending more BR funds on safety, spend zero on safety in their own homes, where most accidents occur. Following fatalities in a 1986 motorway crash, a coach operator on BBC said that seat belts would be too costly! Road transport should catch up on BR standards: effective speeding checks, brakes actuated by traffic lights, deadman's pedals in lorries and coaches, or if these are impractical, double-manned cabs instead of relying on schoolboys to wrestle with the wheel when a coach driver collapses. Vehicles carrying hazardous goods should have to park during fog or falling snow. The 1968 Transport Act reduced the working day for an HGV driver or Coach driver to a length 50% longer than Government had enforced on railways 48 years earlier, and BR has signals and automatic braking, (see Pages 50 & 51).

* Government directed BR to pay higher wages than they could afford due to Government policies, (see also Page 19). In 1951, BR offered increases costing £6¾m, a Government Court of Inquiry sat for six days and lifted this by £¼m - which the Court said was all BR could afford - but which Unions rejected. The Minister of Labour (informed the Cabinet in February 1951, that he told BR that it was a mistake to link pay deals to productivity), met BR and union representatives after which a further £2½m was offered and again rejected. At Government "request", BR resumed negotiations and "a settlement was reached at a cost of £12m". Claims by staff, not involved in the original wage submission, for comparable increases lifted the total to £18½m. Thereafter, it became a practice of unions to approach Ministers to override BR decisions. Following a strike call in December 1953 after unions had rejected the RSNT decision, the Minister of Labour again intervened, after which a new wage offer was made and the strike called off. On 8th December 1954, when the Unions had rejected the final BTC offer, the Cabinet agreed it would "be helpful if the BTC could indicate some possibility of improving its offer". On the 13th December, the MoT told the Cabinet that he had asked the BTC Chairman "if he could make such an offer if Government assured him that the BTC need not be concerned about the size of its deficit". The MoT said this could be justified on three grounds :
* "the Freight Charges Scheme would shortly come into operation"; (It hadn't

been submitted to the Tribunal who had said in 1951 that it would take three years, from submission, before a scheme could be brought into operation).
* "the Government would favourably consider the Modernisation Plan".
* they "believed that Staff would co-operate in efficiency".
The Cabinet agreed a Public Statement: "If the RSNT conclude that the NUR claim should be met, in whole or in part, the BTC will consult with the MoT as to means by which the additional cost should be met". The next day this was modified - the consultation would relate to "any consequences which acceptance of such a recommendation might entail in relation to their statutory duty under the 1947 Act". Following a strike call, the Minister of Labour set up a Court of Inquiry, under Sir John Cameron QC, before the official industrial relations machinery had been exhausted. He pronounced: "having willed the end, the Nation must will the means". He also said "that the statutory requirement that the Commission (BTC) must pay its way, taking one year with another, should not be allowed to stand in the way of legitimate wage claims", and that railway wages should be no worse than those in comparable industries. The Government accepted his report. The Chairman of the BTC was reported as saying that "where the money was to come from was no concern of mine", (The Government having taken over negotiations again, it was interpreted to mean that the Government had given an undertaking to assist the BTC financially - which they did not do).
BTC Minutes in April 1958 record discussion involving the Prime Minister Ministers, BTC and Unions. In 1960, the Government appointed Guillebaud Inquiry awarded increases of 8-10% plus differentials based on comparability with other industries, which the PM informed Parliament on 10th March 1960 was accepted by the Government. In 1965, the Government set up a Court of Inquiry under Jack Scamp into relaxations of the Single Manning Agreement. In 1966, staff costs were increased "by the PM's settlement". "Beer & Sandwiches" at 10 Downing Street had become a catchphrase. In 1967, the Government set up another Court of Inquiry under Professor Robertson. Governments showed that they wished to avoid disputes, and seemed to be prepared to meet Union demands. Left to its own devices, BR would have had to reject increases it could not afford - leading, perhaps, to a one-off strike. Interference by Government encouraged the Unions in brinkmanship. In 1972, the Government, having given way on the miners wage claim, decided, against the advice of BR managers, to use new legislation to compel rail unions to ballot members on the dispute. They voted overwhelmingly to support union leadership and continue the dispute. Throughout, Government has acted precipitously to avert strike action. BR managers believed that failure to face a strike threat would lead to escalating demands, as it did.

Government propelled BR into deficit in 1956 by pricing restraint, higher wages and uncontrolled cost increases, Government then decided to hold down BR prices even further, loaning BR sufficient to cover deficits which Government policy had created and having BR pay interest on, and repaying the loans. But BR couldn't pay the interest - so the Government authorised BR to borrow to pay the interest, meaning they had to pay interest on that loan as well. Picture it, - BR are £55m short, so Government advance £55m, on which BR have to pay £2.75m interest pa. So they have to borrow £2.75m on which they have to pay £137,000 interest, which they have to borrow ....
In due course, they have to repay the capital borrowed at, say, £2m pa, so they borrow and borrow and end up with the enormous losses publicised in the media and criticised by Government whose own policiies created the situation. Had BR been permitted to operate commercially from Day 1 , there would have been no deficit, no "subsidies" and we would have had a better railway. Instead, we had a lesson in unprecedented usury, (see Page 22). The Government failed to recognise that BR had no freight monopoly even after the 1955 ASLEF strike enabled heavy industry to discover that railways were not indispensable. Governments continue to ignore a statement by the Conservative MoT in 1956 that the BTC "have not had and never have had a

complete monopoly of the traffics for which their services are provided",
but still went on treating it as a monopoly. Even today, some still seem to
believe that a definition of a monopoly is a state enterprise with less than
10% of the market. In these psuedo monopoly situations, there are many
avenues for the most trivial complaint. Where real monopoly exists, in the
Private Sector, one gets no help. In my small business, one supplier put up
its price in a series of stages by 38% during 1988, when the RPI rose about
7%, without warning, explanation or apology, - there was no other supplier.
As a private individual requiring a part for a domestic appliance, I found
the sole UK national supplier had increased the price by 1119% in 4½ years.

A major beneficiary of low fares and freight charges and delayed increases
was the Government itself - and hence the taxpayer. Under the Cheap Trains
Act, 1883, Government told railways it would pay a reduced rate for military
travel. Delayed increases, and fares below the RPI, kept down the amount
they paid to BR for duty travel, and for Government freight traffic. In
1948, the total cost of such traffic was £40m, in 1949 - £35m, and it
continued into the late 1950's. Travel by 400,000 Armed Forces personnel at
Bank Holidays and weekends was paid for by the personnel themselves, at
reduced rates. Wives and children enjoyed the same concessions. Had their
fares kept pace with the RPI, the Government would have been under pressure
to increase service pay or fail in its attempt to increase regular strength
to a level which would permit the end of conscription. (The Chancellor of
the Exchequer proposed to the Cabinet in March 1951, that BR should be
relieved of these costs, estimated to be £3m pa. They did not do so).
Others travelled at Government expense in addition to Armed Forces. Keeping
fares down would keep Civil Service pay demands in check. Thus, whilst the
Government refers to subsidising BR, in reality, they were "giving" with one
hand that, which they had taken with the other. Yesterday's travellers,
particularly London commuters, (including many thousands of civil servants)
gained from lower fares - but at the expense of today's travellers, who have
begun to pay fares above the RPI to pay for past underpricing.

Political interference cannot be justified by linking it to the "subsidy".
That was the Catch 22, the subsidy was not to BR, but to passengers. BR
were not permitted to close or price up loss making lines, so Governments
should have funded the consequences of their decisions, 20 years before they
did so. Furthermore, interference was not restricted to subsidised lines.
In 1988 Government gave as reasons for the PSO - the so called "subsidy":-
* To alleviate road congestion in the South East; (reducing road costs).
* To sustain loss making parts of the network, to maintain minimum levels of
accessibility to areas where people have come to rely on rail for essential
local journeys, and local communities are economically dependent on them.
(CTCC 1990/91 Report, page 9: an "eight year policy of reducing the PSO").

Despite creating the organisations, selecting executives, and taking key
decisions, often overriding solicited advice, Governments blamed BR managers
for losses! The BTC with the Railway, and other, Executives below it, was
cumbersome. It would have been simpler in 1948 to create independent Boards
for BR, LT, Road, Canals and Docks. Even worse the BTC was headed, for the
first 14 years, not by a businessman, but first by a retired Civil Servant
and then a retired General. Neither could claim expertise in commercial,
operational, engineering or financial management. The Railway Executive (BR
proper) was headed by professionals who had been running railways since
prewar. But Government withheld from them the essential power to decide
prices. BR was not even directly involved in the tortuous pleading with the
Tribunal for variations in charges - that was in the hands of the BTC. The
Executive had no power over prices, but was responsible for costs, in which
it made economies every year, despite Government interference forcing up
wages which were about 66% of total costs, and suppliers increasing the

balance. No Private Sector business could survive on such a basis. Every Government had the power to replace top managers, if they could find any willing to take office under such constraints and at such ridiculous salaries - when Dr.Beeching was brought in, he had to be paid double his predecessor's salary. MoT inactivity on this score proves that they must have accepted that BR's problems arose externally. In 1953, Government took out the wrong level of management leaving the monolithic BTC in place, as an even more unwieldy organisation. Nine years later, the horse having bolted, they reverted BR to separate status but still withheld essential powers.

MoT's appointed to the Transport Tribunal and the CTCC, people with the apparent knowledge to run BR. They should have given them, objectors and their advocates a chance to carry out the Statutory objective of the industry paying its way, ideally, as a legal partnership - so that, when, not if, they failed due to the impossible hurdles in their path, they would have lost their own money instead of the taxpayers'.

Classified Information
In 1960 the MoT appointed the Special Advisory Group, (Stedeford Committee), to report to him on the BTC. Its findings, recommendations and views were not disclosed to Parliament or the BTC, and were only released in 1991. The papers criticise Government, hence had the papers been made public at the time, they would have been acutely embarrassed. The Inquiry did not affect State Security and should not have been kept from taxpayers who funded it.

The members of the SAG criticised the BTC taking on the role of the Railway Executive in 1953 - "a change which was not for the better - there was no real general management of the railways as a whole - the Railway Executive which had exercised that role had been abolished by Government", who approved the new cumbersome BTC organisation. Government also decided to continue "the unitary nature of finances and other statutory restrictions on commercial operations", which the SAG noted was "one of the major causes underlying the defects of the BTC structure both as regards management and finance". The Treasury told the SAG that if the BTC was to broken up into separate Boards, any surplus accruing in one should be used to offset losses in another - continuing the "unitary nature of finances". Dr.Beeching - a member of the SAG - said that Railways should be run mainly by professional railwaymen. There were then only two among the fifteen members of the BTC. (As BR paid 70% of BTC Central Charges, it was 70% of the BTC; see Page 10).

Much of the investment money being spent was "repairing obsolescence of the past 20-50 years", which in Dr.Beeching's view had to be spent. The SAG criticised the financial justification of elements of the Modernisation Plan, notably electrification. The Plan's forecast return was approved by Government. There was understanding in the SAG that the BTC was motivated by the statutory requirement with "due regard to efficiency, economy and safety of operation and to the needs of the public, agriculture, commerce and industry", that is of adequacy of service rather than what was profitable. In a letter enclosing recommendations to the MoT, the SAG stated that their Report "will not be given to the BTC". This was odd. If the BTC was not applying investment criteria, and was required to do so, they should have been put right at once. Since Government had accepted the Plan, any report critical of the BTC, was critical of Government, which may explain why the Report was not published. The MoT told the SAG that the Modernisation Plan "was an assessment of the best kind of railway which could be provided, no account was taken of commercial outturn, but the Government had nevertheless approved the Plan and had confirmed in a White Paper that the proposals were commercially sound. The MoT said that the "assessments were made 5-10 years ago, since when conditions and prospects for the future had changed considerably". In May 1960, the MoT told the SAG that he had every expectation that there would be increased expenditure on an enlarged road programme which would inevitably affect the prospects for rail traffic, and slow down railway investment. Despite this, BTC minutes in July state that the MoT urged the BTC to 'spend up to its allocation'. (It is notable that road improvements are not justified by increased revenue to the State. The **existing** revenue from road traffic, which the road lobby prays in aid to build new roads, is irrelevant. More real national value for money would come from improved signs to reduce the waste of fuel by misdirected road users, who create extra traffic volume and delay.

The Transport Tribunal President told the SAG that they "took social considerations into account in reaching decisions. No formula was applied and no attempt made to quantify the social element". (The Acts made no provision for 'social considerations' - their remit was to do nothing which would impede BTC paying its way). Of the 1953 Act changes in Tribunal powers, the SAG said there remained a weakness in that the accelerated procedure could only be used if the BTC **proved** that costs had increased - it could not be used to replenish depleted reserves. SAG papers record their opinion that at least "some part of the deficit can be put down to delays in securing authority for fares and charges increases", and that "the level of fares is inordinately low in relation to the general movement of prices since the war. The Tribunal is a symbol that all proposals for increases in fares, rates and charges are unreasonable until proved justified. It is inimical to any imaginative and positive approach by BR staff". Dr.Beeching had strong views on TUCC's, CTCC and the Tribunal and that the "procedure resulted in the least possible benefit to the BTC coupled with the worst possible Public Relations. The Tribunal had allowed increases in fares which had provoked public criticism but which were too small to have any real impact on financial results". The FBI, ABCC and the Chairmen of the CTCC and the Scottish and Welsh TUCC's advocated to the SAG that BR should be free to decide its own prices. The SAG considered "that BR and LT ought to pursue a commercial fares policy both as regards commuters and ordinary passengers without delay or reference to a statutory Tribunal and advocated the abolition of the Tribunal, not the watered down arrangement, the Government implemented in 1962. (Not for the first time, Government, rejected independent advice for which it had asked).

SAG files state that it was necessary to speed up the closure process as the machinery was too slow (two years after the BTC had reported a speeding up of the process). The BTC submitted to the SAG statutory changes which they considered essential to viability :-
* pricing freedom;
* removal of legal obligations to provide facilities which traders used as a minimal convenience whilst making maximum use of road transport, [BTC had put this forward to the MoT two years earlier];
* the requirement to consult coastal shipping on freight charges
* the right to develop land for carparks and other purposes
The DoT opposed some restrictions being removed, notably on rates for bulk freight - the principal field in which BR had volume, and were concerned about freedom on season rates for commuters because of a possible effect on road congestion. They did not advocate money changing hands from highway to railway budgets. The SAG criticised "statutory prohibitions on the use of land and property, the lack of powers to develop carparks; the reason for road haulage being free to charge and carry as it will, whilst BR was under an obligation to consult coastal shipping about rates and charges and be under a risk of reference to the Tribunal. If shipping needs protection, it should not affect the legitimate commercial freedom of BR". BTC minutes, in 1960, record that they "would prefer to be free to run the business as they judge, but they doubted whether such freedom would ever be accorded".

16

When Government handed control of railways to the BTC they were running at a loss, due to Wartime Government underpricing policy (see Page 7), whilst costs were increasing.   Government artificially held prices down in a situation in which making a profit was child's play.   In July 1946, the MoT authorised increases of 33.33% in fares, and 25% in freight rates, after six years of no change with prices 70% higher than prewar; and in October 1947, by 16.25% in fares and 24% in freight rates which together lifted charges to 55% above prewar, well below the increase in costs.   The Wholesale Price Index had risen 116.2% above prewar.   BTC & BRB Annual Reports warned Governments that pricing restraint was creating losses.

BTC 1948 Report, Para 41 refers to the task of preparing Charges Schemes for its road, rail, inland waterway and dock subsidiaries for passenger and freight, which had to facilitate integration and be capable of application to all forms of transport, (The task of designing complex charges schemes simply delayed increases which were unavoidable, despite large economies. Management would have been better used, pursuing a sensible pricing policy currently, rather than pandering to external theorists who saw 'Charges Schemes' as the ultimate Tablets of Stone which would allow the business to run without making a profit or a loss); Para 43: "It is clear that the present level of charges even with increases authorised by MoT in the 1947 Act will not enable the BTC to comply with the directive to pay its way.   It is not possible that any undertaking which is to pay its way should submit to constant increases in the costs of service and commodities which it needs and yet refrain indefinitely from raising its prices to its customers".

BTC 1949 Report, noted the steep rise in cost of purchases from the Private Sector and the consequential need for rises in fares and freight charges. Para 28: A Draft Merchandise Charges Scheme based on integrating Rail, Road & Waterways was submitted on 14th December to the Traders Co-ordinating Committee on Transport, [representing 77 organisations including the FBI and ABCC], before submission to the Transport Tribunal; [Coal will be dealt with later].   A test of a weeks consignments [$3\frac{1}{2}$m items] had to be made to ascertain the effect of the Scheme in pursuit of the statutory concept of integration and a new system of common distances had to be prepared.   Rail charges were still at 1947 levels, which were below 1938 in real terms.   By autumn 1949 the deficit was £70m and an "immediate increase was essential, (they were permitted a freight increase eight months later); Para 200: prices of the index for selected commodities in general use were 145% above prewar by December 1949.   Para 70: applied for 16.66% increase in freight rates which were only 65% over pre war levels.   [BTC 1950 Report Para 57: the delay cost £11m at a conservative estimate].   (The vast organisation, created by Government, founded on undefined integration, meant that BR had to submit proposals to increase BR prices to the BTC for inclusion in the Government's Grand Concept of Integrated Charges Schemes).   An application to increase fares was submitted to the Transport Tribunal in February 1950.

Railway Executive papers reveal that Members agreed that the Chancellor of the Exchequer's announcement of 6th July 1949, on controlling inflation by holding down prices because of a serious dollar and gold reserve crisis, ruled out the possibility of applying to increase charges.   Subsequently, there was disagreement about the course to take on fares, influenced, no doubt, by the Chancellor's warnings.   Some advocated a lower ordinary fare, to create a simpler structure, but others said that the public would expect cheaper fares below that level.   As costs were not being covered, at current fare levels such a concept was ruled out in submissions to the Tribunal.

BTC 1950 Report, Para 31: The Draft Freight Charges Scheme includes coal and coke, but it is improbable that any such scheme can lay down a detailed basis for road haulage rates and charges; Para 49: BTC began without reserves [in 1948]; Para 50: Any organisation working under these limitations [price control and no reserves], is bound to be chronically in deficit; Para 73: reducing fares by 25% requires a one third increase in revenue without taking account of the extra cost of coping with the extra traffic. Para 99: BTC asked for a method of effecting quicker changes in prices to avoid deficits. Para 101: the archaic rail freight rates structure diverts traffic to road transport when the rates are less than rail, but where the rail charge is less than road [and perhaps well below cost] it goes by rail. Remunerative traffic is lost to rail, only unremunerative remaining. Para 102: BTC has announced its intention to propose railway rates which take account of actual costs [for individual consignments]; (sought in the prewar "Square Deal" campaign - see Page 60 - the Rates system which BR had to use under existing legislation precluded this practice). Para 226: By December 1950, freight rates were 81% and passenger fares 75% above pre war levels [after allowing for some reduced fare levels not restored], whereas, prices for steel rails had doubled, copper plates/tubes trebled, sleepers quadrupled, brass & tin quintupled, general timber 3½ times, oil tripled, motor spirit & diesel up 2½ times, uniform clothing quadrupled and coal tripled. Para 228: London area passenger fare increases had been reduced from those proposed by the BTC in a Tribunal decision, which would reduce income by £1m from the projected £3m budgetted due to lower increases on season and day tickets. This scheme was submitted in February 1950, introduced October - Para 57: the delay cost £0.5m (plus an annual loss of £1m). Para 417: The Road Haulage Executive increased rates by 7½% with the approval of the BTC, The BTC could act freely for their road business, but not for rail, (this was absurd).

BTC 1951 Report, Para 48: average fare per passenger mile has fallen : 1948: 1.38d, 1949: 1.3d, 1950: 1.26d, 1951: 1.24d; (the RPI had increased 19%). Comparative fare levels per mile in 1951 were Workmen: 0.72d, Season: 0.77d, Monthly Return: 1.6d, Ordinary Single: 2.44d; Para 94: freight rates increased by 10% in April 1951, roughly double prewar rates, whilst the price of coal was 340% above 1938, having started 1951 280% above, (NCB increases did not seem to be restrained) and oil was 237% above 1938. Other commodities have risen steeply - taking 1938 as an index of 100:

	Steel Rails	Steel Plate	Copper Plate	Copper Tubes	Brass Bars	Timber sleepers
1950	216	207	316	278	520	416
1951	278	244	359	308	536	659

BTC 1951 Report, Diagram 7: at the end of 1951 compared with 1939, fares had risen 77%, goods rates 99%, [overall 93%], costs had risen 150%; Para 197: March 1951, asked MoT for 10% increase in freight rates - authorised on 16th April. Due to further steep cost increases (including wages increased at Government behest), the BTC asked on 17th November for a further 10% with 20% on smalls and 50% on Returned Empties (not wanted by road haulage), the MoT authorised increases at half of those levels on 31st December.

18

Cabinet Minutes, March 1951: "MoT and Chancellor had met the BTC Chairman who had agreed not to pursue Monthly Return fare increases, but must proceed with an application to the Tribunal for main line and London fare increases. The BTC had been unable to balance accounts in 1950 due to wage increases granted by the Railways under pressure from Government [fearing a strike would paralyse industry]. Many economies had been made, e.g., 50,000 staff. When the Transport Act was passed, it was widely recognised that Railways would be unable to pay their way", (not by Managers who did not foresee the scale of external interference). "Railway fares and charges had not risen as much as other charges. As the public would link Government and the Tribunal, BTC should be persuaded to make minimum demands in Charges Schemes placed before the Tribunal. The BTC should be authorised to put to the Tribunal, proposals which would yield only £4m-£5m in London fares instead of £11m contemplated and similarly scale down elsewhere". (The Act did not require Government authority to submit applications to the Tribunal). The Chancellor said "the Act did not contemplate the MoT coming between the BTC and Tribunal", (this did not inhibit him from so doing).

BTC 1952 Report, Para 52: fares in comparison with prewar are up about 90%, whereas prices are up 160%. Para 139: On 15th April 1952 MoT directed BTC not to increase charges beyond those in force on that day - the BTC had to apply the Tribunal's 28% reduction in Ordinary fares [which the BTC had planned to leave unchanged] at a cost of £1m from 1st May but increases, worth a further £2.3m, authorised by the Tribunal must not be introduced, (see Pages 66-71: the Tribunal's Order was supported by the CTCC, but was then subject to political reduction. The £2.3m was mainly increases in seasons and EMR. Monthly returns had been increased in January but were cut back by the Tribunal's reduction in Ordinary fares). Para 141; increased costs added £18m to BTC costs. Para 142: The Road Haulage Executive raised charges by 7½% in February and 5% in December, [the latter simultaneously with BR's 5%]. Road increases did not require MoT authority, but BR's did; Para 144: LT costs were 130% above prewar whilst fares had risen by only 63%; It was not generally appreciated that BR fares outside London were generally higher than those in the London Area. In the Draft 1953 Charges Scheme, BTC proposed increases in Seasons and EMR (which had been held down by Government), because they were much lower than ordinary fares, but for which services were no less costly to provide. Para 32: Outcome of Fares Scheme submitted to the Tribunal on 5th January 1953, awaited on 15th May.

British Transport Review, April 1952, pp 20/21: "The present level of railway freight charges, 120% over pre-war, compares with a level of wholesale prices which is 225% higher. Not long ago, an industrial transport 'expert' was deploring inflated transport charges which he said industry had no alternative but to pass on to the public, after cushioning their impact by economies and improved methods. Many traders have in practice, lost no time in advancing their prices by a proportion estimated to represent the higher cost of freight. Some indeed have put up their prices within a matter of hours. Precisely, it is the nationalised transport which has provided the cushion. After procurring economies on a scale equivalent to millions of pounds annually, BTC have found themselves forced to carry the higher cost of their materials for periods of months and up to a year at a time, before the Tribunal's sanction could be obtained to higher charges. In the case of the last Charges Scheme submitted to the Tribunal in April 1951, it might fairly have been said that transport users - in this case passengers - have been cushioned to the extent of £17m over the last 12 months. More than a year will have elapsed before one of the main groups of higher charges sought by the Commission takes effect".

Cabinet Minutes, 22nd April 1952 : Prime Minister Winston Churchill "would not accept that the BTC should be free, with approval of the Tribunal (that was free?), to adjust railway rates without any intervention by Government or Parliament, and he did not consider that Railways should be obliged to recover from revenue all their costs including capital invested in them". (Despite this, the Government retained the concept of the BTC paying its way in the 1953 Act). The Cabinet was discussing a draft White Paper for the 1953 Act [to denationalise road haulage], in which it envisaged that "the BTC would be free to decide its own charges". (passenger and freight). The Cabinet decided that "words should added to make it clear that the BTC would remain subject to the overriding power of the MoT to give such directions in this matter as the National Interest might require". (It was amended - see Page 9). The Prime Minister also called for exceptionally favourable treatment of a bus company "before BR gets its freedom", (see Page 49. The already drafted 1953 Act did not give BR freedom, perhaps the PM meant '15 years before BR gets its freedom' - a strange definition of freedom!).

BTC 1953 Report, page 6: A Passenger Charges Scheme was lodged with the Tribunal. In February 1953 the LCC had challenged the Scheme's legality in the Court of Appeal. They put it back to the Tribunal on March 9th, considered 24th April, ultimately confirmed and operated from August 16th. "Meantime the submission for increased bus fares were granted in whole or in part with comparative expedition". Para 47: BR will be free to quote freely and competitively for traffic provided they do not exceed maximum charges; (This was freedom? Road transport was free without let or hindrance).

BTC 1954 Report, page 2: "The fall in working surplus is due to the fact that fares and freight charges were never able to catch up quickly enough with rising price levels. When there are no margins in fares and charges which will meet rising costs until a readjustment is possible a deficit is inevitable"; Para 16: The average fare was 1.38d per mile in 1948 and 1.35d in 1954. Compared with 1948, Industrial earnings in 1954 had risen by 45%, the RPI had risen by 32%, but BR fares had fallen by 2%. Page 4: "BTC 1951 Report had said a Draft Goods Charges Scheme was to be lodged at the end of 1951. It was delayed when the Government asked the BTC to consult coastwise shipping and then withheld owing to a change in Government Policy later embodied in the 1953 Act. By this, Schemes must provide, not for fixed or standard charges previously envisaged by the Government, but for maximum charges below which BR could vary at discretion the actual charges being made to individual companies. Hence BR had to start work on an entirely new Draft Scheme which was completed by 15th December 1954"; Para 27: "It is imperative to have a free system of charging and to adjust rates to attract traffic to rail which is suitable", (confirms that the "freedom" mentioned in the 1953 Act was not real freedom since they had to submit a new scheme).

BTC 1955 Report, Para 5: "London fares went up in December 1955 by 4% but were still only double prewar, whereas the RPI was up 2½ times; Para 21: Freight rates increase authorised 5th June 1955 [7½% full loads and 15% for smalls] but Freight rates were still below the index of wholesale prices. BTC's road haulage rates varied according to circumstances. It would benefit BR if they had equal liberty to adjust charges, and would assist them in attracting to rail, goods for which that medium is suitable, whilst transferring the unsuitable to road; Para 22: BTC put a new Freight Charges Scheme to the Tribunal on 22nd March 1955 following months of consultation with representatives of rail users and other interested parties". Despite this, "28 objections were lodged with the Tribunal whose Public Inquiry opened 10th October 1955 and after 44 days of hearings adjourned to 7th March 1956; BTC is still without that greater freedom to charge, and hence to compete, which Parliament had intended them to have"; Para 35: "the main explanation for £70m deficit over 8 years is the persistence of inflation. In 1955 BTC could see an increase in charges was inevitable to preserve its position in real terms and took action to secure approval. Delays involved on each of these occasions before such increases, or modified increases, were sanctioned produced a loss of over £50m. The BTC are prevented from keeping any margin in newly adjusted charges to provide against further price movements against them in the period lying ahead. Thus in the intervals before an application became inevitable, the BTC were carrying increased and uncovered charges totalling £50m. Hence it is now apparent that inflation has cost £100m. This compares and more than explains the accumulated deficits of £70m. The levels of railway wages and charges compared with the corresponding wage and price levels in manufacturing industry prove that far from themselves starting an inflationary process, public transport has, from the beginning, been dragged into the spiral. Receipts per passenger mile are now well below prewar allowing for the fall in the value of money; Para 36: Another factor is the growing volume of competition from privately owned transport, coupled with unequal terms on which BR are expected to meet this competition - BTC are still hedged about with a variety of restrictions and obligations not shared by competitors, leaving the BTC providing many types of services at controlled charges that fall short of the individual cost of providing those services; Diagram 6 of the BTC Report compared price changes since 1938 - average earnings by 1955 had risen 50%, rail fares had fallen by 34%! Diagram 7a of the BTC Report shows Freight charges had also fallen:-

Price Index	1938	1955	Corresponding BR index
Manufactured goods	100	102	
	100	84	Merchandise rate
Iron & Steel	100	115	
Building materials	100	118	
	100	98	Mineral rate
Coal	100	162	
	100	108	* Coal rates

* including use of a wagon which prewar was an extra cost, mainly for non railway owned coal wagons; (The indices prove industry created inflation).

On 9th March 1955, the MoT told the Cabinet that he "was seeking authority to tell the BTC that they may proceed to hold a Press Conference to say they have deposited a Draft Merchandise Charges Scheme, announce a fare increase and that an application has been made to him [MoT] to increase freight charges". (Government had announced BTC's freedom in 1952 but it appears that they could not even take these actions without MoT authority).

Addressing the **Royal United Service Institution** [February 1956], the BTC Chairman said "the 1947 Act required the BTC to integrate inland transport. The 1953 Act reversed that and the work of those years and directed a return to competition between various modes of transport. The Commission were promised freedom of charging on railways and release from restrictions on the rates which they may quote. Because of the cumbersome procedure which has to be followed before approval can be had to a new Railway Freight Charges Scheme, railways have not yet achieved the flexibility in charging which the Act promised, meanwhile the competition of privately owned road transport grows daily. The country must make up its mind whether public transport should be run as a commercial enterprise, self supporting financially, and as free to run its affairs as any commercial enterprise under private ownership, or as a service bound to minister to every want of the community, however uneconomic that might be. That inevitably would mean subsidising it from taxation". The BTC view was that "we must never fall back onto the heroin shot of subsidy". (Government's 1953 promise was not implemented until 1962, giving denationalised road transport a golden opportunity to consolidate an unassailable position).

In March 1956, the MoT said that he had asked the BTC to defer increases in fares "to put a stop to continually passing on this sort of charge to the public". An Opposition MP pointed out that fares and freight charges had risen less than the RPI or Wholesale Indices. (As Indices are averages it was impossible for fares and freight charges, which were below these averages to be the cause of inflation. See page 88 for a comparison of BR charges and these indices. Published data proved that BR charges had been anti-inflationary since 1941. BR was perhaps the only industry – which had not been "continually passing on these charges". The MoT was preventing BR from increasing ordinary fares to a level which was below 1947 in money terms, and below prewar in real terms, having not reverted to the level from which the Tribunal had disastrously reduced them. Some of the enlightened media saw time lags in BTC price increases as the cause of unprofitability). The MoT told Parliament in July that "by applying the ordinary principles of enlightened private enterprise, I am hopeful that we are going to show how they [BR] can make a profit". (BR managers who believed that he was about to free them to act commercially, like their competitors and the rest of industry, were quickly disillusioned. For a thwarted attempt by BR to practice 'enlightened private enterprise practices' see page 40).

1956 MoT Paper: "Proposals for Railways", Para 1: BTC applied for an increase in freight charges on 21st February. MoT said on 19th March "As an essential part of that decision [upon the application] a reassessment of the economic and financial future of the BTC would be undertaken in the next six months"; Para 6: "The BTC have not and never have had a complete monopoly of the traffics for which their services are provided"; Para 16: "It remains the Government's view that every effort to avoid continued cycles of price increases in the basic industries is essential to break the spiral of inflation – any general increase in railway charges should be avoided". (BTC Reports show that BR was the victim, not the the source of inflation. In contrast to the MoT's directive to the BTC, Government were satisfied with less firm assurances from industry: the National Union of Maufacturers had an "uncontrollable element in manufacturing costs", the British Employers Federation: "will make every effort to avoid increasing prices"); Para 20: MoT advocated carrying "substantial deficits until 1961 or 1962"; Para 21: "During the next 5 or 6 years the BTC may impose selective increases in freight charges. They may well make adjustments to passenger fares from time to time"; (the word 'may' infers 'may not be allowed'); Para 25: "Government will [as the price for preventing increases in fares and charges] loan to BTC £250m on which it will pay interest"; Para 26: "The BTC will be empowered to borrow to cover the first three years' interest". Published as part of the MoT paper was a BTC Memorandum to the MoT; Para 1: "It is Government policy that Nationalised Industries should seek fully to reflect their costs, but Government was asking the BTC, in the national interest, to follow a course which would involve an exception to this general policy. The increases for which they had applied .... were reduced or postponed for a period of six months, during which, a fresh assessment would be undertaken, followed by such special action as seemed appropriate at the end of that period. It was on this clear understanding that the BTC agreed to the course proposed; Para 4: BTC earned a working surplus in every year since they began operations, on the other hand, in several years the surplus was not sufficient to meet financial charges on the fixed interest borrowings, which constitute the sole source of external capital. They started without reserves and never obtained increases in fares and charges large enough to permit their creation; Para 7: A lapse of several months in putting up charges cost £10m in 1955. Para 9: The accumulated deficit at end of 1955 was £70m, due mainly to time lags in putting up fares and charges, largely on traffics such as London passengers, rather than weakness in the competitive field; Para 71: First among all statutory restrictions and obligations which have fettered railways ..... must rank restrictions on freedom to fix fares and charges; Para 73: The Freight Charges Scheme (which was supposed to give BR the same freedom Road Haulage had had for 35 years), was 'appreciably restricted' by the Transport Tribunal, (this was freedom?); Para 83: The standstill on charges was conditioned by an expectation that Government would implement a course of action which would enable the BTC to meet its statutory obligations. (Events disappointed the BTC; Doubts expressed in the Memorandum regarding risks of increasing prices do not sit easily with references in the BTC 1955 Accounts - published mid 1956 - to the widening gap between Price & Wage Indices and those of fares & freight rates, and suggest the BTC were unconvinced about restraint - see also BTC Minutes below). Para 101: The BTC forecast that this economic policy would cost them £6m pa rising to £20m pa in 1961 in interest charges, (still creating no reserves) and these charges would continue to at least 1970"; (the MoT, in his part of this MoT published Document did not disagree, contradict or dissociate himself from the BTC comments). BTC Minutes March 1956: "in deference to MoT wishes, the BTC postponed for six months an Application to the Tribunal for increases in certain fares and would not increase Ordinary fares within existing powers".

The MoT told the House of Commons in December 1956, that BR were offering competitive terms to attract traffic in the Suez Crisis: "it was BR policy to quote commercial terms which will encourage movement of traffic by rail". (How they were to do so as rates were still held in the paralytic grip of the 1921 legislation pending implementation of the Freight Charges Scheme, which was to apply from July 1957, was not explained. The only rates which BR could legally offer were those which road haulage had been undercutting for 30 years, (see Page 58). Had BR been given freedom by the Government even as late as 1953 when road haulage was denationalised, BR would have been able to be selective in securing good paying traffic on medium or long term contracts, during the Suez Crisis. BR was denied that opportunity and could not adjust prices at will, as hauliers did to reflect costs and maximise profit. BR were still bound to offer "reasonable facilities" to all, which meant they could not pick and choose). Road hauliers were totally free, and used BR to carry traffic for the latter part of a journey - to eke out fuel rations - whilst the haulier remained as the carrier to individual companies keeping BR at arms length from senders. Some companies transferred 'C' licence traffic at short notice to BR in the Crisis, and had it moved currently, but after the Crisis reverted to past arrangements. As common carriers BR could not refuse any traffic from competitors or traders.

BTC 1956 Report, Para 45: "financial worsenment is due to freezing of fares and charges to combat inflation, plus loss of freight business mainly due to C Licences; Para 46: Abstained [at MoT 'request'], from making increases in 1956 although the prices of coal, electric power and steel had risen considerably. In agreeing to make no increase in charges, BTC hoped that suppliers would exercise restraint .... but were perhaps over optimistic". (Others had not acted in the national interest); "BTC felt obliged to ask MoT in February for 10% in freight charges - the MoT granted 5% in March.

The Transport [Railway Finances] Act 1956 was to "enable the BTC to meet interest and other revenue charges by borrowing and modifying the 1947 Act

23

as to the sufficiency of BTC revenue to meet revenue charges". Government set aside £250m to cover Government created deficits. (BTC should have had total commercial freedom avoiding subsequent losses, instead of forcing them to borrow, shackling them as debtors to the Treasury in perpetuity. In October 1956 the MoT said the £250m to cover Railway Deficits was a "Tough Bargain", (a gross understatement); "Alternatives were to carry deficits or impose heavy increases on heavy bulk traffics, which may drive traffic away – and would be a serious addition to industrial costs and it was against the national interest to do the latter". (This was absurd, if higher freight rates may drive traffic off BR, they could not be an addition to industrial costs). Having claimed there was a case for holding down freight costs, he requested the BTC not to proceed with an application to increase **passenger fares** for the rest of the year, when had it gone to the Tribunal, it would have taken that length of time anyway. It is incomprehensible how he could say that to overcome present financial difficulties, "it is vital the BTC should be able to take advantage of freedom Government have given them to vary charges in accordance with sound principles, and that the Government view was that passenger services should be run at reasonably remunerative rates", when the Tribunal and Government were holding fares below the RPI. Freedom on BR freight and passenger charges was given respectively 6 and 12 years later. The MoT said the BTC could not be expected to keep down prices if faced with further large increases in costs which are not counter balanced by a corresponding improvement in efficiency and output. He was saying that BR should improve efficiency to enable them to contain the higher costs which industry, by inference, had not been able to contain by efficiency. How much further did he want BR fares and rates to fall below the RPI, Wholesale or Manufacturing indices? BR fares and rates had been well below comparable price indices since the war, hence BR was losing money, and the Private Sector were not. The first step to put BR into line with the Private Sector was pricing freedom. Contemporary media reports saw the effect of the Government policy on prices in Electricity, Coal and Rail would be to put money into consumer pockets to spend on imports and inflate prices. How could the MoT believe that BR fares were inflationary in 1956, when fares were then at 4% above 1948, against the RPI which was 45% higher? The MoT had authorised freight increases in 1956, when the 1955 level of freight rates was 54% above 1948, still 20% or more below industrial price indices. There was no logic in his decisions. Had BR been free from 1948 to decide its own prices, and allowed to tie its fares to the RPI, it would, by the end of 1956, have been £280m better off, see below:

Year	Actual Average fare	Inflation linked Average fare	Actual Passenger Receipts #m	Inflation linked Receipts #m	Lost Revenue (in year) #m	Lost Revenue (in 1956) #m	Cum. Lost Revenue #m
1948	100	100.0	122.6	122.6	0.0	0.0	0.0
1949	93	103.8	114.0	127.2	13.2	17.6	17.6
1950	91	106.7	106.6	124.9	18.3	23.7	41.3
1951	89	119.4	107.0	143.5	36.5	42.3	83.6
1952	93	120.2	111.9	144.6	32.7	37.6	121.2
1953	96	122.1	114.8	146.0	31.2	35.3	156.5
1954	96	126.3	116.6	153.4	36.8	40.3	196.8
1955	100	134.1	118.1	158.4	40.3	41.6	238.4
1956	104	138.3	127.5	169.5	42.0	42.0	280.4
					£251.0	£280.4	
					======	======	

Freight rates tied to the Wholesale Price Index would have produced £159.8m:

Year	Rates index	Wholesale index	Receipts freight	Inflation linked	Lost in year £m	Lost at 1955 prices £m
1948	100.0	100.0	180.5	180.5	0.0	0.0
1949	97.5	104.9	178.9	192.5	13.6	20.1
1950	107.5	119.6	198.9	221.3	22.4	29.1
1951	119.5	145.6	227.9	277.7	49.8	53.1
1952	134.5	149.4	250.5	278.3	27.8	28.8
1953	138.5	149.6	263.1	284.2	21.1	21.9
1954	148.0	150.5	272.8	277.4	4.6	4.8
1955	154.0	155.2	274.2	276.3	2.1	2.1
					£141.3	£159.8
					====	====

Freedom on prices and closures would have increased reserves and modernised assets, generating more revenue. No loan would have been needed to support price restraint and the BTC would have been over £400m better off.
CTCC 1956 Report, Para 57: "increase in fares .... only 86% above prewar in the London area, 90% for the whole country compares most favourably with the price increases for almost every other service and commodity".
BTC 1957 Report, Para 166: the average level of real fares was 0.76d per mile in 1938, and 0.57d in 1957; Para 180: BR average fares are about double prewar - other [external] prices are three times the prewar level; Para 181: the cost of travel compared to personal incomes showed that the time taken, to earn the fare for a 20 mile journey [then the average journey], was:-

Year	1938	1949	1950	1951	1952	1953	1954	1955	1956	1957
Minutes	51	44	42	36	35	34	33	32	31	29

Freight charges had also fallen - Diagrams 3 & 4, BTC 1957 Report :-

Price Index	1938	1957	Corresponding BR index
Manufactured goods	100	101	
	100	81	Merchandise rate
Iron & Steel	100	124	
Building materials	100	116	
	100	99	Mineral rate
Coal	100	184	
	100	108	* Coal rates

* including the use of a wagon which prewar was an extra cost.

25

BTC 1958 Report, Para 163: "Fares are still well below prewar levels in real terms with average earnings keeping ahead of fares; wages in 1958 were nearly double 1948, whereas fares had hardly changed; Para 151: no general increase in fares or freight charges, but there were selective increases; Para 179: The gap between prices and costs compared with prewar is 20% for merchandise and even more for coal". (Couple these with the real fall in the cost of passenger travel and one wonders how the Government and industry could possibly have believed that rail prices were creating inflation).

PEP 1958 Report 'Paying for Railways', Page 281: "Passenger fares appear to have been well shielded from the effects of inflation"; Page 294: "maximum freight rates must still be authorised by the Tribunal even after they had approved the 1957 Freight Charges Scheme" (which was supposed to give BR the equality and commercial freedom it had sought for over 20 years); and that they could not refuse expensive-to-handle marginal traffic at rates below the cost of carriage, which C Licence operators dumped on them.

BTC 1959 Report, Para 165: Some fares are still below prewar levels in real terms per passenger mile. Comparative averages were - BR, excluding London area: Prewar 0.78d, now 0.57d; BR & LT London area: Prewar 0.56d, now 0.55d. Para 166: the discount of quarterly season tickets against ordinary fares at 70 miles, was 70-75% [these passengers were paying as little as one quarter of the standard rate for travelling at peak times due to statutory control of fares]". At 20 miles it was 50-55%. Para 179: "Compared to 1954 [then the current base year for Indices] BR freight charges had risen less than wholesale prices, BR merchandise rates being below 1954 levels, other rates had increased but were well below industrial prices. The Government would reconsider the financial structure dominated by fixed interest charges which are large in relation to the working surplus. The printing strike from the end of June to mid August had an adverse influence on revenue as it seriously affected the advertising of excursions.

BTC 1960 Report, Para 3: "In 1956 when the Government introduced deficit financing the BTC didn't increase prices to levels contemplated. The 1958 recession in coal and steel cut revenue by £30m in 1958 & 1959. Steel has recovered, but not coal"; Para 14: refers to a drift of staff away in London and Midlands "where industrial wages have risen sharply". (It reminded me of two men who applied in 1961 to become trainee Guards at Coventry. When they were asked to complete an application form, one did so, but the other couldn't read or write, so we only recruited the former. A week later, the man we employed asked for his cards, because his illiterate friend had got a job at a motor company at twice the wages); Para 182: "Fares are still not at parity with prewar; Para 183: The long drawn out processes of public enquiry and argument about the price of road and rail facilities has given this [fares] a special significance in the mind of the public and has affected the willingness of the public to pay reasonable fares. The Government stated that people must be prepared to pay more for rail travel. Increases are needed not only to offset changes in the value of money but to compensate for costly trends in problems of transport; (one of the problems was a 50% increase in peak hour travel). Earnings are still racing away faster than fares - well over double 1948, whereas fares were +20%. Fares went up by one sixth in two stages - November 1959 and mid 1960".

1960 MoT Paper : Reorganisation of Nationalised Transport Undertakings, Para 10: "The commercial capability of the railways is circumscribed by outmoded statutory obligations and restrictions on their trading operations; Para 12c: The Government have decided to give maximum practicable freedom of operation in their commercial affairs" (Not total freedom, like their competitors and suppliers); Para 50: "The Select Committee had recommended that unremunerative services run by BR for social needs should be met by grants from public funds, but the MoT proposed to leave this concept in abeyance", (concealing social costs in deficits); Para 57: "BR were to be freed from statutory control over fares, except the London area". Dr.Beeching, the new Chairman of the BTC, was "looking forward to fewer restrictions on railway charges and greater flexibility in their fixation"; - Para 58: "statutory restrictions on the development of BR property will be suitably relaxed" (relaxed - not abolished).

Select Committee on BR, March 1961, Para 2: "The comparatively small deficit at that time [1955] could be attributed to inflation and the delay in securing authority for adjustment of fares and charges; The financial position of the BTC was seriously worsened by the economic changes in 1958 when the carryings of coal and steel fell sharply, losing £30m". (Had BR had commercial freedom from the start, they would have built up reserves to cover such fluctuations - £30m was 5% of annual revenue, provision for such a small amount would not have been difficult to build up over nine years); Para 15: "The Tribunal can now be required to give reasons for decisions"; (hardly timely as Government intended to reduce the role of the Tribunal. This implied that they had been deciding without giving reasons).

BTC 1961 Report, Para 259: "Important changes have been made in the levels of fares since 1959, in the autumn of which the first of a series of steps to improve the financial position of rail passenger services was taken. Substantial increases in revenue have been obtained, which have been required to meet additional costs incurred in the meantime due to higher costs, [materials and fuel prices], and for increased depreciation charges" (the increases could not clear deficits, nor create reserves); Para 260: "years of statutory control and the publicity arising from the processes of Public Inquiry have given currency to the belief that higher fares are an important inflationary factor, that the cost of travel is an important item in the family budget and that fare increases have been excessive. In fact, during the first 15 years of the inflation which began with the Second World War, passenger fares rose much less than would have been necessary to compensate for the fall in the value of money. Even with the rise in the past 10 years, the average level of fares remains at or below the prewar level - though it is widely accepted that prices of services in a modern economy must be expected to rise faster than the prices of manufactured goods". (This was not from a career Railway manager - whom the media would doubtless assume was not trying, but from Dr.Beeching imported from that icon of the Private Sector - ICI). Para 263: "discounts in season ticket prices compared with the 2nd class Full Fare, on the basis of 5 return journeys per week at the end of 1961 - at 10 miles was 40%, and at 70 miles was 70%"; Page 63: from 1952 to 1961, the index of earnings showed that commuters' salaries had risen every year [9 increases], always ahead of rail increases [8 increases], half of which were very marginal. (These were the passengers forcing BR costs through the ceiling). Diagram 4 of the BTC Report shows that the receipts per passenger mile, at constant prices, taking 1952 as a base had by 1961 risen 26%, whereas 1938 fares had been 31% higher than those in 1952 - hence fares in 1961 were below 1938 in real terms; Para 278: "transport charges have been falling in comparison with delivered prices of commodities" (the latter includes transport charges, which traders said had caused their increases); Para 295: "over a half of the increase in working expenses was due to increased price levels and the cessation in 1961 of the Government contribution towards the cost of upkeep of road bridges over railways and level crossings".

Transport Act, 1962, Para 18: the Government has decided that "Each of the Boards [BRB, LTB etc] shall so conduct their business as to secure that their revenue is not less than sufficient for the meeting of charges properly chargeable to revenue taking one year with another".

British Transport Review, April 1963: BTC will be dissolved, finances reconstructed, and maximum practicable freedom given to the various undertakings - BRB, LTB, DB, BWB, and the Holding Co of which Bus Groups, BRS and Thos Cook were to be subsidiaries; Page 110: the Act appears to involve a considerably increased degree of ministerial control, in that there are a large number of measures to which his consent is necessary. Page 114: The White Paper said 'the present restrictions on the ability of the railways to adjust quickly and adequately their freight charges and passenger fares are in the Government's view, no longer justified in present competitive conditions. The Railways will, therefore, be freed from statutory control over their charges, (also promised in 1952, 1953 and 1956), **except** for the London Passenger Transport Area', which included BR lines. It also said that the Boards shall not be regarded as common carriers by rail or inland waterway nor bound by enactments which authorize the revision of freight charges on complaint by competitors or traders', Coastwise shipping retained its protection against rail competition, (railways had never had the right to object to competitors rates). The effect is to reduce the functions of the Tribunal which now concerns itself with rail & road fares in the London Passenger Transport Area.

BRB 1963 Report, Para 130: Working expenses include items from which BR derives no benefit - manning and maintaining crossings and maintaining overbridges, and costs for CTCC/TUCC of £60,000 pa, (which began in 1949 and continued until 1969 when responsibility for CTCC staffing, financing and accommodation was transferred to the MoT).

BRB 1964 Report: Para 82: "BR applied to the Tribunal to bring fares on the LT&S line, beyond the LT area, up to BR standards elsewhere, by increasing Seasons by 5%, replacing Day Returns by reduced off peak and weekend fares. The Tribunal only agreed to the Day Return alteration"; (LT&S benefit again)

BRB 1965 Report Para 50: "BRB required by Government to give early warning of changes in a wide range of passenger and freight transport charges", (an unusual form of freedom). "In November BRB did so in respect of increases to be introduced in early 1966". Para 107: Deferred an application for a fare increase at Government request worth £1.4m.

BRB 1966 Report Para 3: "Government restraint prevented implementation of increases in fares and charges, some of which had either been approved by the Transport Tribunal or were provided for in commercial agreements. Most [increases] were delayed long enough to be frozen".

MoT's Transport Policy Review, 1966, Para 8: "BR are struggling to reconcile two mutually contradictory objectives: to provide an adequate service for the public and to pay their way", (due to Government policies); Para 14: "Commercial viability is important but secondary; Para 16: Government must decide now the right role for BR". - (what had they been doing since 1947?); Para 29: A Joint review will be set up to study issues.

BRB 1967 Report, Para 3: "The Government refused, 'because of the freeze' to allow certain increases in fares and charges, including some approved by the Tribunal for the London Area as long ago as July 1966. The Government referred the proposals to the NBPI from whom a decision was still awaited at the end of the year [1967]; This highlights the perennial problem of fares and charges always lagging behind increases in costs - agreement to any increases comes too late and allows too little margin to build up reserves to combat the next cost increases. There is an urgent need for headroom to be granted in advance to enable costs and charges to be kept in step".

BRB 1968 Report, Para 5: refers to a new policy - of pricing not on mileage, but according to 'market conditions'; Para 6: "while the necessary research was being completed BR applied for a general fares increase to ensure a continuing flow of revenue, and asked for powers of headroom for future rises"; which - Para 7: "in September of 1967, the MoT had referred to the NBPI, who approved a 10% increase in ordinary fares, and 7½% in season ticket fares in the London area. The 10% was later reduced by the Transport Tribunal. The NBPI rejected a general increase for the rest of country telling BR to pursue the BR plan for variable fares which would take many months; Para 8: BR accelerated its research and the first stage was ready by September 1968, gaining £70m in a full year"; (NBPI delay cost about £50m).

NBPI Report May 1968, Para 1: "In the spring of 1967 the BRB informed the MoT of a wish to raise fares outside London. Following the PM's announcement on 7th September 1967 that all future price increases in the nationalised industries would be referred to the NBPI; these proposals were referred to us [NBPI] on 3rd October; BR proposed increases in 1st class fares: 8.2%, 2nd class: 4.6%, coal: 6-10%, sundries: 7½%, parcels: 6%; Para 31: The proposed increases would raise the RPI by less than 0.04%; Para 33: In the event of our [NBPI] approving the London proposals, they would then be submitted to the Transport Tribunal, which considers fares in the London area". (This merry-go-round was unparalleled outside BR and LT).

MoT Paper "Transport in London", July 1968: the lack of viability is "because of the financial structure; control, and external intervention in fares in the face of rising costs"; Page 14: "subject to financial objectives, BR should themselves determine fares on the network - London Passenger Transport Area - but proposals for major increases should be referred to the NBPI"! Page 57: "there is no reason why future travellers should pay so that today's passengers can continue to travel at less than the cost of the services provided for them", (this had been happening for 20 years); "In these circumstances relating charges to costs seems not unreasonable; Page 61: recommend that LTB should be free to fix fares, and Transport Tribunal duties relating to London fares should be abolished. LTB should develop pricing based on peak costs - when they have the freedom!"

BR Management Quarterly, October 1968 on Selective Pricing: "The impression was given that BR was trying to hang onto a sterile system of standard tariffs. In fact BR had asked for headroom to make selective price increases, but this was rejected by the NBPI". (The NBPI had told BR to pursue its own plan. The BTC 1958 Report mentioned selective increases).

NBPI Report, December 1969 [London Area proposed fare increases], Para 6: "No forward estimates of the London commuter network beyond 1970 had been made by BR". (It is difficult to see the value of long term plans, which were undermined by 'U' turns. A 1961 Select Committee pointed out that Government required three year plans, but did not approve them beyond the first year! In 1973, an approved five year plan lasted three weeks); Para 9: "The Minister issued guidelines to BR limiting the amount by which fares should rise", reducing the proposed increase by 28.8%. "The NBPI were asked to look at how the smaller sum should be raised. It told BR to raise it by varying prices on different routes, where **justified** on cost grounds"; (what happened to freedom?); Para 16: "A move to uniform rates could be at variance with the different degrees of road congestion which will vary from one area to another. This points to lower fare increases on relatively under used lines; BR to determine which lines should pay higher increases".

BRB 1970 Report, Para 3.5: "The unprecedented rate of inflation caused steep increases in costs".

BRB 1971 Report, Para 1.9: "A CBI initiative to keep price rises at 5%

within 12 months of the last increase" (not a problem for the Private Sector which had not experienced real price restraint and for whom it was a voluntary policy). "BR had to accept the Government directive and would have to borrow money at 8-9%. Government advanced BR £27m for 1972 to cover overdue rises they were not allowed to make". (This increased BR losses; eventually prices would have to reflect that 8-9% - was this one of the MoT's "principles of enlightened private enterprise" - see Page 22 - to borrow to keep prices down?); BRB said that "the effects of artificial restraint can never be recovered. BR's 1971 fuel & power bill was 13.25% higher than 1970; materials, supplies etc were +17.4% - wages were up 6%". (CSO Annual Abstract of Statistics: industrial wages rose by 12-13% in this period; contradicting the belief that BR increased wages faster than the Private Sector. So much for 'voluntary restraint' in the Private Sector).

BRB 1972 Report: "Although the Board was compensated for price restraint during the year, restrictions on price increases will inevitably have an effect for years ahead making further compensatory payments necessary".

BRB 1973 Report: "The Board still suffers from and is bound to suffer in perpetuity from the effects of past price restraint. The adverse effect on BRB finances of restraint on the levels and timings of necessary increases has been very considerable. The effects of this restraint are in present circumstances permanent for BR is, as a result handicapped to a place behind the start line (again) for increases made necessary by the rising cost of materials and living. A year of unprecedented inflation".

BRB 1974 Report: "1972 costs rose by 10%, but we were allowed to increase prices by 8%. In 1973 costs rose by 6%, but we were allowed to increase by 3%. In 1974, the Chancellor gave BR the freedom to price up, but by that time the price base was so low that the market could not take the increase needed - costs rose by 33%" (note that 5% had also been lost in the preceding two years), "and we were able to price up only 16%. At constant prices, present earnings per passenger mile are in fact slightly lower than they were in 1969", [1.09p compared to 1.10p]; "Unpleasant economic facts do not go away if you ignore them they always get worse. BRB foresaw financial problems stemming from the support arrangement adopted by the Government and gave early warning of their forebodings. In the spring of 1975, these forebodings are being realised at a higher level than they were first seen because like all such problems they are aggravated and distorted by inflation and by the rolling effect of past pricing restraints".

MoT "Transport Policy", 1976, Para 2.1.2 : "the peak has been a factor in keeping unit costs high"; (the understatement of the post war period); Para 2.5: "rail freight shows up well at 1.2p per tonne kilometre, road is 8.5p - but best to avoid comparisons"; Para 3.6: "It is the higher income groups who use railways the most regularly for travel to work and business journeys, while those on lower incomes travel by rail much more sporadically"; Para 2.14: "The trend of growing losses has continued since the 1950's despite revenue and capital grants"; (In fact, it was **because** grants were introduced as an alternative to price increases). "Since the early 1950's railways have experienced successive financial crises and been rescued by successive subventions from the taxpayer", (that is standing history on its head - crises didn't happen, but were caused by defective Government policies. The form of rescue was as helpful as throwing a colander to a drowning man, after having pushed him in at the deep end. Had BR been given a fair remit in 1948, together with commercial freedom, revenue deficits would not have arisen in the first place. They took money from the public to give it back to the public - it did not benefit BR, it was a disbenefit to BR; This is borne out by Page 20 of the Report): Page 20 Para 4a : "There is no evidence that the real fare increases that occurred between 1970 and 1972 were accompanied by any significant change in the pattern of rail use"; Para 4c : "A reduction in fares without an increase in subsidies would be unlikely to pay for itself through increased ridership"; (revenue deficit financing as an alternative to commercial pricing was a deliberate Government policy, one consequence being to remove the ceiling on wage increases which would have existed had BR's remit been to be profitable. When BR management attempted to keep wage increases within bounds, they were undermined by others: Government Pay Inquiries, PM's decisions, local authorities who created the wage explosion and the Private Sector who could and did pass on their wage increases to consumers which included BR - a large scale consumer of Private Sector goods); Page 13, Para 3.6 : "subsidies were effectively going to the better-off, rather than the less well-off, as the former group use rail to travel to work"; Page 17, Para 3.25: advocates asking the passenger whether they preferred a slightly faster journey or a better buffet, (The MoT does not advise what to do when the inevitable lack of agreement arises. In fact, BR carried out far more market research than most realise). Para 7.5: "Costs have risen much faster than revenue particularly during the period when fares were held down as part of a counter inflation policy from early 1971 until early 1974", (The penny may have dropped, but not far enough - for 1971 read 1948!); "Rail fares rose less than the RPI" (for the 26th year); "There were substantial rises in the cost of energy and other resources" (why was the cost of energy, other resources and the RPI allowed to increase while rail fares were held down?); Para 7.25: "The key to success lies in the identification of those areas where specific tasks can be dispensed with ....." (and then replying to external criticism after doing so, not least from some MP's); Para 7.31 "Recent fare increases have had remarkably little effect on the volume of traffic. Despite a rise of 50% in fares during the year, there was only a marginal drop of under 5% and Board's earnings increased by £90m, with a further £30m expected". Para 7.36 refers to underpricing of season tickets (due to external interference); Page 61 compares the user of passenger coaches of BR and other railways, despite BR coaches being generally shorter than those of European and other Railways (the penalty for being first), and Japanese Railways employ staff to push passengers into coaches. Table 1, page 93, shows the static level of rail transport compared to motoring. Had the car not existed, travel would not have expanded to the extent it has. People are making journeys by car because they have the car - a trip into the country or to shopping centres. Whilst BR has lost a share of the market, a major part of the expanded market is unsuitable for rail and would not exist without the car.

BRB 1976 Report reveals that fares had really been falling. At constant prices, taking out the effect of inflation, the earnings per passenger mile were for the years 1972 - 1976 inclusive were: 1.5p, 1.46p, 1.34p, 1.44p, 1.54p. (As a result of interference in pricing, fares fell by 2½%, 10%, and 4% respectively, before finally advancing a modest 2½% - which did not recover preceding losses. The fall in fares 1973-5 was equivalent to a loss of £45m had the real cost per mile merely remained constant).

BRB 1977 Report: "Our January 1978 proposals for fare increases were referred to the Price Commission who duly recommended that there should be no restrictions on the notified increases", (a flag day).

Select Committee Report, 1977, Para 357: "rail fare increases have lagged behind inflation in the early 1970's" (they had lagged behind since 1948). "Taking an index of 1972 = 100, RPI at end of 1974, reached 127, and Rail 120, but at end of 1976 both were equal at 184", (so what? The 7% margin is never recovered - related to revenue, it amounted to £63m); Para 425: "BR becomes dependent on the Government for further loans - £63m in 1975 alone"; (I had calculated a £63m loss due to the gap between RPI and fares from

1972, before reaching this paragraph, 15 pages later); Para 359: "fares should not increase for at least the next five years by more than the average RPI", (unless the private sector did likewise - history would repeat itself); Para 279: "BR say: from June 1971 to 1974 rail rates were constrained by severe price restraint measures". Para 328: "London and South East passengers benefit disproportionately from Government support, about £16 per head of population in 1975 compared with £8 elsewhere in England and Wales". Paras 371 & 369: proposed a tax on employers with a specified minimum number of employees, as in some European countries, [making employers contribute to the peak costs which they create], and proposed a tax concession to users of public transport for travel to work. "The Treasury response was negative". Para 288: The National Bus Co complained of having "its entire capital treated as repayable debt - since there is no prospect of such repayment from profits, repayment instalments are met by taking out further loans at high interest rates, thus placing an increasing burden upon the company whatever level of efficiency is attained by management". (This was BR's position since 1948 and a major factor in its financial collapse. No Private Sector company is required to repay its entire share capital to shareholders, if a company collapses, shareholders get nothing); Para 90: makes productivity comparisons with foreign railways, (irrelevant as they operate under different criteria - Government should compare BR with UK companies which face similar economic and labour circumstances. Many will know from personal experience that many UK companies were overpricing, failing on quality and giving dissatisfaction.

Price Commission Report February 1978 [Fare increases]: Page 2 Para 11: The "Board should ensure divergence from average rates per mile for comparable journeys are kept within moderate limits", (so much for pricing freedom!). Page 3: dismisses conventional beliefs that fare increases lose business or that reductions would solve BR's problems. Para 15: "Past experience of resistance to price increases shows it is usually temporary". Para 16: "Over the past decade fares have been market oriented and the BRB estimates it produces 6-10% more revenue. Para 18: It is clear to us from the wide ranging studies made by both the Board and outside bodies that there is no prospect that general reductions in fares as distinct from the Boards practice of making selective reductions might increase revenue. Para 19: BR have successfully developed marketing techniques for this purpose" [filling empty off peak seats], (Had BR been allowed similar "freedom" from 1948, even with the reins which existed in 1978, there would have been no losses).

BR 'Facts and Figures' booklets 1978 and 1980, reveal that the index of BR fares was below the RPI from 1947 to 1972 - 26 consecutive years - by up to 20% in a year. (The loss represented by a fares policy disastrously enforced on BR could never be recovered. The extra interest paid on Government enforced loans was the final straw).

BRB 1981 Report: Fares held steady for a full year; Average increase of 9.5% applied from November 29th was over 2% below the annual rate of inflation.

Requiring the BTC to submit Charges Schemes caused delay in matching prices to costs in the first 14 years, whilst BR and LT remained chained to fares control in the London Area for the next 6 years. This gave the public an expectation that State owned railways could keep prices static - something that the private sector did not do. Instead of being grateful for the opportunity to pocket cash saved by fares declining in real value, when increases were sought, the public and their advocates sought to delay and reduce overdue increases. BTC was under pressure to hold prices down and avoid passing on the increases in costs which they faced, and to pay regard to social implications, which was the role of Government. Had BR been run independently, they would have demanded their overdue pricing freedom in

1946. Government experts and economists should have seen the dangers of their policies which were covertly subsidising passenger travel - notably commuters. Government were using taxpayers money to give commuters and others subsidies via the BR accounts. The honest policy would have been to allow commuters to treat their travel costs as tax deductible expenses - it would still come from the Exchequer. BR's practice of reducing some freight charges in the late 50's and early 60's to recover or retain traffic until modernisation could improve the service, was advanced as a reason for dismissing the complaint that Tribunal and Ministerial control of freight rates prevented pricing up. The theory misses the point - had Government given commercial freedom, equal investment, equal allocation of restricted materials and an independent identity to BR in 1948, BR would not have lost so much traffic to have had to resort to low prices to recover it. BR would have been able to build up essential reserves which were never achieved. Government gave BR's freight competitors more than a head start until 1962.

The effect of pricing restraint was such that if passenger fares alone had kept pace with the RPI, by 1982 BR would have earned, at 1991 prices, £8.7 billions more than they did, (see the table on page 34). It may be argued that sales resistance would have prevented any fares increase from yielding the full amount of the percentage increase. In fact, the Transport Tribunal thought the BTC was being unduly pessimistic in expecting a 1% loss of yield in some submissions. Deducting this percentage would still have left the net loss at £8.6 billions. When BR obtained freedom on fares after 1968 and began to price selectively to maximise revenue, independent reports (see above and Page 154), showed that sales resistance was short lived. Significantly, this evidence came to light when competition for passenger traffic was considerably greater than it had been in the earlier years. By 1989, the gross loss of passenger revenue arising from enforced under pricing, at 1991 prices, was down to £7.8 billions, due to the belated application of real price increases. Even so, as I have shown on Page 154, the scale of real industrial wage increases so outstripped the RPI, that comparable BR journeys required a smaller percentage of earnings in 1988 than in 1938. It requires little imagination to see what service improvements could have been provided from such an enormous sum, and that so called "subsidies", initially described as loans upon which interest had to be paid, would have been avoided. Had BR been permitted to price selectively and above the RPI as other industries were doing, the gain would have been far higher than £7.8 billions. Traffic losses would have been diminished or avoided, given pricing freedom and improved assets purchased from extra revenue. Additional business would have generated even more revenue. Without doubt, the £1 billion Government gained from railways in wartime should have been paid to the owners rather than to BR, but BR has a greater claim to it than the Government. At today's prices that sum would be worth about £150 billions, whilst the interest thereon is incalculable. UK Governments - and hence the taxpayer and general public - have had far more than 'a pound of flesh' from this country's railways.

In the table on page 34, the years to 1982 inclusive were calendar years, those after 1982 were fiscal years, hence 1983 refers to 1983/84, 1984 refers to 1984/85 and so on.

Year	Actual Average fare	Inflation linked Average fare	Actual Passenger Receipts #m	Inflation linked Receipts #m	Lost Revenue (in year) #m	Lost Revenue (in 1991) #m	Cum. Lost Revenue #m
1948	100	100.0	122.6	122.6	0.0	0.0	0.0
1949	93	103.8	114.0	127.2	13.2	205.2	205.2
1950	91	106.7	106.6	124.9	18.3	276.8	482.0
1951	89	119.4	107.0	143.5	36.5	493.3	975.3
1952	93	120.2	111.9	144.6	32.7	438.9	1,414.2
1953	96	122.1	114.8	146.0	31.2	412.3	1,826.5
1954	96	126.3	116.6	153.4	36.8	470.2	2,296.7
1955	100	134.1	118.1	158.4	40.3	484.8	2,781.5
1956	104	138.3	127.5	169.5	42.0	490.1	3,271.6
1957	106	144.7	138.9	189.6	50.7	565.3	3,836.9
1958	106	147.4	138.0	192.0	54.0	591.0	4,427.9
1959	108	147.4	140.0	191.1	51.1	559.2	4,987.1
1960	120	150.1	151.3	189.2	37.9	407.5	5,394.6
1961	129	156.7	157.5	191.3	33.8	348.0	5,742.6
1962	140	160.6	161.1	184.9	23.8	239.1	5,981.7
1963	141	163.6	161.8	187.8	26.0	256.4	6,238.1
1964	143	171.5	167.2	200.5	33.3	313.4	6,551.5
1965	159	179.3	173.5	195.7	22.2	199.8	6,751.3
1966	165	186.0	179.4	202.2	22.8	197.8	6,949.1
1967	177	190.5	179.7	193.4	13.7	116.0	7,065.1
1968	169	201.7	185.2	221.0	35.8	286.4	7,351.5
1969	190	211.3	205.3	228.3	23.0	175.6	7,527.1
1970	205	227.8	227.8	253.2	25.4	179.9	7,707.0
1971	238	248.4	261.0	272.4	11.4	74.1	7,781.1
1972	259	267.3	274.1	282.9	8.8	53.1	7,834.2
1973	274	295.7	297.3	320.9	23.6	128.8	7,963.0
1974	291	352.3	328.8	398.1	69.3	317.4	8,280.4
1975	390	440.1	428.8	483.9	55.1	202.0	8,482.4
1976	490	506.4	505.1	522.0	16.9	53.8	8,536.2
1977	559	567.9	593.4	602.8	9.4	26.7	8,562.9
1978	631	615.5	701.8	684.5	(17.3)	(45.4)	8,517.5
1979	690	721.5	799.7	836.2	36.5	81.6	8,599.1
1980	831	830.7	954.0	953.6	(0.4)	(0.8)	8,598.3
1981	919	930.8	1,022.8	1,035.9	13.1	22.7	8,621.0
1982	931	981.1	924.1	973.8	49.7	81.7	8,702.7
1983	1,041	1,033.2	1,149.5	1,140.9	(8.6)	(13.4)	8,689.3
1984	1,133	1,080.5	1,226.7	1,169.9	(56.8)	(84.8)	8,604.5
1985	1,207	1,142.1	1,331.1	1,259.5	(71.6)	(101.2)	8,503.3
1986	1,279	1,184.5	1,427.5	1,322.1	(105.4)	(143.6)	8,359.7
1987	1,345	1,228.3	1,603.5	1,464.4	(139.1)	(182.7)	8,177.0
1988	1,431	1,311.5	1,780.0	1,631.4	(148.6)	(182.8)	7,994.2
1989	1,569	1,412.6	1,882.7	1,695.0	(187.7)	(214.4)	7,779.8
					£262.8	£7,779.8	
					======	======	

MoT 1956 Paper "Proposals for Railways": "During the War, the railway system, its equipment, and rolling stock was subject to workloads well in excess of design and kept in use long after normal renewal dates". The BTC said "it was impossible to provide resources to maintain railways except to the very minimum to keep them running, whilst they were subjected to the increased strain imposed by heavy war traffic and wartime operating conditions". So far as normal wear and tear was concerned, the Government decreed that all wartime maintenance was to be charged to a control account on the basis of the average expended in 1935-6-7 allowing for the increased cost of carrying out the work during, [not after], the war - but not for the heavier wear and tear. In 1941, under the Second "Agreement" the Government established a Trust Fund into which was paid money chargeable to expenditure which would have been spent on maintenance had materials and labour been available. These Funds were not a Government gift, but part of the chargeable expenditure before the Government was left with £1 billion of profit and discounts. The Trust Funds were to be paid out at the end of the control period. By 31st December 1946, the Funds amounted to £147m plus interest of £5.26m. A report published in 1944, to mark the "Coming of Age of Railway Grouping" (the 21st anniversary of the enforced grouping of main line railways in 1923), shows that the Trust Fund had reached £92.25m by December 1942, and that this represented the cost "of more than one year's maintenance at current prices". The final total of £147m would, therefore, represent nearly two year's maintenance, a formidable backlog to arise from six years of Government control. Little wonder that the MoT said that "railways emerged from the war with most of their equipment out of date and all of it run down". Having sequestrated railways in 1939, the Government had a moral duty to return the infrastructure and assets to the state in which they found them. Had Government repaid the gratitude which Ministers voiced, (Page 7), they would have put railways into even better condition as a reward for its wartime efforts. Archaic Industrial methods, particularly in the Steel industry, many unchanged since the industrial revolution, led to the shortage of materials needed to renovate war torn railways.

Unsatisfactory standards are unquestionably a result of Government policy. To improve quality in any industry, capital, profit, and reserves are essential. Without them they die. BR didn't die, despite being denied these essential ingredients, but was kept on a minimal life support machine. Governments continually delude themselves that they can run industry but prevented the creation of reserves which would have given the birthplace of railways a system second to none. Having created losses by their policies, Government loaned sufficient to "balance the books" from 1956. Reserves cannot be created in that way. The phraseology of the 1947 Act - carried into other Acts - "pay their way taking one year with another" was absurdly dangerous and inadvisable. Its' meaning was unclear, even to experts (see Page 8), and produced opposition to price increases (which would have created reserves), in the hope that next year the sun may shine. Those who make detrimental comparisons between BR and other Railways overlook the different rules to which they work. For instance, on a study tour of Italian Railways, we were told that income and expenditure was not matched at any level. Their Ministry of Transport funded expenditure and receipts went direct to the Government. French Governments long ago decided that Railways would be subsidised as a policy, and changes of Government lead to no 'U' turns, as applies here even when the same Party remains in office.

BTC 1948 Report drew attention to the excessive wear and tear arising from minimum maintenance standards since 1939 (which had arisen because the Government abstracted around £1 billion - worth £150 billions today - from the Railways, whilst they had to operate a system being run into the ground by unprecedented traffic levels). The Report mentioned "Arrears of war damage, large numbers of temporary speed restrictions due to condition of track and bridges" which together with "Poor quality of locomotive coal causing loss of steam pressure and locomotive failures" had undermined standards of service. The UK Government gave priority to housing, and some other industries - notably the motor industry, which repaid them by losing its domestic market share and world position as an exporter. The BTC Report refers to the **Government Economic Survey** [Cmnd 7647] for 1949 which affected rail investment; Para 30: "The general level of investment which has been prescribed by the Government has been largely governed by the availablity of the principal controlled material - steel, and both allocation and delivery have been matters for grave concern to the BTC". The Summer service operated with 4000 fewer coaches than pre war - 3000 less in the fleet due to war damage losses etc., (including some sent abroad by the Government), plus 1000 more than prewar undergoing repairs after excessive wartime usage. To make up some of the shortfall 355 coaches which had been condemned had to be repaired and kept in service for 2-8 years. Due to a lower steel allocation, new rolling stock construction had to be cut back, "and this will apply in 1949 & 1950 also"; Para 111: "poor quality and uneconomical sizes of timber used in wagon repairs during and since the war placed a heavy burden on repair capacity. It will be years before the pre 1939 repair figures are achieved. Shortage of nuts and bolts impeded output throughout the year; Paras 111/2: on 1st January 1948, BR acquired through the Act 544,000 privately owned wagons, mostly over 40 years old and in poor condition. 55,000 were scrapped in 1948! 260,000 were repaired by BR and a further 87,000 by private wagon repairers. (544,000 - 55,000 scrapped - 347,000 repaired left only 26% fit for traffic. BTC was told by Government to buy these for £43m - a bad nationalisation bargain); Para 119: "Hopes of overtaking [war] arrears [of maintenance] within a short time were 'modified' by the Government White Paper on Capital Investment for 1948, that supplies of materials for the permanent way must be "reduced to current needs, about the same as prewar without overtaking arrears". Materials shortage especially, steel, timber and electrical cables governs the rate of tackling arrears; Paras 246/7 wagons Under & Awaiting Repair was 16.62% in September 1947, due to wartime material shortages and had been reduced to 9.8% by December 1948. The **Economic Survey** also stated "Arrears of track renewal were to be overtaken only to the extent necessary for safety" (prolonging speed restrictions, wasting money and helping competitors); "The shortage of passenger coaches was acute, 1949 will be the same as 1948".

BTC 1949 Report: heavily preoccupied with the task of acquiring road transport as prescribed in the 1947 Act; Para 23: At Government request, the BTC prepared forward estimates for expenditure - 1950: £100.2m, 1951: £114.8m, 1952: £123m. Government reduced these to £95m for 1950, rising to £100m in 1952. Subsequently, the figures were again reduced, and the repair of the permanent way was excluded, despite warnings that this would seriously impair efficiency. BTC powers to raise capital for investment were put in abeyance.

BTC 1950 Report, Para 51: Such projects as electrification are only practicable if capital resources are available. Public transport counts itself fortunate if the ration of capital expenditure allowed to it (by Government) is sufficient to patch and maintain existing apparatus, let alone permit introduction of large schemes of capital improvement; Para 54: Accounts are in balance, but there are no reserves to meet rising costs of replacing assets".

CTCC 1950 Report: for BR "to become more up to date requires substantial capital expenditure which it is hopeless to expect can be found out of revenue".

Cabinet Minutes, 12th March 1951, MoT stated: "Government refusal to allow Railways to carry out much of the Capital investment which they thought to be necessary had resulted in an accumulation of higher costs".

BTC 1951 Report refers to arrears of maintenance and the "sheer scale of this would take away resources from revenue earning tasks"; "Until BR can be assured of sufficient steel to carry out maintenance and renewals no return to prewar speeds is practicable; Only 96 bridges repaired, two thirds of the year's programme"; Para 3: the effect the shortage of steel was having on building new rolling stock : 340 locomotives built - 447 planned; 1923 coaches built - 2764 planned; 37796 wagons built - 45190 planned. Control on expenditure [including renewals and certain maintenance] exercised by Government has continued, in addition to control on supply of materials. Government had initially reduced the BTC investment requirement from £114m to £95-£100m, then further reduced it to £81.5m. The actual investment was £76.1m: the underspending was mainly due to material shortages.

The secret 1960 SAG papers show that in 1951, the Railway Executive had given six months notice to private wagon repair contractors at outstation depots that BR would cease to place wagons for repair. The contractors had appealed to the Government - BR withdrew the notice. The private repair companies described BR's policy of building new higher capacity coal wagons "as over wagonning, leading to the scrapping of thousands of wooden bodied wagons". (It is incredible that a policy to replace 19th century, life expired, wooden grease box wagons by steel wagons of 33-100% higher capacity could be seen in such a light. If this was the philosophy of UK industry, little wonder they lost a world lead in so many fields - see Page 129).

BTC 1952 Report refers again to steel shortage affecting replacement of rolling stock. Government allocated steel 20% below BR needs. During the first half of 1952 deliveries did not reach even the reduced allocation. Locomotive building was 67 short on the programme. BR was compelled to repair life expired carriages 40-50 years old. Since 1949 BR has spent £600,000 on such repairs, and is having to continue this wasteful practice. New coach construction fell short by 920 [1923 planned], and wagons 9200 short [37,796 planned]. Government had nationalised 544,000 old wagons with grease lubricated axle boxes which could only run at low speeds, would often run hot and sometimes catch fire; Government control on investment in 1952 limited to £76.6m for Railways and £7.2m for LT. [in 1949, Government had reduced BTC's planned £123m for 1952 to £100m, and now it was less than £84m despite inflation]; Para 34: There are still no reserves, (Not surprising, in view of Tribunal and Government control of prices and Government interference in wages which were about 66% of total costs).

BTC 1953 Report, Para 125: referring to arrears of development, "explanation lies in the effect of past restrictions and shortages of materials. Position is far more serious in relation to Railways than in Road Transport, not only as regards rolling stock but civil engineering works also, on BR the arrears of maintenance due to intensive use made of Railways during the war have hardly yet been made good; Para 126: Discouraging and disruptive effects of constantly changing limits upon capital investment - all combined to hinder progress. Still having to "make do and mend". Accumulated arrears of passenger coach building: 3600, wagon building: 12,000 short [29%] and locomotive building 39% short. Steel shortage is the cause".

BTC 1954 Report, Page 8: "although progress on repairs is at highest level since the war, BR are still having to keep old vehicles in use; Page 31: war arrears were still not cleared by the end of 1953; Para 120: A condition to undertaking this bold plan [1955 Modernisation] is that the enterprise must not be allowed to get into a position of irredeemable balance meantime.

BTC 1955 Report, Para 102: "despite steel shortages, wagon output included 41,739 16ton wagons. This will permit the withdrawal of 87,300 [13ton capacity] grease box wagons [formerly privately owned].

The Modernisation & Re-equipment of BR (dated December 1954, but known as the 1955 Plan), drawn up with Government blessing, envisaged an expenditure of £1240m over 15 years - to be funded by the BTC, not the Government. The Plan would improve track and signalling to enable speeds "of at least 100mph" to be achieved - well ahead of world standards, ('experts' often comment on prewar test trains which achieved 100mph+, over short distances - the Plan would provide general service trains of that speed). Freight services would be improved and depots modernised. Some lines would be electrified, and others would have diesel traction. Office systems would be modernised. A return of £85m pa was forecast, which must be seen alongside prevailing interest rates, the probability that BR prices would continue to be held down, whilst suppliers' prices would not, and the need to reverse past asset dereliction due to Government policy. This Plan should have been funded directly by the Government to redress its neglect during the War, also in acknowledgement of the part played by railways in the war effort and the vast amount the State gained, (see Page 5 - "Wartime control"). The word "Re-equipment" was particularly significant - referring to a long overdue re-equipment after the Government had nationalised "a worn out bag of assets" (the view of Dr.Hugh Dalton, Chancellor of the Exchequer), with which BR were to provide a service. The Plan envisaged more line closures. Since the Government bound BR into a constrictive closure procedure, directed retention of loss making lines on social grounds and controlled prices, they could not reasonably expect a better return. (At a Cabinet meeting on 22nd April 1952, Prime Minister Winston Churchill said that "he did not consider that the railways should be obliged to recover from revenue all their costs including capital invested in them". This must have had a bearing on the acceptance by the Government of the Plan). On 21st January, 1955 the Cabinet "was cautious, the Railway future was doubtful, roads and aircraft would take over much of the rail traffic. On the other hand, it was pointed out that railways had been starved of capital for many years".

The ink was barely dry on the Plan before Goverment reduced the investment. The "Plan" was widely seen as being beneficial to UK industry, both in terms of regeneration of production and as a "shop window for exports" - UK suppliers having long complained of a lack of opportunity to prove their products in the home market. In July 1960, British Insulated Callenders Cables placed an advertisement in the Times: "The modernisation of BR has given British manufacturers valuable practical experience in the most up to date forms of traction and is assisting them to secure export orders in the face of intensive competition". BR was criticised for buying British diesel locomotives because some did not live up to expectations. No word of criticism was levelled against those whose product was unequal to the task. Whilst main line electrification was more costly than dieselisation, BTC would be influenced by experience that electric traction had already been proved reliable, (subsequent experience revealed that diesel traction had not reached similar levels of reliability in the UK). BTC Minutes reveal that they also preferred electric traction, because its use of home produced fuel would help the balance of payments problem.

MoT White Paper "Proposals for Railways" 1956, Para 13: BTC "have ... inherited the position in which they find themselves. For 30 years railways have been unable to undertake ... modernisation, or keep up an adequate programme of replacement .... owing to the challenge of road transport. During the war .... impossible to provide resources for maintenance except to the very minimum extent ... increased strain of heavy war traffic .... emerged from war with equipment out of date and all of it run down". Para

20: "in the interest of national economy, BTC were asked at the start of 1956 to reduce capital investment by 15%." also "It will take time to overtake decades of under investment". (The "challenge of road transport" was capable of being fought by BR but Government policies had prevented that). Included in this **White Paper** was a Memorandum from the **BTC**, Para 5: "The controls over capital investment have prevented the replacement of out of date rolling stock, buildings and equipment, and have led to excessive maintenance costs", (waste arises from trying to keep clapped out equipment in service). "Competitors had up to date equipment". Para 11: "It is significant that most Western European nations gave priority to railway reconstruction in their post war plans".

Speaking to the **Royal United Services Institution**, February 1956, the BTC Chairman said that BR "are not working at full efficiency, mainly because they have been prevented from keeping equipment up to date". With this "they are expected to accept the skimmed milk, while others walk off with the cream of the traffic. BR are expected to carry awkward consignments for remote destinations at standard charges, while those for easily accessible destinations are carried by firm's own road transport", (due to 24 years of Government inertia on freight transport rates - see Page 60).

BTC 1957 Report, Para 167: "A further contribution to the containing of inflation has been the restriction on investment, although these have damaged the railways' commercial position. Here again, railway transport and the roads, but not road vehicles, have since the war borne the brunt of the Government restrictions imposed because of shortage of resources and materials, particularly steel".

BTC 1959 Report, Para 10: "Government debated the Reappraisal of the Modernisation Plan accepting a shortfall due to circumstances outside BTC control, (the only time I have read anyone conceding that could happen - not admitting of course within whose control it had been for 11 years!), and said the Plan would be speeded up, (but not for long!)

BTC 1960 Report, Para 10: Government slowed down the Modernisation Plan; Para 82: "The Select Committee said that the Plan is a whole and neither physical benefits nor financial results can be judged in isolation until all has been completed".

Select Committee on BR, March 1961, Para 14, the BTC "are asked to forecast investment for three years ahead - but budgets beyond the first year were not given approval, and the BTC has been unable to forward plan [on a basis] that future requirements will be met." (This is priceless, Government ask for plans, which cost time and money to prepare, and then neither approve nor reject them. A few years later BR were being asked for 20 year plans, when five year plans were only accepted for three weeks). In 1960 the MoT asked to see all schemes over £½m before they were authorised which meant that the Railways Regional Area Board, the Works & Equipment Committee, the BTC itself and then the MoT were considering each scheme. It is surprising, therefore, that the representative of the MoT told the Select Committee "we have no technical experts at all - and could not check what they [BR] were proposing to do technically".

BRB 1966 Report, Para 27: "The political decision not to proceed with the full implementation of the 1962 Act has already been taken, although the new Act [1968 Act] will not be effective until 1969.

BRB 1968 Report, Para 6: "the inherent capabilities of rail are not achieved due to the frequently changing statutory position and different Government views on integration or competition".

MoT Paper "Transport in London", 1968, page 34, Para 23: "It is unlikely that any community, even a prosperous urban one, would be willing to pay for a service so adequate that hardly anyone ever complained"; (Despite this, the MoT says four pages later): "the concepts of viability and adequacy of service are irreconcilable, though they remain desirable objectives"!

BRB 1971 Report, Para 6.12: BR set up a leasing arrangement so that much needed rolling stock could be obtained over a five year period and paid for from revenue rather than capital, (an innovative concept for BR, practised in the Private Sector). By this rolling stock built by BR Workshops was sold to Leasing companies for use by BR. BRB 1972 Report: £14m worth of rolling stock sold to leasing companies; BRB 1973 Report: £16.9m worth of stock sold to leasing companies; BRB 1974 Report: no further assets can be taken under these arrangements - the Government had terminated the practice. (Such arrangements were operated by companies which used wagons on BR lines which they had leased in exactly the same way. So much for commercial freedom on BR. Perhaps a Privatised BR will will be allowed to revive the concept. In July 1956, the MoT had told Parliament that "by applying the ordinary principles of enlightened private enterprise, I am hopeful that we are going to show how they [BR] can make a profit", (see Page 22). Leasing assets is a common Private Sector practice - but when BR applied this ordinary principle of the Private Sector, they were soon stopped).

BRB 1973 Report: "Within three weeks of an announcement that investment in BR for five years would total £891m, a 20% reduction in investment was imposed as part of a cutback in the public sector".

BRB 1975 Report, page 3: "October 1975 - MoT confirmed reduction in investment levels. This is an explicit abandonment of the interim rail strategy propounded by the Board in the December 1972 Rail Policy Review to the MoT which formed the basis for the 1974 Act. No alternative strategy was agreed with the Government"; Page 4: "Public Expenditure Paper [Cmnd 6393] : Investment is pegged in real terms 30% below the level accepted by the Government as recently as 1973".

Transport Policy Document 1976, Para 1.8: The Government have "decided to limit the growth of public expenditure in the interests of higher exports and investment generally, requiring a painful re-appraisal of the priority accorded to transport against the competing claims of housing, education and the social services" - (it sounded like this is going to hurt me more than it hurts you. How reducing transport expenditure helps exports was not explained, all goods - export or domestic - require transport); Paras 7.23 & 7.24 "investment options are: track & signalling, product improvement, electrification, slower introduction of HST and APT, a less comfortable and slower service. Only the BRB have the detailed knowledge necessary to choose between the various relevant factors, but it will be open to Government in the light of the outcome of the present consultations to give broad guidance between, for example, freight and inter city; or between manpower saving investment and higher quality rolling stock", (the BRB have the expertise, but the Government will decide anyway!).

Report of the Select Committee, 1977, Para 24: individual schemes are scrutinised and appraised by the DoT from a list of major projects submitted by BR, normally schemes costing less than £2m are not scrutinised; (all were vetted at three levels on BR); Para 386: "The investment criteria used by the MoT in approving schemes was open to question. On 8th November 1976 the Department announced approval of a scheme to electrify Bedford - St.Pancras - Moorgate at a cost of £80m, but no rate of return was specified, whilst they had not approved the Picc-Vic scheme in Manchester which claimed a 12% return and was above the minimum level required"; Para 387: "The Bedford

Scheme was with the DoT for over a year. BR and other witnesses complained of delays in approvals which prevented BR taking advantage of investment opportunities. This would appear particularly to be the case in highly competitive areas such as roll-on, roll-off shipping and hovercraft operation. They [BR] also suggest that one reason for the delay in entry into service of the HST on the Western region was the time taken by the MoT to authorise the scheme - 15 months"; Para 47: criticises a lack of high speed trains (BR had more daily 100mph trains than any country and it is the residents of Kent who have opposed TGV through their backyard); Para 406: "BR have placed an order for 60 Class 56 locos, 30 in Romania. The constraint in Britain appeared to be the difficulty of getting design facilities. Even allowing for the unsatisfactory state of the British Engineering Industry, it seems surprising that even the task of adapting existing design work could not be completed here"; Para 264: "new freight facilities applied for by private sector companies under the 1974 Act [to transfer freight from road to rail] are being delayed or rejected by Local Authorities on enviromental grounds" [eg 18 schemes in the Western Region's London Division]; Para 55: "Demand forecasting for freight is much more difficult than for passenger traffic" (MoT 1963 Paper, "Transport Needs of GB in the next 20 years", Para 33: passenger forecasting is more difficult than freight). The Committee recommended that the DoT should have a Transport Policy Unit strengthened by staff with practical expertise in transport planning and management, (confirming a lack of expertise).

Price Commission, February 1978, page 8, Para 1.25: called for "a 20 year time scale of freight strategy to achieve sustained viability", (as industry did not plan so far ahead whence would BR get the data? Given such a plan, for how long would Government accept it - 3 weeks?).

BRB 1981 Report, page 7: "Our 1981 Corporate Plan for 1982/86 had to be revised in December [1981] following a decision by the Government to fix our External Financing Limit at the same level for the next three years". (Three years earlier there was a call for a 20 year strategy!).

CTCC 1981 Report refers to the "London Evening Standard" survey: "passengers are not prepared to pay now to improve quality of service nor to accept lower standards for stabilised or reduced fares". Evidently passengers want what they cannot get from the Private Sector - improved quality at lower prices. In the past they were not even prepared to pay to cover working expenses, much less provide for depreciation and investment.

Investment in improving BR infrastructure, unlike roads, required financial justification:
* by cost reductions in staff or maintenance savings,
* by funds arising from road improvement schemes which involved the purchase of BR land and rerouting of tracks,
* from quantified new revenue.
There were instances of replacements of infrastructure on Grant Aided lines, without a commercial return, but these, were usually like for like, and not improvements. Even these had to be justified within BR because of expenditure limits imposed by the Government. Most Grant Aided routes had low traffic volumes and were not in competition with road transport, (See Chapter 1, Part IV - BR had to subsidise buses when lines were closed proving a lack of business potential). On routes where BR was in competition with road, I can recall no instance of investment without financial justification. Government missed a golden opportunity for using social criteria to justify rail improvements on the North Wales Coast which local authorities asked to be electrified, but which BR could not justify financially. The cost would have been less than the cost of the Conway estuary tunnel, which was but a small part of the upgrading of the A55.

Post war Britain seems to believe that closures were a new concept. In his "Review of Railway Developments, 1928-38" to the Railway Rates Tribunal on 14th June 1939, Sir Wm Wood, Vice President of the LMSR, stated that "In the 11 years, 235 miles of track and 223 stations have been closed to all traffic and 951 miles and 412 stations to passenger traffic only". Post war opposition to closures received political support, locally and nationally, causing costly delays to essential rationalisation. (see also Pages 97-99).

The 1947 Act made no reference to a special procedure for railway closures. The Act specified procedures in respect of proposed abandonment of canals, and intended cessation of any regular road goods transport service. The Act stated in Sec.2 [7]: that the BTC may dispose of any part of the undertaking which in their opinion is not required by them for the discharge of their duties under the Act. It empowered them under Sec.2 [2] to do all things which in their opinion are necessary to facilitate the proper carrying on of the business of the BTC. Since railway companies had been closing lines to reduce losses, it was reasonable to assume that the practice would continue, since road competition was set to increase. Hence, those concerned with passing the Act should have included provision for public hearings by Consultative Committees if that was their intention. Unfortunately, the 1947 Act gave Consultative Committees wide powers "to consider any matter". The 1953 Act which was intended to "give BR its freedom" (see Pages 9 & 20), did not address this growing problem. The 1962 Act reduced, but did not eliminate the involvement of Consultative Committees in this aspect of BR's commercial policy. What began as the BTC responding to a CTCC request to consider one closure, soon expanded with costly consequences.

BTC 1949 Report, Para 196: A standard procedure has been introduced of **advising** Local Authorities before closures of lines, to take account of any representation they may make before a final decision is made, (simply a matter of good Public Relations).

BTC 1950 Report, Para 11: "The closing of uneconomic branch railways has the general support of the CTCC; Para 30: BTC are criticised for not closing a large number of branch and secondary lines, yet when after careful study a decision is reached that a line should be closed, local opposition is well organised and strong protests are made. It is noteworthy that those who protest are never able to offer a solution to the problem of securing enough traffic".

CTCC 1950 Report records that they "are glad to note the BTC are closing unremunerative branch lines; but they asked BTC to postpone closure of the East Kent line pending investigation by the CTCC".

BTC 1951 Report, Para 11: BTC and Railway Executive satisfy themselves as to alternatives [before withdrawing services]. With the setting up of the Area Committees [TUCC's], all important proposals are now referred to them for their views, (This did not seem to envisage public hearings and long delays would follow, and it referred to 'important' proposals. Subsequently, they were to have all cases put to them. **BTC Minutes** 29th May record for the first time "Chairmen of TUCC's to be consulted in certain cases"). The BTC could not have foreseen that this would lead to them subsidising privately owned bus companies to carry passengers displaced from closed branches until 1968. It was analogous to a corner shop, closed by the opening of a hypermarket, having to subsidise a competitor to serve former customers).

CTCC 1952 Report, Para 7: The CTCC called for more BR information to justify each closure. (No other business had to justify closure decisions).

The following sample of closure cases illustrate the nature of the problem:

CTCC 1953 Report:
* Isle of Wight lines, hardly used for nine months each year, were losing £0.27m pa. The 38 objectors briefed a QC (the first time this practice was adopted), extending to four days, the TUCC public hearing, which was followed by an "exhaustive inquiry". The TUCC recommended closing the Newport-Freshwater line, keeping Cowes-Newport-Sandown for two years, closing Whippingham and Wootton stations, but were undecided on the 2¾mile Brading-Bembridge line, which had only one sixth of the passenger volume of competing bus services operating over a shorter route than the railway. The CTCC supported the TUCC recommendations and in addition recommended that the Brading-Bembridge line be closed. They were "surprised by the unwillingness of the County Council to consider improving the Island's roads as it seemed that it would be advantageous to have up to date facilities for the progressively increasing number of holiday visitors who provide a principal source of revenue to the Island. Road improvements were overdue and should be undertaken without delay. Fares should be increased on the Island to reduce or eliminate the loss, but this required special legisaltion as the present maximum charges would be inadequate to permit the raising of fares to an economic level, which would be justified". (The inadequacy of fares to cover costs on this Island should have been a clear pointer to inadequacy of fares to do likewise on the national scene).
* The Wivenhoe - Brightlingsea line, losing £8000 pa, was cut by sea storms, so the TUCC said it was not the fault of residents (it wasn't BR's fault either). The TUCC considered whether "we should recommmend an additional expenditure of £4500 for repairing the line, which we were satisified could only be operated at a substantial loss. There was no justification, but it would be reasonable for rail facilities to be restored as soon as possible and kept open for three years and that the road system should be brought up to date". They recommended reinstatment for three years at a cost of £4500 capital plus costs of £8000 pa. The CTCC concurred. (10 years later, it was listed for closure under the Beeching Plan - see Page 47).
* The Woodall Jcn - Horncastle line was poorly used: 21 passengers per train, and closure would save £6300 in wages alone. Objectors agreed residents had done little to support their case by using the trains. The TUCC recommended keeping the line, but the CTCC disagreed. BR had proposed it for closure in July 1952, it did not close until September 1954.

CTCC 1954 Report: "there is rarely sufficient traffic to provide both road and rail services with an economic return where branch traffic is light and railway stations happen, for historical reasons, to be inconveniently situated". (The "historical reasons" were usually that lines had been laid remotely from towns and villages because of the 19th Century NIMBY factor). Para 12: In no cases are withdrawals of unremunerative services recommended unless suitable alternative road facilities are available or will be made available (invariably at BR cost).

BTC 1954 Report: "Only limited progress during the year in freeing the undertaking from the heavy burden of uneconomic categories of passenger services"; Para 18: "A survey of train services clearly shows many slow and stopping services fail to cover direct costs by many millions of pounds pa, there is no remedy except withdrawal and substitution of road services. Local opposition to this is still very great". Para 182: "In progressing closures BR have to ensure that alternative road services are available or could be made available".

BTC 1955 Report, Para 9: "the 1954 Report mentioned that since the TUCC's were set up they had examined 102 closure schemes with economies of £0.9m derived. Since then a further 28 schemes had secured economies of £0.53m".

"Use of Lightweight Units on loss making lines as an alternative to closure were constrained by safety requirements and many stations are a long way from the nearest community" [CTCC agreed]; Paras 10/11: "Delay in obtaining MoT approval to closures recommended by TUCC's and CTCC widened the gap by £8m".

BTC 1956 Report, Para 39: CTCC/TUCC's accepted that DMU's would not have turned loss into profit on lines already closed.

Addressing the **Royal United Services Institution** in February 1956, the BTC Chairman said "These local and stopping services represent a loss to the Commission of many millions of pounds a year. In the make up of our annual deficit no one seems to care very much about these losses; it is taken for granted (by the Government and Public) that they should be made good out of our earnings on other services, though for myself I confess I cannot see the justification for such cross subsidies." (Had BR not been directed by the MoT to keep loss making services and delayed in closing others, the money used to subsidise them would have improved other services competing with road). He said the time had come to "concentrate on express and suburban passenger routes, the middle and long distance hauls of full wagon load freight, yielding an excellent return for the capital employed". (Six years before Beeching).

BTC Minutes, March 1956: MoT requested to direct TUCC's to expedite closure proposals and curtail requests for additional data where the closure case was clear. He responded in April that he had done so. It was not until a further approach to the MoT in 1958 that the BTC reported an improvement.

British Transport Review, April 1956, page 58: "We are running passenger trains whose costs are more than five times receipts, so that if we halved costs and doubled receipts, they would still lose money; Page 64: the Licensing Authorities would not permit BTC buses to replace trains on a route on which the BTC buses did not already operate".

MoT Paper "Proposals for Railways", 1956, BTC Memorandum, Para 50: closing loss making services was an essential part of the Modernisation Plan.

CTCC 1957 Report, Para 16: there are services which, however well modernised, will never pay in any circumstances at all. There is a tendency to think that all services can and should be dieselised or electrified forthwith, but the magnitude of capital cost is not generally realised. The Report referred to closure of the 'Bluebell line' [Lewes - East Grinstead] "which BR's Southern Region had never intended to electrify, as it was too expensive, and there was no traffic potential". Objectors were represented by a QC and hence, so were BR. Ten members of the public appeared personally and eleven objectors had written, (if this was the scale of use, little wonder the line lost money). A special 36 page **CTCC Report in 1958** on the closure included 28 pages of detailed financial data from BR, and revealed that nine members of the CTCC, (which seems excessive) 'took part' in the Public Inquiry on 9,10,11th October 1957 and agreed the report on 10th December. The MoT had directed the CTCC to hold an Inquiry on 13th May (BR had concluded in 1953 that the line was irretrievably unremunerative - it was closed in June 1955). In August 1956, BR had to reopen the line when an objector pointed out that the original Act of Parliament specified that closure could only take place with the sanction of Parliament. Savings were assessed in 1953 at £67,936 gross, net £59,736, plus avoidance of renewals. BR said losses had increased since 1953 which in view of inflation was indisputable, but the CTCC were critical that "no estimates [of the increase] were submitted". The objectors case was that losses were greater than they need have been, and could be reduced (not eliminated) and "it was

44

assumed that a line of this kind was never intended to pay for itself". (It is inconceivable that shareholders built any line with this objective. Obviously those who promoted this line, expected it to pay, if it didn't they would have lost their investment. Presumably users in 1955 expected travellers elsewhere to subsidise them). Objectors claimed that Zonal C&D services for small packages were not as good as a rail service (proving that they did not understand the concept - it was speeding transits and reducing costs. Zonal vehicles took packages direct to main railheads instead of local depots, expediting transits by 24 hours at each end). BR estimated costs of a new DMU service at £45,000 capital plus £40,000 pa, there being no diesels in the area, maintenance would be costly. The CTCC knew that DMU's were not turning loss into profit on many loss making lines and agreed that they were not a solution, but argued that the 75 year old station buildings were adequate (attitudes changed in later years), to dismiss needs for renewal costs. CTCC said that as the BTC had no depreciation fund, it was unreasonable to allow for renewals and depreciation, (but Government had prevented creation of reserves and from 1956 was making up losses from taxes. Renewals cost money whatever paper transactions may show. What would be used instead of money to renew the trains? Perhaps they thought all trains would give timely and simultaneous warning of their final demise giving BR time to recommence a third submission for closure). The line closed for the second time in March 1958, after further avoidable losses.

BTC 1957 Report, Para 20: TUCC's supported closure of ten branch lines and sixty stations, (mostly remote from communities), e.g., Merthyr-Abergavenny: eleven Local Authorities, seven public bodies and 1125 residents objected causing a long delay before the £59,000 pa savings were achieved. The TUCC listened to deputations, considered the matter at four meetings in five months, inspected the line, dealt in detail with every objection and finally agreed unanimously with the BTC proposal.

BTC Minutes, December 1958: "again seeking alleviation of the closure procedure from the MoT".

BTC 1958 Report, Para 8: In 1958, TUCC's approved 236 closure schemes: with savings of £0.9m [1957: 70 schemes: £0.14m] "The average time to deal with each case was 9-10 months, but has now been reduced to 8-10 weeks." (by 1965, BR were again complaining of three year delays); Para 9: the largest single proposal for closure was the 189 mile M&GN with a minimum saving £640,000, submitted September. There were objections from 51 Local Authorities - County to Parish, Chambers of Trade & Commerce, Local Authority Associations, individuals and private firms. By mid November, the TUCC had approved closure, and on 25th November the CTCC considered and confirmed closure, all in ten weeks, (10 weeks losses would be £0.12m, with further losses for the time preparing papers for a hearing and the time taken by the MoT to authorise closure). The line closed 28th February 1959.

BTC 1959 Report, Para 11: 60 TUCC meetings dealt with 49 withdrawals or reductions of facilities and 230 individual station closures saving £0.86m.

CTCC told SAG that by June 1960, "of 919 closure proposals submitted to them by the BTC, 521 were unopposed, 25 had been rejected (almost certainly pursued again in the Beeching Plan), whilst 55 were 'modified'"; (Even unopposed closures incurred delay and avoidable losses).

BTC 1961 Report, Para 13: early railway development led to "a dense network to minimise horse transport; even then there was excessive construction and many services did not pay. Stations were serving a radius of 2½ miles; Para 19: Stopping passenger services produce almost 50% of the loss for 10% of the revenue"; Para 22: If such services were discontinued at small

45

stations it would save £75m pa; (Government did not act quickly to make savings – all schemes had to go through the time and money consuming closure procedure).

CTCC 1961 Report – proposed closures considered :
* Oxford – Witney – Fairford: "Seven of the eleven stations are in the depths of the country, some distance from the towns or villages whose names they bear, but have never properly served";
* Barnard Castle – Penrith: withdrawal of passenger and rerouting of freight trains. Two TUCC's considered it on twelve occasions and CTCC on four occasions over two years. Objectors claimed that rerouting freight was not in the best interests of customers. Major freight customers said they were satisfied with the rerouting !
* Westerham branch – 4½miles long, used by 167 passengers; TUCC considered it "at great length in 1960" and recommended closure, but CTCC put it back to TUCC to reconsider and they changed their minds. CTCC supported, but MoT decided to close – the first time the MoT had ignored a CTCC recommendation.
* Colne Valley Line – TUCC "faced with more objectors than used the line" recommended deferring consideration for 2-3 years to await the effect of main line electrification. CTCC disagreed as the main station in Colchester was not in the town centre, but the bus station was. "The number of rail passengers was never very high and has halved in the last 20 years".

BTC 1962 Report: "From September 1st to the year end, 18 'hardship' closure cases were put to the MoT by TUCC's, who decided that 14 had little or no hardship [BR must subsidise buses in three cases], four with severe hardship were to remain open"; Para 21: "Since 1954, 44 bus services were subsidised by BR as a condition of closure", (Government wanted the public to have buses at the taxpayers expense, but concealed the cost in BR losses); "Bus services are reviewed annually, eight have been discontinued, since it is not justified to support them in perpetuity because the area once had a train service. (Withdrawal of these bus services caused criticism of BR!). Savings on schemes subject to a bus subsidy were £1.5m less subsidies of £86,000"; Para 22: "CTCC are interested in converting stations to unstaffed halts".

CTCC 1963 Report: "We see no reason why station buildings not required for other purposes should not be demolished, let or sold".

BRB 1963 Report, para 4: "a third of the system carries only 1% of rail traffic". (This should have changed attitudes on closures, but didn't. One reason for keeping unprofitable lines is strategic – Defence of the Realm – and is a matter for Governments to fund, the other reason is Social and should be for local authorities to fund, as they do for buses); Para 130: "Bus services operated in lieu of closed rail routes were subsidised in 1963 by £92,000".

In July 1963, when the Haltwhistle-Alston line was considered for closure, objectors stated that all roads were blocked in the previous winter's freeze-up for weeks, and the line was the only means of communication; bread was taken daily to the snowbound villages. (This was a not uncommon basis for objecting to closure of loss making lines. Spring and bad memories quickly ended support for the line, until closure was threatened).

In September 1963, 15 members of the TUCC (which seemed excessive), held a Public Inquiry into the proposed closure of the Ringwood line [Brockenhurst – Bournemouth], and Fordingbridge line [Salisbury – West Moors]. There were 60 people present, including the TUCC, BR representatives, journalists and "a strong team from Dorset CC". After lunch, attendance fell to 30. A petition signed by 900 people had been submitted from Wimbourne, which contrasted sharply with an average of 59 people using the station each day!

In 1963, the Brightlingsea-Wivenhoe line was again being considered for closure, after BR had been compelled to reopen it, when it was severed by sea storms, (Page 43). Objectors said that shipyard workers travelling to Wivenhoe would have to pay an extra one shilling per day (5p) by bus - so much for high rail fares; had fares kept pace with inflation, many lines could have been kept open. Users wanted to 'have the penny and the bun'.

BRB 1964 Report, para 150: MoT refusal to agree to closures cost BR £1.5m in 1964, plus the realisation of land value and other assets which could have been made available for disposal or use elsewhere.

CTCC 1965 Report mentions a line in Yorkshire which was severed to avoid heavy engineering costs. BR had to provide a bus link for the severed section and then submit it for closure. (This further proves BR interest in the cost of assets contrary to media opinion).

BRB 1965 Report, Para 16: refers to "The protracted procedure for withdrawing loss making services; 400 had been called for in the 1963 Reshaping Plan and others added since. At the end of 1965, 275 cases had been decided, and 60 were awaiting MoT approval. For some closures recently announced, the procedure took about three years. During 1965, two further steps were added. The MoT now scrutinises all proposals before statutory announcement to the public is begun. All proposals are [also] referred to the new Regional Economic Planning Councils and Boards. These two steps add still further to the length of time proposals have to await a decision. Others must await the results of various provincial conurbation studies initiated by the MoT during the year. Closure cases outstanding at the end of 1965 involve losses of £7m pa. Para 18: Withdrawal of some services which were approved for closure were delayed to establish bus services which the MoT required as a condition of closure. Para 122: five train services, approved for closure in July 1965, were still awaiting provision of Licences to Road operators [when the BRB 1965 Report was published 12 months later] - one depended on road improvements first being carried out! In some cases this resulted in indefinite postponement. These [delays] cost the Board £1m pa. Subsidies to buses were running at £350,000 pa; Para 19: From the Reshaping Plan [1963] to the end of 1965 consent on 21 lines, 6 parts of lines and 3 stations had been refused, continuing a loss of £2m pa. Para 20: The work involved in preparing submissions and progressing them absorbs considerable management effort which could be directed at positive measures to improve efficiency and reduce costs of the Board's main services.

Government White Paper "Transport Policy" 1966: "There are services which have little or no prospect of becoming directly remunerative - on the basis of revenue from users"; Para 21: each closure proposal "will go through the normal procedures, including consultation with the Regional Economic Planning Councils." (which played no part before 1965. Thus we had, TUCC's, Economic Councils, MoT, and Treasury involved) Para 25: "BRB had refrained from proposing some commuter and cross country services for closure because of their social and economic importance"; (Having been prevented from closing lines with strong cases, BR knew a dead horse when it saw one!).

BRB 1966 Report, "in 1966, the MoT approved 25 of 92 proposals put to him, after public hearings. He did not approve 26, or did so in part only. Losses of £3m pa were incurred on services where the MoT refused consent, and BRB also paid £0.5m in subsidies to bus companies as ordered by the MoT as a condition of closure."

MoT Railway Policy Review, 1967, Para 4: BRB cannot be expected to break even if "accounts are burdened with losses on socially necessary lines for which they are refused permission to close."; Para 8: "The time has come to face this fact squarely: the services which require long term assistance will be identified and separately costed so that a conscious decision can be made whether the social benefit obtained from the maintenance of a particular service is sufficient to justify the cost of continuing it; the MoT not the BRB will decide". (after 20 years! The MoT, not BR, had taken decisions on closures throughout that period). "The Ministry was already making a start on the work". (Beeching made a list 4 years earlier); Where the MoT decides against a grant, BRB may submit an application to close". (Events proved that a Grant would not be made until the closure case was refused, following the usual TUCC hearing and other delays, leaving BR with considerable losses). Para 9: "Best estimate of grants is £40m in 1969, £35m in 1974"; (this implied agreeing to closures). Page 21: "Payments to bus operators for services provided as a condition to withdrawal of rail services cost BR £500,000 in 1966. (No justification existed for inflating BR losses in this way).

BRB 1968 Report, Para 32: at the beginning of 1968, 51 cases were awaiting a decision, whilst a further 34 were submitted in 1968 – making a total of 85. Of the 34 cases, the Government had withheld Grant Aid on 10 services, (this is astonishing – having introduced the concept of Grants for loss making lines which BR were not allowed to close, here was the MoT refusing Grants on such lines. Most of us at the sharp end had believed that the purpose of Grants under the 1968 Act was to relieve BR of an unjust burden, and "to be quick about it"). By the end of the year, 52 cases were still awaiting decision by the TUCC or MoT. Page 31, Para 10: Subsidies to bus operators for the provision of road services in substitution for rail passenger services cost BR £1m in 1968.

BRB 1969 Report, Para 4.26: At the end of 1968, 47 passenger services were under consideration for closure; by the end of 1969, the MoT had reprieved sixteen closures, authorised eighteen and was undecided on thirteen. (The pace of dealing with closures was appallingly slow).

Transport Consultation Document 1976, Para 7.9: "BR have found it necessary to take some unpopular measures – in 1975 they cut the level of some under used services – weekends and closing on Boxing Day." (In 1947, as a Junior Booking Office Clerk at Rotherham, I noticed that the revenue on Christmas Day did not pay the wages of a much reduced station staff, much less all other costs, even when there were few alternatives, yet there was an uproar when BR closed on that Day. Boxing Day eventually became as quiet as Christmas Day had been, due to longer industrial breaks and the growth of car ownership, but complaints followed closure).

CTCC 1991 Report: expresses concern that MoT has not directed BR not to make pre-emptive cost saving closures as this was creating a dangerous precedent – quite so – they would be acting like Private Sector companies, by applying one of those "principles of private enterprise" which the MoT was advocating in 1956, (see Page 22).

48

In stark contrast to Government treatment of BR was their attitude towards
BR's competitors.   In 1956 the MoT asked the BTC to help ease city
congestion by special measures to attract motorists, no funds were offered
for longer trains or stations, carparks, assets or staff; and 1956 was the
year in which the MoT had "requested BR not to increase fares".   In 1957, he
went further asking that BR assist competitors by increasing parking space
in central London when parking meters reduced street parking! No funds were
promised for deploying valuable land to such a self defeating purpose.   BR
would have to borrow from the Government whose policies had created BR
deficits of over £50m in both 1956 and 1957.   The BTC Minutes in November
1957, curtly record that "this is not in the BTC interest".

In March and April 1952, the Cabinet was deciding whether BR should be
"free" to implement the watered down fares increases which the Tribunal had
authorised under its statutory powers.   Without justification, Government
asked the CTCC to reconsider their decision.   The Cabinet discussed another
statutory decision by the Licensing Authority to refuse a licence to a
Scottish bus company following objections by other bus operators and the BTC
(which operated buses and rail).   Government sought to enable it to operate.
Cabinet Minutes, 7th April 1952: "steps to be taken to facilitate new bus
services to compete with BR before BR gets its freedom".   These buses were
not competing solely with BR, but also with other bus operators.   Moreover,
it is noticeable that BR was not given freight rates freedom before road
haulage got its freedom.   On the contrary, Government stated that BR (and
the Tribunal), should be subject to the overriding power of the MoT.

Whilst BR was supposed to gain pricing freedom first in 1953, then in 1962,
it was not until 1968 that they were finally relieved of the statutory need
to ask the Transport Tribunal to raise fares.   This happened just in time to
be hit by a general Government restraint.   Meanwhile, Government had
reminded BR in 1964 that they were still subject to coastal shipping
objections to "unfair freight rates", when the MoT compelled BR to increase
freight rates for china clay from Cornwall to Kent following an objection by
shipping interests.   Not once in Railway history had Government compelled
road haulage to increase rates when railways objected to unfair competition.

Equipment

Whereas BR were denied raw materials in the early years of nationalisation,
even at the reduced level which the Government had decided BR should have
for building new and repairing war worn rolling stock, the supply of road
vehicles to UK companies exceeded Government limits by a wide margin.   BTC
1948 Report: the Economic Survey 1949 [Cmnd 7647], "restricted supplies of
material to BR, and limited the total of new Public Service Vehicles to 6000
in 1948.   The bus industry got 8000 and in 1949 would get 7700!   Road
freight were supposed to get 50,000 new vehicles in 1948, - they got 85,000!
The national lorry fleet was 700,000, 180,000 more than prewar and 250,000
more than 1945".   (Competitors were getting more new vehicles than specified
in the Government Plan, whilst BR were getting less steel for rolling stock
than Government had allocated, placing BR at a serious disadvantage as they
had to make do and mend with 40 year old wagons.   The extra 38,700 vehicles
sold to UK operators should have been sold abroad to help the export drive).

BTC 1949 Report: Due to steel shortages, BR had to operate the 1949 service
with 4000 fewer coaches than prewar.   BTC 1952 Report: Government allocation
of steel [reintroduced 4th February 1952] allocated BR 20% below needs.

BTC 1953 Report, Para 125: There was virtually a complete post war
re-equipment of road fleets - both passenger and freight - but on BR even

the arrears of maintenance due to intensive use made of Railways during the war have hardly yet been made good.

BTC 1956 Report, Para 45: "the financial worsenment was due to freezing of fares and charges to combat inflation plus loss of freight mainly due to C Licences" (operated by companies to move their own goods, and who had adopted the concept of creaming off themselves). **BTC 1959 Report**, Para 174: For every 100 'C' Licenced road vehicles over 6 tons capacity in 1948, there were 338 in 1959; For every 100 Public Road Transport vehicles in 1948, there were 110 in 1959; whereas for every 100 BR wagons in 1948, there were only 70 in 1959.

Most Bus and Coach operators do not have to provide the terminal facilities which BR are expected to provide. Bus shelters and bus lanes are a cost to the community, whether or not they use public transport. Some operators even live off the backs of BR, as was evident by a letter from a coach driver to the Liverpool Echo, in 1984. He complained about the condition of Lime Street station men's toilets, into which he had taken it upon himself to conduct his female passengers, when the station was under reconstruction. I replied that there was little wonder that coach companies could offer low fares if they didn't provide basic passenger facilities at their own cost.

Pre war attitudes by Government towards rail and road were similar. In 1935, the Government, in an endeavour to reduce unemployment and improve the economy, decided to spend £100m on roads, but offered to loan about £60m to railways to be spent with UK industries. Railways had to repay the loan together with the same rate of interest which the Treasury would pay to raise this sum. Not surprisingly, railways limited their use of these funds to Works which would be self financing.

Safety

I suspect that many accidents are caused by haulage vehicles. In wet weather they throw up a Niagara like spray, blinding motorists, and drive above their speed limit, with inadequate braking distance behind others, which when they are behind cars is very intimidating. Many pull out as you pass their rear end. I was intrigued by chunks of tyres on roadsides until 1991, when overtaking a string of nose to tail juggernauts on the M1, there was a loud bang, then a cloud of dust under the vehicle next ahead in the left hand lane, followed by chunks of tyre hitting the front of my van. Fortunately, my windscreen was above the point of impact. In a car, I would have had my windscreen shattered, resulting in instinctive deceleration, rear end collision and curtains. As I edged towards the hard shoulder to check for damage, the offender carried on. That did not surprise me because in January 1982, I was on a coach on the M1 when a loud bang was heard from under the coach. A passenger told the driver, who shrugged his shoulders, saying it was only a tyre, and he didn't even slow down throughout the rest of the journey. Lorries carrying materials which may blow off should be sheeted in the interests of the safety, and after unloading should be thoroughly cleaned so that no debris remains to cause broken windscreens. I suspect that many unexplained road accidents have arisen from such causes. There are other safety measures which ought to be enforced on vehicles conveying hazardous goods - (see Pages 12 & 114). There is a situation which is worse than a juggernaut throwing up a Niagara like spray, and that is two juggernauts doing so side by side as one driver tries to screw an extra ½mph more out of his vehicle in a selfish attempt to overtake.

The Government line with BR on safety, despite their high standards, is usually tougher than for other transport. BR was given six months to resolve a complaint that coach door handles may have caused deaths. (No similar tight time restraint was placed on improvements to ships, aircraft, coaches, lorries or cars following heavy death tolls). Within 24 hours of that edict, the MoT said that BR would not be allowed to close, without notice, stations which BR regarded as unsafe.

Drivers' Hours

White Paper "Transport of Freight" 1967: the working day for an HGV driver to reduce from 14 to 11 hours per day with not more than 9 at the wheel compared with 11 hitherto. The **1968 Transport Act** was less stringent - reducing hours at the wheel to 10, and allowing for up to a 12½ hour working day; (Traincrews had an 8 hour day imposed by Government in 1919 and now have various safety devices on trains. With competitors:-
* allowed longer working hours by law,
* having uncontrolled pricing freedom,
* empowered to refuse unprofitable traffic,
* using vehicles whose cost is kept low by lack of similar safety devices,
* able to cut costs quickly in a recession by de-licencing vehicles, suspending insurance and laying off drivers, whose training period was a fraction of BR drivers,
it can be no surprise BR lost so much freight traffic).

MoT Paper "Public Transport and Traffic" 1967, Para 108: "legal limits on working hours of professional [PSV] drivers have remained unaltered since the 1930's"; Para 110: maximum length of the working day will be reduced from 14 to 11, except for stage services which may spread 11 hours of work over 12½ hours; there will not be more than 9 hours at the wheel; the rest period before work will be increased from 10 to 11. On one day per week, it may be 9½ instead of the present 8 hours. There will not be more than 60 hours per week. Many bus and coach drivers are working hours substantially in excess of these limits", (even the proposed hours did not seem to be very conducive of road safety).

Report of Select Committee 1977, Para 134: "The Association of Metropolitan Authorities pointed out that passenger miles generated per member of rail staff was 82,500 compared with 128,000 for bus staff of four PTE's". (They mention one man buses but not the longer hours which the law allows bus drivers to work, which alone could account for the difference. BR passenger train drivers were invariably only 8 hours on duty per day as against a bus driver's permitted 12½ hours. They ignore BR station staff in the equation, which if withdrawn, produce protests by Councils. Neither do they take account of manpower engaged in maintaining and renewing BR's 'highway' whilst their highway is maintained by others); Para 260: "One argument used about fair competition is that the Government is not taking an impartial attitude between road and rail freight - it is phasing out rail subsidies and not implementing EEC regulations on drivers hours and the use of tachographs"; Para 261: "The Secretary of State regarded neither as affecting competition"; (which was quite incredible).

Charging System

Against this background, BR had to prepare a comprehensive new Freight Charges Scheme to replace the system forced on them in 1928. Despite prewar evidence that rail had lost freight to road because of its archaic rates structure, BR were not allowed to introduce commercial pricing in 1948, but had to prepare a scheme which would be subject to legal argument and debate - not merely with its customers, but also with its competitors, whilst no other industry was subject to such restraint. There was no justification for those who transferred easy deliveries to their own new vehicles objecting to BR increasing charges based on averages of good and bad paying loads, to compensate for being left with the residual awkward loads to the remote corners of rural UK. One can imagine the outcry had the boot been on the other foot, BR taking the easy loads and leaving manufacturers with the residue. The control of BR rates prevented BR increasing prices to an economic level, or adopting private sector practice to price uneconomic business out of the market. Suppliers increased prices but objected to BR doing likewise.

The BTC Chairman, speaking to the Royal United Services Institution in 1956: "BR are expected to carry odd and awkward consignments of merchandise for remote destinations or split deliveries, and at standard charges, while the larger consignments and those for easily accessible destinations are carried by firm's own road transport".

Proposals for Railways MoT 1956 Para 74: The Freight Charges Scheme (which was supposed to give BR the freedom which Road Haulage had had for 35 years), was "appreciably restricted by the Transport Tribunal". (There was no justifiable reason to denationalise road haulage in 1953 without immediately giving BR equal freedom on freight rates. Nearly ten years later when all industry was supposed to be subject, for a time, to pricing control by the NBPI, their effectiveness with road haulage was at variance with that of BR, who dare not fail to give the NBPI all the data it required. In contrast, the NBPI meekly reported that it had sought from the Road Haulage Industry "information on costs and charges, but the poor response made firm conclusions impossible". When the NBPI approved BR price increases, they were then reduced and delayed by another Government body - the Transport Tribunal - this did not apply to any other industry).

BTC 1957 Report, Para 176: dismisses opinions that road fuel duty is a major cause of the problems of bus companies. "In fact it is less of a burden than it was six years ago when it was raised to its present level; in those six years the general level of prices has risen by 24%. Road taxation which the bus operator pays, averages about one sixth of a penny (the old penny) per passenger mile. If railways were taxed at this rate in return for the free provision of the track, their working expenses would be greatly reduced".

BRB 1974 Report - BRB's solution was to seek support for the infrastructure of the whole railway over which the the Board in most cases would run passenger and freight services on a commercial and competitive basis. Both outgoing and incoming Governments rejected this in favour of a totally supported passenger railway with commercial freight superimposed on the passenger system. [BRB proposed Government paying for infrastructure as they did for road instead of making grants for loss making lines].

In the "Streak for Size", protagonists of bigger Juggernauts overlooked that they have to come into towns, where they damage pavements and streets at no cost to themselves, double park in main roads and cause horrendous delays.

In a BBC TV programme the MoT in answer to a question from the BBC presenter said that, unlike road transport, BR pay no taxes. Governments have never allowed BR to get into a position where they could earn a profit from which to pay tax. There is, however, no reason why the Government should not put BR on the same footing as road and have BR pay taxes, on the following basis, instead of BR paying for infrastructure costs itself directly. I have based costs on 1989/90, to avoid distortions arising from using recent data. Had BR been relieved of the direct cost and responsibility of maintaining the infrastructure, paying tax in the same way as road haulage, they would have saved licence duty by laying up rolling stock during the current recession. As it is not practical to make a fair assessment of the scale of such a saving, it is more meaningful to use pre-recession data. (Using current duty rates would cost only £19m more; the duty for tractive units and buses/coaches has not changed since 1989).

1. **Vehicle Excise Duty** (on a similar basis to road vehicles):-
901 freight and parcels locomotives at £3100 each pa (the highest
rate for road tractive units.   Duty unchanged from 1989 to 1992).   £ 2.79m
No duty on passenger locomotives, licences to be levied on seating
capacity of passenger carrying coaches (as applies with road).

21970 wagons at £355 each pa - as applies with road trailers.   £ 7.80m
1319 coaching stock (parcels and mail) vehicles at £355 each pa   £ 0.47m

Passenger coaches on the same basis as buses and motor coaches
  - 9606 with 60 seats or more at £450 pa, (unchanged since 1989)   £ 4.32m
  - 2879 with less than 60 seats at £300 pa (unchanged since 1989)   £ 0.86m
Less loco and coach licences surrendered when "off the road", in
main works - undergoing major maintenance, repairs (estimated 10%)   £ -1.62m
TOTAL VEHICLE LICENCES   £ 14.62m

2. **Duty on diesel fuel :-**
BR's consumption of gas oil for Traction purposes is 628.5m litres
pa. Approximately 17.5% of locomotives are on Maintenance & depot
shunting duties. As the former would be debitted to infrastructure
costs, the Operators would not pay for that fuel, whilst that used
for shunting inside depots would be analogous to unlicensed motor
vehicles engaged on internal depot movements, and would pay only
gas oil duty.   In 1989/90, the duty on derv was 19.02p and that
on gas oil, 1.18p per litre, a difference of 17.84p. BR's dutiable
consumption of 518.5m (17.5%) litres of derv would cost   £ 92.50m
TOTAL VEHICLE LICENCES & FUEL DUTY   £107.12m

BRB 1989/90 Report, page 41 expenditure on the infrastructure was £758.6m.
If BR had paid duty of £107.12m with Government funding the Rail "Highway",
but BR received no Government Grant (the so called "subsidy" - Government
paid £500.8m in 1989/90, - BRB 1989/90 Report, page 1), BR would have had a
net profit of £150.68m. BR's cash balance would have been very substantial,
had this method been introduced in 1948, and BR allowed the same pricing and
commercial freedom as other businesses: about £7.8 billions more passenger
revenue - see Page 34, plus reduced losses from earlier closures). Given a
form of taxation similar to road transport, the Government would not have
had to provide any subsidy to passengers. (Contrary to recent claims in the
media, the original idea for the infrastructure being owned by the State
came from the LNER, in 1946, as an alternative to Nationalisation.   BR
revived the concept in 1974). If BR (whether privatised or not), were put
on this footing, then Government would have to accept that major loss making
routes would be closed and some under utilised services would be pruned,
whilst others would be priced up, (standard private sector practice),
creating bigger profits for Government to tax. It would be open to local
authorities, (in many marginal constituencies) or others to fund
unprofitable services if they wished to have them continued. If Government
or local authorities wished to reduce road congestion, or avoid costly road
works, money should change hands to justify BR providing or retaining
services, which BR, not others, assess would be otherwise unprofitable.
There have been too many "experts" telling BR they could operate with less
income, none have ever had the courage to back their opinions with their own
money or career. Neither Government nor local authorities can expect "to
have the penny and the bun". If BR is privatised, wholly or partially, such
principles would form the basis of future operations. Hence, if BR is not
privatised, the same course should be pursued on the grounds of equity.

Transport Research Laboratory Reports show that wear and tear of of roads
caused by a ten ton axle is 80,000 times greater than that caused by a car.
The relationship is further widened by the higher annual mileage of the

typical lorry. Car tax is £110 pa, and that of the heaviest vehicle is £3100 - 28 times as much. The motorist is heavily subsidising road haulage. Commercial vehicles should have a separate road system for which they pay.

Other Infrastructure costs

BTC 1951 Report, Para 17: The BTC brought to the attention of the MoT the amount of the liability of the BTC on bridges and level crossings.
Cabinet Minutes, 12th March 1951: "BR should be relieved of the cost of overbridges and burdens which dated from when they had a monopoly".
MoT Paper "Proposals for Railways", 1956 points out that BR could not even try out modern methods for level crossing design and operation to reduce their mounting costs unless the law was altered. (Thus it could not reverse the increase in costs arising from heavier road competition. Three years later, after repeated protests regarding the costs of maintaining surfaces of bridges and crossings which were subjected to ever increasing wear and tear by road transport, the Government conceded an underwhelming £2m pa. BR had reported that level crossing staff costs had increased from £200,000 pa to £1m pa, due to increased road traffic. Deducting this increase left £1.2m to cover maintenance costs at 33,000 overbridges and 2800 crossings, equating to £33 pa per location or about 5p pa per square metre of surface.

MoT Paper "Railway Policy", November 1967, [Cmnd 3439], Page 19: "BR costs in 1965 of Road Bridges: £1½m, and Level Crossings: £1m (£1½m is mentioned on page 51); Page 51: for 2½ years up to 1960 MoT had agreed to pay BR £2m towards the cost of bridges and level crossings; it was stopped because it was thought administratively more convenient (presumably for ministers or civil servants), to deal with this through the revenue deficit, (concealing the cost). In contrast, "if the bridges were transferred to local authorities the compensation would be £100 to £500 pa" (between £3m and £16m). In addition to these figures, "the Board pay £40,000 pa to the MoT for trunk road bridges, and have to find £327,000 pa for road surfaces of bridges". The Paper recommended the payment of £40,000 to MoT [which began in 1946], for trunk road bridges be discontinued and responsibility for surface of overbridges be borne by Local Authority (it was absurd that the BR was paying for the section of road on a bridge and its approaches); Recommended that costs of bridges and crossings "be taken into account in recapitalisation", (concealing the problem and future increases). "The present statutory framework for bridges and level crossings is complicated and unsatisfactory. The main disadvantages are that there is a lack of clearly defined obligations .... and [external] administrative difficulties which often prevent the removal of bridges which are no longer necessary". Bridge surfaces became a highway authority responsibility in the 1968 Act.

Report of Select Committee 1977, Para 19: BR are entitled under EEC regulations to half the cost of providing and maintaining level crossings. This contribution amounted in 1975 to £9m.

BR had to maintain 40,000 miles of fencing in the 1940's - which, because of route closures, has reduced to about 22,000 miles today - along its 'highway' whereas this charge does not fall on road users, (see Page 12).

Unlike road transport, BR has also had to maintain historic buildings and structures, which include many which have no operational purpose, (Page 12).

Footpaths crossing main lines are an unnecessary hazard to pedestrians - and sometimes lead to trains being delayed by accidents or vandals. When a motorway is built, no difficulty seems to arise in diverting or closing off footpaths. Similar attention, with appropriate funding, should be given by the MoT to all existing footpaths across railways.

Repetitive calls from Government or their Agents for information could only distract management from running the railway business. 'U' turns by Governments and enforced organisational changes take the eye off the ball. The constant need to submit investment decisions to the Ministry, (who admitted a lack of expertise - see Page 39), pricing and closure decisions to Government agencies created a workload which should have been employed on improving the business.

BTC 1953 Report: reorganisation proposals put to the MoT, in response to a Government directive, at the end of 1951 by Government Order had still not been discussed by 8th May 1952.

Speaking to the Royal United Services Institution on 1st February 1956, the BTC Chairman referred to political control, pointing out that when the national corporations were set up, "Parliament deliberately denied itself the right to exercise [direct] administrative control over them. Yet MP's seek information; query the conduct of the undertaking, even down to quite local matters". (This was bound to cause some to consider the political reaction of sensitive changes, which consequently delayed or prevented improvements).

BTC 1959 Report: Government set up an Advisory Group and a Select Committee" (more days preparing paperwork, answering questions, etc).

Government Paper "Railway Policy", November 1967, Page 13: the White Paper in July 1966 [Cmnd 3057] set up a Joint Steering Group headed by an MP, which "always envisaged that it would take about a year to report"; page 4, Para 13: "The Steering Group considered BRB forecasts for the years 1969-74 were too optimistic. They estimated the BRB would be in deficit in 1974 to the extent of between £5m and £55m", (A considerable margin for error - why they believed that they could forecast more accurately than BR was not made clear. Most of their forecasts later proved to be inaccurate).

BRB 1976 Report: "an almost obsessive amount of top management time has been taken in the processes of discussion and debate, involving the 'Consultation Document', and special enquiries of both the Select Committee on Nationalised Industries and of the National Economic Development Office Study. The latter said 'The relationship of BR and Government is historically described as overlapping and and confused and what each expects of the other is ambiguous or unrealistic'".

BRB 1977 Report, Page 5: "A period of unprecedented scrutiny - even for an industry as exposed as ours. The NEDO analysis, the Report of the Select Committee on Nationalised Industries on the role of BR in Public Transport, the Government's response thereto, the Price Commission and a White Paper on Transport Policy."

Monopolies & Mergers Commission, October 1980, reported on BR's London & South East Commuter Services, Page 178: "Some of the problems encountered by BRB result from the anti-social behaviour of a minority of travellers". (A minority is less than 50% - the true scale is shrouded in mystery. BR suffers also from the misbehaviour of non passengers). Page 181: "There is a general resistance by the unions to any net reduction in the total number of staff", (This could be expected of any unionised UK industry, and especially in the Private Sector, even to this day. Having been at the sharp end of management, I personally made substantial reductions in staff in the two Regions in which I worked, as former staff representatives would bear witness. Other colleagues made similar economies and it would be surprising if managers in the South East had not done likewise); page 183: "The Board should consider urgently what economies could be made through a reduced use of rolling stock where this could be done without unreasonably affecting the quality of service"; (This is a ridiculous objective - reducing rolling stock which does not affect quality of service can be precisely assessed. Doing so where the service is worsened "but not unreasonably" begs the question as to who will be the judge as to whether it is unreasonable - BR, MoT, Select Committee or individual passenger) "The Board should be continuously employing a variety of measures ranging from shortening trains, taking out trains and altering stopping patterns"; (BR management have been doing this in perpetuity, and often been publicly abused for so doing; moreover demands from the CTCC for consultation on alterations to services can only hinder this practice. Page 186: "It appears to us that it has only been in periods of severe financial restraint that determined efforts have been made to build in cost reduction", (Most BR managers pursued cost reductions, every year. I did so in every management post I held. It is only the Private Sector which reports an attack on costs during recessions, with prophecies of emerging "leaner and fitter" - had they remained "lean and fit" throughout, we would have had less inflation, and no balance of payments problem).

Responding to the **Serpell "Review of Railway Finances", January 1983:** the BRB said that "there were two Reports - which are in some ways contrary - and this means there is a danger of increasing confusion". On network size, the BRB said "the mathematical model on which the options are based is, in the Board's view, inadequate to form a basis for public policy decisions. The [Serpell] committee were too unsure of it themselves to discuss it with BR". (This is incomprehensible). The minority report included the paragraph: "There was insufficient time to develop different kinds of high investment options. But the results of the one investigated indicated ..... that a combination of certain network options with increased investment could prove beneficial. The Board regrets that the Committee did not have time to pursue this line of enquiry. (What was the value of an investigation which didn't have enough time?)

There were politically sponsored re-organisations which involved losing part of BR with some of our staff. Each created a major workload for managers and staff. With Freightliner, we had the disturbance of losing the activity, and then a few years later, getting it back. Thus it was that someone discovered an 'Ancient Manuscript' which seemed to be particularly apposite:
** "We trained hard, but it seemed that every time we were beginning to form up into teams we would be re-organised. I was to learn later in life that we tend to meet any situation by re-organising, it is a wonderful method of creating the illusion of progress while producing confusion, inefficiency and demoralisation. - Gaius Petronius BC 66."

The most recent distraction is the Citizens Charter. Some labour under the illusion that it introduced the concept of performance targets. Targets have been in use for at least 30 years for monitoring performance at all levels. If they have not produced the results politicians think they should, it is largely because one cannot make bricks without straw, and Governments have been less than helpful in that direction. For years, BR performance data has been publicised via the CTCC and TUCC's and on some stations. What has changed is that data is now given even more publicity. This contrasts sharply with the private sector, which ought to have been leading the way by displaying the preceding day's performance data of the maximum queueing time and the number of complaints on the walls of supermarkets, banks, building societies and public reception areas of all businesses. A Citizen's Charter should start at the macro, not the micro level. Hence, it should address Citizens' rights at the constitutional level - which should include free speech and, therefore, a right to have published, a reply to media criticism. Then it should address our rights with regard to the greater part of our expenditure long before it concerns itself with the minor part - it would thus address motoring : manufacturers, garages, insurance; then all other retailing etc until after several stages the concept eventually worked down to the micro level which is railway travel. Of course, that would not have the same political impact and would mean accepting that the Private Sector has a long way to go before it can claim to be setting an example in the field of customer rights for the public sector to emulate. My experience with the private sector must have been mirrored by millions who, because of lack of publicity, assume they are just the odd unlucky person. Most have doubtless realised that there are no real watchdogs protecting the 90+% of their expenditure, - where prices can leap by seven times (or currently, 30 times), the rate of inflation "due to circumstances beyond our control" - but many watchdogs obsessed with the minor part. The media mentioned that the Charter gives no compensation for dirty trains and stations. The reason is perfectly obvious: compensation would fall to be paid to BR by offending passengers, and at stations, also by non passengers who demonstrate their social attitude by distributing litter like confetti, by spraying graffiti, by vandalism and by feet on seats. One man said on a radio phone-in that compensation should be paid by the managers and staff, instead of falling on other customers. If that policy applies in the Private Sector, I now understand why I frequently fail to obtain compensation or refunds for inferior service and defective products from that quarter.

In marked contrast to the rights of a citizen against BR are the limited rights against the Private Sector. The Consumer Protection Act 1987 gives the consumer protection only where "the safety of the product is not such as persons are generally entitled to expect. A product is not considered to be defective because it is of poor quality".

Control of railway rates

From the beginning, railway rates were controlled by the State. In 1826,
the Liverpool and Manchester Railway Act, Sec.128 provided that when a
dividend on shares exceeded 10%, statutory maximum tonnage rates were to be
reduced in the following year by 5% for each 1% paid in dividend in excess
of 10%. The Act set out maximum rates of carriage for passengers, goods and
livestock. The Railway Clauses Consolidation Act 1845, enacted that all
should pay the same charges in like circumstances. The Railway & Canal Act
1854 compelled railways to provide reasonable and equal facilities to all
without undue discrimination. The Regulation of Railways Act 1873, obliged
them to publish rates and keep them available for public inspection at
stations. The Railway & Canal Act 1894 imposed severe restraint, requiring
railways to prove costs had increased to justify increases in rates. Whilst
there was little competition, these conditions were fair. But in the 20's
road haulage found inherent weaknesses which they ruthlessly exploited.
Rail rates were based on the formula that low value goods would have rates
below cost and high value goods, rates above cost. In 1928 the Government
enforced a continuation of their pack horse formula. That alone was deadly
enough, allowing road haulage to "cream off" higher rated traffics which
were subsidising low rated traffic, but railways were tied by the 1845 and
1854 Acts. Road haulage was allowed to be totally discriminatory. As if
this poison chalice were not enough, railways were compelled by the 1873 Act
to open rate books to competitors. Thus road haulage knew by how much to
undercut rail - no question of "blind tendering" for them. Had rail been
entitled to similar rights, they were blocked from undercutting rates to
compete anyway. Road Haulage could even object to rail rates. The right of
road haulage to know rail rates did not extend to inspecting the books of
other hauliers. From 1932 railways pleaded for road to be subject to the
same form of regulation and when this fell on deaf ears, in 1938 appealed
for a "Square Deal" - for their rates to be confidential, on the same basis
as road and all traffic at "cost plus" instead of the archaic "what the
traffic would bear" which was so vulnerable to "creaming off". Had the law
been changed then or immediately after the war, rail would not have lost its
core freight traffic. The Railways were trapped in a legal maze.

The Railway Rates Tribunal (RRT)

The 1921 Railways Act provided for a Charges Scheme which was unique in
industrial legislation. It was devised by the Government appointed Railway
Rates Tribunal - a Court of Law, which took until 1928 to implement this
monopoly based strait jacket at the very time that Railways ceased to be a
monopoly! The Act specified that the four new Railway companies formed by
enforced amalgamation under the Act should be able to earn the annual net
revenue [the "Standard Revenue" - £51m in aggregate], earned 15 years
earlier - in 1913 by the railway companies forced into amalgamation by the
Government. Inputs to the Tribunal on the proposed scheme were made by
industry, agriculture, traders and railways. It perpetuated the concept of
the pack horse formula. The RRT was required to review charges each year
[the MoT could order no review after the first two years], and to adjust
rates to ensure that Net Revenue was achieved, taking account of whether
railways were being run as efficiently or economically as possible. If they
were not, the RRT would not authorise an increase even if the standard net
revenue was not being achieved : 1921 Act, Sec.59.3: "If on any review, the
Tribunal find that the net revenue obtained, or which could with efficient
and economic management have been obtained by the company, is substantially
in excess of the standard revenue of the company, they shall modify charges
so as to effect a reduction of that company in subsequent years to an extent
equivalent to 80% of such excess, unless the RRT are of the opinion the
excess is not likely to continue". This would return the excess to users in

the form of lower charges. How the RRT would assess whether four of the largest industries in the UK were inefficient, was not prescribed. (Sir Josiah Stamp, President of the LMSR described that company as the largest privately owned organisation and largest employer of labour in the whole of Europe. In April 1953, during the hearing of the BTC Draft Passenger Charges Scheme, the President of the Transport Tribunal said that "this body is not a proper body to examine the efficiency of the LTE" - a much smaller organisation than any of the four prewar main line companies). Efficiency improvements arising from amalgamation, which improved net revenue would result in a claw-back so railways would be denied a major part of their economies - Sec.58: "In determining the Standard Charges, and to encourage economies from amalgamation, the RRT shall make a fair allowance in respect of economies achieved not exceeding one third of such economies". The RRT had a legal obligation to adjust charges from year to year, to ensure the earning of net revenue, but never did so, despite the fact that in no year was the Net Revenue produced. There appears to have been no valid reason to prevent the RRT from increasing low rates and decreasing high rates to achieve the statutory objective and resolve the unfair competitive position of road haulage. Then, as now, it seemed a case of heads the railways lose, tails they don't gain. (1961 SAG papers: "the RRT was inflexible and railways were placed at a disadvantage in meeting competition from a growing road haulage industry"). In the 11 years preceding the Second War, the annual shortfall was between 12% and 78%, amounting to £172m, or 3½ years total Net Revenue lost from 11 years of activity. By virtue of their privileged status allowing them to charge a special discriminatory rate for every job, after first exercising a legal right to check their rail competitor's rate, road haulage, creamed off 24% of merchandise traffic in 1937 and 26% in 1938. An appreciation of the wide margin for undercutting rail rates is illustrated by the following typical example:

The 1928 Rates Book, was unaltered until a 5% increase in 1937, but its basis remained unchanged until 1957, except for percentage increases. Hence, its vulnerability to "creaming-off" was undiminished throughout that time. A rate increase brought more traffic within the attack zone. Rates for 1928 show that for 100 miles, the rate for class 1 traffic, was 9s11d per ton (approx 50p) and for class 21, the highest class, was 90s7d per ton (approx £4.53p) both including wagon provision. Thus the rate for class 21 was nine times that for class 1, whereas the cost of carrying, ton for ton would be broadly the same. Before the onset of road competition goods were, in aggregate, carried at a profit, the carriage cost per ton being somewhere below the midway level of rates - say for purposes of illustration about 39s (£1.95p) for 100 miles. All below that is subsidised by all above that level. When road began to cream off the upper layers offering 2s6d (12½p) below the rail rate, rail lost profitable traffic which was subsidising the loss makers. In 1928 rail carried: Coal £33.5m, Minerals [Class 1-6]: £15.3m, Merchandise Class [7-21]: £49.4m, Livestock £1.9m. Road attacked classes 7-21 and between 1924 and 1935 increased its share from 13% to 50% of the total market. These complex Standard rates were imposed on railways, who may offer "Exceptional Rates" [to all, not discriminatively] at 5% below Standard, and upon application to the RRT may secure approval for up to 40% below, requests for over 40% reduction required MoT approval, by which time the traffic had moved by road. 40% below a Standard rate of £4.53 was £2.72, say, 39% above cost, but reaching this level was constrained, so road could always win on price. Sir Wm.Wood said to the RRT in 1939 that "railways were told that packed confectionery and packed explosives are carried at the same rates by road and that the same must apply to rail, although the rail rate for explosives is, at 50 miles, double the rail rate for confectionery. No suggestions were received from consignors that the converse should apply and the rates for traffic in the lower classes increased to the level of road rates. The General Classification of

Merchandise (GCM), listed every item known to man, and was described by the RCA as a 'Nonsense Novel', because it prescribed for example, that in sending fish products, you had to separate oysters from periwinkles and from crabs because all go at different rates. Goods - say shoes, packed in different containers - hampers, sacks, casks or cases go at different rates". Nominally, there were 21 classes, but due to sub divisions there were really 60. The RCA said that the classification system was clearly applicable only where the transport organisation using it was a monopoly. Had the onset of war been deferred the railways might have been too run down to meet wartime demands. There was a story circulating many years ago, that, before the War, the LMSR had threatened the Government that it intended to file for voluntary liquidation if the Government did not act on its claim for fair treatment. When addressing the Glasgow Chamber of Commerce in February 1939, Lord Stamp, Chairman of the LMSR, said "the need for the Square Deal was now or never - if the out of date laws were not changed the railways would succumb". Even with the average rail rate below road rates, higher rated traffic remained vulnerable to "creaming - off". To alter the GCM, or to include new products, Railways, or Traders, applied to the Tribunal (up to 1957). RRT costs were recoverable from the Railways.

Rate Relief
It is relevant to note how Government treated railways in pre war Rate relief. Industry and agriculture were given relief from Municipal Rates to reduce production costs. The apparently corresponding relief to railways, including their factories, was transferred to the RRT to use to benefit coal, iron, steel and agricultural industries by railway freight rebates. Government stated that railway derating was to assist those industries not to assist the railways. In November 1949, the BTC asked for the Scheme [set up under the Local Government Act 1929 amended by Railway Freight Rebates Acts 1936 and 1943], to be wound up. The BTC said that of derating relief paid into the fund, 20% was used for rebates on railborne livestock and milk, whilst the rest went to the MoT to subsidise coal and merchandise by coastwise shipping (which was empowered to object to lower rail rates). BTC had to agree to continue on a voluntary basis for milk and livestock, at the existing rate of 12½%, pending the introduction of the new freight charges scheme. Between 1948-50 the total rebates credited to the scheme averaged £3.8m pa. The Railway Freight Rebates Regulations 1950 wound up the Scheme from 1st January 1951 and paid the balance back to the BTC.

The "Square Deal" Campaign
A 1928 Royal Commission recommended in 1931 that a Transport Advisory Council (TAC) be set up to advise Government on co-ordination. On 8th March 1932 the Railway Companies asked the Government to give them the conditions enjoyed by road competitors, stating that the road industry was unduly favoured and that as Rail transport were bound by Statute, Road transport should also be regulated. Railways estimated that in 1930 they lost £16m in net revenue to road - one third of the profit the law stipulated they should be allowed to earn - despite cuts in costs. Railways called for an end to the favoured treatment which road transport received. In April 1932, the Association of British Chambers of Commerce called for the removal of disablities and restrictions on railways which made it difficult for railways to compete efficiently with road transport. (Had these events taken place today, Railways would probably have tested the archaic law as some companies test illogical Sunday trading law now. What could the Government have done if the four main line companies had pulped the GCM and Rate books and charged on an unfettered commercial basis on exactly the same lines as road haulage?). In July 1937 the TAC said that all forms of transport should be rate controlled. The Government accepted the Report but did nothing, so in 1938 railways proposed in their "Square Deal" Campaign that statutory control of rail rates be abolished to put them on a par with

road haulage. In November 1938 Railways placed proposals to the MoT for removal of legal restrictions on freight charging powers, saying "The extreme urgency is apparent". The MoT asked the TAC to consider the proposals, saying that there was a prime facie case for relaxing statutory regulations. In January 1939 railways submitted proposals to meet traders' fears, offering to accept a five year experimental period. Agreement was reached on 6th February 1939 between Railways and Road Haulage, who withdrew objections to the 'Square Deal' campaign. (It is incredible that the railways needed competitors, who were using the law to poach traffic, to agree that railways should have the same freedom as themselves). A Joint Memorandum of Agreement was submitted to the TAC, proposing a consultative committee of the two industries to establish agreements on rates to be charged by road and rail. These would require the approval of the RRT, supplemented by a member experienced in road goods transport, which would hear objections by traders or road carriers. The parties said that there were safeguards to protect industry and trade and there would be no interference with the right of traders to use C licence vehicles. Objections of coastal shipping, canals or traders would be considered before the TAC reported to the MoT. The Report on 19th May 1939, made unanimous recommendations, based on agreements reached between railways and other interests, except coal mining. On the publication of railway rates the TAC made no recommendation. The main recommendations were:-
1. The present system of control of railway rates to be abandoned.
2. railways to be entitled to make such reasonable charges as they think fit, subject to safeguards.
3. Safeguards for trade & industry should take the following form :-
[a] a periodic conference on a voluntary basis;
[b] current charges only increased by agreement, (by the appropriate conference in the case of a general increase or by traders concerned in the case of an individual increase), or by authority of the RRT;
[c] right of appeal to the RRT on the reasonableness of any charge;
4. Safeguards for other forms of transport should be :-
[a] a periodic conference on a voluntary basis;
[b] agreement as to rates with the road haulage interests [subject to the provisions of 3b above];
[c] certain specific provisions to prevent unfair competition.

The TAC said that a material relaxation of statutory control of railway goods charges was necessary, but because of the ultimate [Government] objective of the co-ordination of all forms of transport, recommendations were to be regarded as a temporary measure and should be for not more than five years or such shorter period as might be necessary to establish adequate co-ordination. The proposals did not meet the basic demands of the railways, but were beginning to indicate a prospect of a new understanding. It is an excuse to say that war postponed change, which should have been made in the mid thirties. Railways asked for equal legality with their competitors. Government moved quickly enough in passing complex Defence Laws but were paralysed by this crisis. They quickly established, before the war that Railways would play a vital part in evacuation, and could move 100,000 persons per hour from London, on top of the movement of war and industrial traffic, and millions travelling to work by train. Railways moved 1.3m evacuees in the first four days of September 1939. Neither is there reason to believe that the war precluded action since the Government busied itself with post war plans long before they knew that the war could be won. A postwar national health plan was debated, housing plans were developed, the Cabinet considered more Civil Service leave. The change railways sought could have been contained in a simple Act of Parliament - on one piece of paper, for implementation at the end of the war, for this problem was not going to go away and would only get worse. Government was thinking ahead about the pressing need for post war exports to repay enormous debts and pay for the welfare state. Ensuring that rail did not lose more traffic to road would have released road vehicles for export and killed two birds with one stone. Rates freedom could have been embraced in the 1947 Act. Giving post war BR the power to decide its own pricing strategy in line with the rest of industry would have been just. Instead, Government compelled BR to devise Charges Schemes which would be subject to Public Inquiry in a Court of Law to prevent BR exercising the monopolistic power they had lost 20 years earlier! The RRT was renamed the Transport Tribunal, but its powers were more constrictive, having power to review and change its own earlier decisions, unlike its predecessor. Worse, there was no annual NET REVENUE to attain, instead the Tribunal would consider whether price increases were necessary to enable the BTC to balance their books "taking one year with another". This, despite all the evidence of prewar diversion of traffic to road, and a major expansion of road transport taking place. Heads firmly in 19th century sand, the Government told the BTC to prepare "Charges Schemes" for passenger and freight businesses, submitting them within two years, for consideration, to the Transport Tribunal - whose predecessor had taken seven years to produce one freight scheme.

Transport Tribunal

The Court of the Transport Tribunal, to give it the title used on the headings of its Reports was set up by the Transport Act 1947 which refers to it only as the "Transport Tribunal". Its duties empowered it to consider Charges Schemes submitted by the BTC. (No reason has been advanced for having "Charges Schemes", BR's competitors and all industry managed quite well without them. BR did not ask for them, Parliament decided to have them - ours not to reason why, ours but to do and get into debt). The BTC had to publicise proposals. Objections to schemes could be lodged by "any body representative of any class of persons using the services or facilities to which the scheme relates". For passengers this included Local Authorities, and a multiplicity of Travellers Associations which were created for this purpose. For freight schemes, traders using services could object. "Any body representative of any class .. providing .. services .... similar" to those under review could also object - viz competitors - road, canal carriers, coastwise shipping. No other industry was placed in the position of having competitors legally empowered to object to its charges. Worse was to follow, as the Act stipulated that if a Draft Scheme or Alteration to a Scheme provided for charges which were unduly low, competitors may object. In respect of existing charges applicable until a new Charges Scheme was implemented, if the BTC wished to "increase a rate which was unduly low by reason of the competition of road haulage, canal carriers or coastwise shipping, any trader aggrieved by raising the rate may appeal to the Tribunal". Thus whilst a competitor, finding itself offering a rate well below rail rates would be free to increase their rate to narrow the margin of undercutting, BR could be prevented from doing likewise. BR's customers could take action to make BR hang on to unprofitable traffic! The Act stipulated that neither the BTC nor the Tribunal should do anything which, in their opinion, will prevent the BTC from discharging its duty to pay its way. The Act did not prevent the MoT from so doing, nor for resolving the inevitable situation when the opinion of the BTC and the Tribunal were in direct conflict - BTC saying it needed certain increases and the Tribunal saying it didn't. The Act required the BTC, within two years from the passing of the Act to prepare and submit schemes relating to its services - BR Freight, BR Passenger, Road Freight, Road Passenger, Canals, Ports and Storage. The Act was passed on 6th August 1947, only six months before the organisation came into being, leaving 18 months for these tasks.

When I first perused the Proceedings of the "Court of the Transport Tribunal", I was surprised by its full title, amazed at the volume and minutiae of Proceedings and looked to see if BR had pleaded guilty of trying

to balance its books.   In the following cases "advocates" means the number
of Kings/Queens Counsel, barristers or spokespersons.

Passenger Fares
A Draft London Area Interim Passenger Charges Scheme, was submitted by the
BTC to the Tribunal on 23rd February 1950, covering LT and BR-London lines
including the whole of the LT&S - a scheme for the rest of BR would follow
separately.   Its object was to create a new common level on BR and between
BR & LT, involving some increased and some reduced fares; to replace
Workmen's Tickets (a 19th century anachronism) by EMR (Early Morning Returns
- higher fare - but below ordinary, and available to all, unlike Workmen's
tickets), and to increase revenue.   The forecast yield was £3.6m on £74½m
(4.9%).   The BTC forecast accumulated losses by the year end at £40m, plus
£10m to replace wasting assets, pointing out that London passengers were
paying less than prewar compared with increased prices, that LT fares were
abnormally low and full of anomalies.   BR season holders were paying 55%
above prewar, and LT passengers 25%, (both well below other price
increases).   The LT&S Act 1852 had provided limited powers - fares of ½d per
mile compared with the usual 1d per mile.   The Southend Railway Travellers
Association were told by the BTC they had long enjoyed a specially
privileged position and were still the cheapest at 0.55d per mile.   Nine
Local Authorities and 100 organisations had objected.   The hearing occupied
26 days from 9th May to 26th July.   It was the first considered by the
Tribunal under their 1947 Act powers.   The evidence of 32 witnesses lasted
5½ days.   The MoT was represented; 39 Advocates appeared, representing 57
objectors, including the National Union of Ratepayers and 23 Ratepayers
Associations, (why all need be involved was not evident); the TUC, Light
Railway League, Heston & Isleworth Tory Association, New End Primary School
P&TA, Northolt Grange Residents Association and Mr.S.F.Oldland appeared on
his own behalf - when called to speak, he expressed surprise.   Counsel for
City of London Corporation said that estimates were drawn up "too much on
the safe side because of a period of rising costs and to add a little for
safety" (in line with Private Sector and Local Authority practice).   BTC
were asked if it wouldn't be "prudent to wait until taxes are reduced and
wages unfrozen before starting to set up reserves", (any industry doing so
would quickly go bankrupt).   The TUC said that if shift tickets were
withdrawn, workers may refuse shifts which would interfere with industry.
Objectors said that many couldn't afford to pay more and it would affect
wage claims, (irrelevant and at odds with the facts set out in the BTC 1957
Report - see Page 25), or that the increase was not needed anyway, (despite
a submission forecasting a deficit).   Objectors warned of refusals to pay,
of strikes and an end to the wage freeze.   One union representative said
compensation paid to former shareholders should be reduced by 25% and their
interest rate cut from 3% to 2½%.   (The Tribunal had no power to consider
this issue, and one wonders how he would have reacted had the Government
decided to nationalise all privately owned property - including his, on such
terms.   The BTC 1951 Report, Para 55 revealed that the dividends of former
shareholders had fallen to about one third of the 1938 level).   The BTC had
to respond to an irrelevant proposal that they should receive a subsidy -
eventually the Tribunal ruled this point out of order, as being outside the
Act, (the same suggestion was made at Hearings held in subsequent years).
NALGO claimed their wages were up by 35% since prewar against 80% increase
in the RPI.   (Much 'evidence' and objections were irrelevant - the remit was
not conditioned by any effect on the economy or of hardship).   The London
Rail Passenger Association said BR had not cut costs (in 1950 BR shed 19,000
jobs), and that the 1d fare (introduced 120 years ago) should be
reintroduced.   Objectors also said that as the BTC was not in credit,
provisions for replacements and reserve would be a "contribution to the
liquidation of deficits" (was that wrong?).   On 13th July, the Tribunal gave
a Preliminary Decision that the Scheme would "produce £1m more in a future

normal year than the contribution which the London area ought to be called on to make" (subsequent events proved they were wrong). They said that "EMR fares would impose hardship on travellers and that [23,000] London shift workers should not be the only ones to be deprived of cheap travel facilities", that reductions should be made in proposed EMR fares, and that 'shift workers' tickets should be retained on railways (but not buses) at EMR rates. They directed the BTC to alter the Scheme to cut the yield by 25%. The Tribunal said that "it was improbable that the right contribution London ought to make to total BTC revenue can be determined accurately at the present time, (after two years of study?), and considered that a present assessment possibly too low is more justifiable than one too high". The BTC revised proposals reducing the yield to £2.77m were considered on 26th July, and the Tribunal made further alterations to reduce the yield to £2.68m. The Tribunal handed down its final Judgement on 23rd August. Proceedings covered 648 pages. The amended scheme was implemented on 1st October, [The BTC said that the delay cost £0.5m]. (The RPI had risen 6% since 1948, the Fares 'Index' had fallen 9%).

The 1951 Draft Passenger Charges Scheme, submitted 7th April 1951, covered BR-LT&S, BR-London Area, LT rail & road, BR outside London, and revoked the 1950 London Area Charges Scheme, which had been an Interim Scheme. It addressed the rest of the UK (where there had been no increases since 1947). It sought to create equality for comparable journeys and to increase sub standard fares to standard levels :-
1. London Area - further adjustment to sub standard fares and the average level raised by 20%;
2. Outside London:
[a] monthly return and day return increases;
[b] standard seasons raised by 3%-20% and sub standard raised to these levels. This meant some sub standard seasons would be raised by up to 50%, but the revenue from these involved £0.27m compared to £2.26m proposed increase in season revenue. The average season increase would be 16.6%;
[c] workmen's tickets replaced by EMR for arrivals up to 08.00;
[d] withdraw Traders Season tickets [which did not promote BR business being mainly used for residential travel], Commercial Travellers tickets [which were 1/6th below the 1928 standard rate] and Bulk Travel tickets.

The forecast yield was: London area £11m [LT £8m, BR £3m], outside London £6m, but this would still leave a shortfall of £15.7m. Had the Scheme not provided for raising sub standard fares up to a common standard level, but all fares had been increased by the same percentage, the application would have been for over 20% to produce the same revenue. (Whilst 20% sounds high, many fares had not been increased for four years, whilst the RPI and average industrial wages had been increasing annually). On BR outside London and the LT&S, seasons would be on a similar basis to the London Area "but generally raised less than 20% as rates are at present higher than the London Area". The BTC demonstrated that LT fares as a whole had, since 1939, risen less than on main line railways: LT about 43% up on 1939, BR London Area 51%, the rest of BR 55%. If the application was approved fares would be 75% above prewar in the London Area and 90% outside London. On 12th June, the BTC handed in 54 pages of Statements & Exhibits, with 180 statistical tables (which would be specially prepared). In making its application the BTC stated some passenger rates were as low as 6% of the public rate and added that it hadn't so far been able to put a penny into the reserves. Despite its statutory remit, the Tribunal did not remedy that situation. BTC said that, in the case of EMR where traffic was the heaviest, the increase was very small - 1d per day for 41.3%, 1½d per day for 14.4%, 2d per day for 31.4%. (It is incredible that objectors and Government could become wound up at such trifling increases, when wages were clearly outstripping fares). The BTC mentioned that "the amount for Forces and Police travel is negotiable with Government and BTC hoped to get a considerable amount out of this". (In fact, little was gained from either).

There were 204 objections lodged. The variability of objecting bodies was such that the President of the Court said that "It seems even the Red Headed League had a right to be heard". Among objectors were the Ski Club of GB, and the Traffic Committee of the Federation of the Ratepayers Association of Kent whose Chairman "calculated that we had between 25,000 and 30,000 members" (imagine the criticism had BR statistics been as vague). The Tribunal sat on 17th & 18th July to decide whether each objecting body had a legal right to object. 109 bodies appeared and 84 speeches were made. The Tribunal decided that 75 of the original objectors did not have a legal right to object under Sec.78 of the 1947 Act.

The main part of the Inquiry began on 8th October, and ended on 3rd December, having sat on 32 further days. The hearing involved no less than 70 advocates, 99 objectors [local authorities and others], and the MoT was represented - a point of some significance later. On 10th October, the BTC asked for a variation in the Scheme to produce £4m more in London and £½m outside London to meet cost increases since the scheme was lodged six months earlier, [the average season increase would be 18.5%; and the average fare per mile would be 1.38d in the London Area and 1.48d outside London]. BTC witnesses were in the witness box for 15 days and were asked 4858 questions, 45 speeches were heard together with oral evidence from 24 witnesses. Objectors mainly advocated no increases or proposed reductions (some were trying to take fares back to 1d per mile, which was less than the Liverpool & Manchester Railway rate in the 1826 Act). Objections were made on the most incredible grounds. An Adviser to local authorities said "passengers were being asked at the present time to suffer increases greater than would otherwise be the case so that BTC might be in a position to renew assets without raising as new capital the full cost of new assets; there was no need to provide for obsolesence". He prophesised that "the working expenses of the BTC would reach a peak next year and then decrease", (events proved him hopelessly wrong). The British Legion suggested free seasons for war disabled and all other disabled at 50% discount (roles for the War Office and DHSS). The KC for Corporation of London said that "increases should be limited to cover only working expenses, any contributions to the general reserve should be left until times were better". The KC for Southend Corporation and the local travellers association said "there should be no increase of fares on LT&S until electrification was completed - or a lower fare offered for seasons and EMR (those pushing peak costs through the ceiling); the line should be regarded as a special problem, there was no basis for a uniform rate per mile - there was no logic in uniform rates" (it was obvious that they were paying below standard or they would have argued for equality). They also said the district was built up on favourable traffic facilities and people had placed reliance on such facilities" [viz sub standard fares subsided by the rest of the UK. One wonders if their council rates had been more favourable in earlier days). The KC for Middlesex CC said "there should be no question of a reserve being set up whilst there was a bottomless pit of a deficit. (BTC would never rid itself of a deficit with this philosophy). There was no point in BTC asking for an increase in fares which led to no increase in the number of passengers carried". The KC for London Trades Council: "nothing should be done detrimental to shift working which was in the national interest" (that was for employers to pay wages which would attract staff to shift work, not for BR, or its staff, to subsidise them); "no increases could be afforded without giving up some other expenditure: in 1949 the wages index was 111, and cost of living 109, now they are 120 and 129 respectively" (the fares index had fallen to 89). The KC for LCC referred to the increase of 48% in revenue from electrification to Shenfield, totally ignoring the formidable capital costs, and said the BTC should find "a fare level which was commercially and socially the right one - which yields most revenue, and enables the greatest number of people to travel" - (that was not BTC's remit). The BTC stated that "despite extension of cheap tickets in the past year producing 26% more journeys, and 19% increased receipts on cheap tickets - total receipts actually fell". The LCC disagreed with the BTC who had stated that on the grounds of equity there was no justification for sub standard fares. West Ham Trades Council urged that EMR be extended to 09.00 (lowest fares when costs were highest - one doubts their members were selling below cost). One MP objected to fare increases only one year after the previous one of 3% (that was the first for three years and applied only to London), when other industry was increasing prices annually. The Proceedings of the Inquiry covered 782 pages. In January 1952, after the Inquiry had concluded but before the Tribunal had issued its conclusions, the BTC said that if the Scheme was confirmed as submitted, they forecast a deficit of £16-17m pa. There was an accumulated deficit of £40m.

The Tribunal issued a document entitled "Conclusions" on 17th January 1952. This was followed on 27th February by a more formal Order entitled the **1952 Passenger Charges Scheme** - it began as the **1951 Scheme**. This Inquiry, which was hearing an Application for an increase, was notable for reducing ordinary fares below existing levels, which were already below prewar in real terms. It was even more notable for placing LT&S fares to a level lower than the general reductions so that a 40 miles journey on LT&S would cost 48d, whilst all other BR lines were to be 70d for the same distance until January 1953 and thereafter 80d, an LT&S discount of 66%. They were able to maintain this privileged position of lower fares for many years thereafter. Todays travellers on the LT&S must blame their forebears if the current standard of service is unsatisfactory since it arises from sub standard fares for which they fought. They can hardly begrudge better trains in areas which paid higher fares. The Order stated that fares in London Area would be raised from 2nd March, and that revised fares including seasons would come into effect throughout the rest of Britain on 1st May. The Order approved uplifting sub standard fares by more than 20% to bring them into line with other discounted fares being lifted by 20%. To mitigate hardship which might be caused if all existing fares and charges were immediately brought up to permissible maxima, BTC was prohibited from increasing any fare by more than 42% (these were the ultra sub standard fares) for 12 months. They reduced ordinary fares, which the BTC had planned to leave untouched, from 2.44d [about 1p - the 1947 level] to 1.75d per mile, [the 1940 level], and back up to 2d from January 1953, [18% below actual 1951 rates and still below 1939 in real terms], which would lose revenue as BR provincial ordinary fare sales being mainly single journeys, would not generate more traffic from a fare decrease. These and their reduction in LT ordinary fare from 3½d at 2 miles, to 3d, cost £4m. BR's Monthly Return fares had been increased by 10% in January, having been deferred at Government request (see Page 19), because they were well below the statutory level, and the hearing was so prolonged. These were the first increases since 1947 outside London, and the first increase of Monthly Returns in the London Area. Reducing Ordinary fares meant that Monthly Returns, at 1.33 times the original single fare would exceed double the new single, and be above the new statutory maximum. They had to be reduced from 1.78d to 1.75d per mile producing a further loss in revenue. Since monthly return fares then became the same as ordinary return fares, monthly returns were abolished, (the 10% increase had been cut back to 7.7% - after five years of no increase). Increases authorised would yield £16.6m, including £3.2m on Monthly Returns (down from £4.5m implemented in January), to be implemented on 2nd March in the London Area and 1st May in the Provinces. [BTC 1951 Report, page 77: Tribunal changes in Ordinary fares reduced the projected yield by £4m].

Worse was to follow. Following public criticism, the Government issued a statement on 7th March stating that "the decision was not that of the Government, but by the BTC under authority of a Scheme confirmed by the Tribunal, an independent judicial body, and that legislation does not require the consent of the MoT". (The Scheme was substantially altered not confirmed). In response to objections by MP's on the increases, MoT said on 10th March that "it was inconsistent with the purposes of the Act for me to interfere, or to require the Tribunal to review the operation of a Scheme they had just confirmed, and that no other action other than reference to the CTCC is open to me", (in fact, the Act gave him powers to ask for a review by the Tribunal, at any time). He said that "Fare Stage alterations could be referred to the CTCC". Fare stages related only to road services, but he referred the whole Scheme to the CTCC on 11th March 1952, saying the "Alteration of fare stages and fares in relation to them" were a "main cause of complaint"; and mentioned "considerable public comment on an increase in passenger fares recently made by BTC under authority of the Order dated 27th February 1952, by the Tribunal under the BTC Passenger Charges Scheme 1952. He asked the CTCC for "conclusions and recommendations". The CTCC decided, in view of the large number of protests against increases all over the country, to incorporate in its Report both the matters referred to it by the MoT and the whole question of increases sanctioned by the Tribunal. Following an enquiry in which no less than 17 members took part, the CTCC produced a special report on the Charges Scheme, replying on 8th April [and published as a White Paper, Cmnd 8513 on 17th April], that it was "in the national interest" that the BTC should pay its way. In order to do this it "must increase its charges for transport if they are insufficient to meet this obligation", under the 1947 Act. In this connection, the CTCC accepted the Decision of the Tribunal that the revenue which the BTC sought to obtain from passenger fares was necessary. They said it was "fair to the travelling public" and opposed staged increases for those facing the biggest percentage increases to bring sub standard fares into line; "staging increases would cost £1m pa, which was essential to BR". They said the scheme proposed to bring all fares including sub standard to one level, and had this not been the basis but a fixed increase applied, the general rate of increase would have been above 20%. They pointed out "that the Tribunal accepted uplifting sub standard fares and that the decision was right, although it was not for them to challenge". They said that the sudden introduction of a limitation of arrival on EMR to 08.00 hours - which the Tribunal had approved - was too severe and recommended extending it for the time being to 08.30 hours, which would take them into the peak. In regard to complaints of hardship arising from increases in seasons and other reduced fares, they said it was "not to be expected that any undertaking, nationalised or otherwise, should provide concessions to a few which must be paid for by the many. They could not overlook that the 1952 Scheme London fares were 86% above prewar, and 90% elsewhere, which compares most favourably with the increase in prices for almost every other service and commodity". On the subject of fare stages they said the new stages should remain. Thus on the two grounds on which the MoT had put the issue to the CTCC, viz fare stages and national interest - under his 1947 Act powers, they argued that the scheme was fair. They criticised BTC for not publicising details earlier because "charges were sub judice until a decision had been made by the Tribunal". This I could not comprehend. The BTC had publicised its application in the media. The details of the scheme had been given to all 200 objecting organisations and had been subject to prolonged debate in public, and comprehensive reporting in the media. It is difficult to see what more the BTC could have done except publicise that the Tribunal may approve their requested increases, grant absolutely zero, anything in between or something totally different.

On 17th March 1952, the MoT was asked to "ensure that this burden is equally shared in all sections of the country", but replied that it would "not be proper to issue directions such as those to which the question referred", (and yet he issued on 15th April a Direction which interfered with a Tribunal decision of which he had known since 17th January). In Cabinet on 16th April, the PM said that some further delay must be imposed before the introduction of the new fares outside London in relation to the general scheme of transport reform which they had in hand (the denationalisation of road freight haulage which had absolutely no bearing on passenger fares). The terms of reference for the CTCC "would be drawn in such a way as not to bind them to recommendations which were consistent with the BTC duty to meet their expenses out of revenue". The CTCC had reported on 8th April - this indicated an intention to refer it to them again. The CTCC stated that they "had not yet heard from the MoT, but it was difficult to foresee what it would be asked to consider - the recommendations of the Report of 8th April had dealt with all problems both in and outside the London Area, including the abolition of workmen's tickets and increases in seasons". CTCC Annual Reports do not mention a further review.

Despite the Statutory Decision of one ministerially appointed body and the advice of a second, on 15th April the MoT directed the BTC not to implement increased charges due to come into force on 1st May 1952 - charges outside London - beyond their existing level, but permitted the Tribunal's decreases to stand. "Whilst not wishing to prevent the BTC from increasing charges to meet increases in costs as had been done by other Nationalised Industries, he considered that certain charges inflict substantial hardship on some sections of the community and should be carefully examined", (the Tribunal had done exactly this, although the Act made no provision for them to do so. It was later estimated that the cost of the Direction was £5.5m pa (Increases authorised by the Tribunal from 1st May being worth £4.5m and Tribunal decreases cost £1m, the decrease being implemented, but not the increases). The MoT said that he "was not fettered by recommendations of the CTCC", (which begs the question as to why he asked for their recommendations). He made this Direction under Section 4 of the Transport Act which empowered him to give the BTC directions of a 'General Character' in relation to matters which appear to him "to affect the national interest", and shall only be given after consultation with the BTC. Opposition MP's were not convinced that consultation had taken place. The Direction on proposed increases in fares, excluding the decreases, seems to have been of a very specific character, rather than of a 'General Character'. It was very selective in the fares which were later subject to reduction by the MoT. It is inconceivable that it would benefit the national interest to hold some fares down at an artificial level. Quite the reverse - since freight rates would be forced to bear a disproportionate burden - which is what happened, thereby affecting exports as the BTC was a significant carrier of export goods at the time. (The MoT remarks of June 16th on freight are particularly revealing, see page 70). At a Cabinet meeting on 16th April, 1952 the Chancellor of the Exchequer said that "although it was right to step in to prevent the unreasonable fare increases which would otherwise take place outside London on 1st May, railways would have a serious financial deficit if fares were not adjusted soon to reflect increases in costs". On 16th April, Ministers told the media that "it intended to secure adjustments in rail and bus fares in operation in London after referring those outside London to the CTCC", (which seemed to be pre-judging the outcome of any reference).

On 21st April, the Prime Minister stated that "the principle of sub standard fares should be preserved and not unduly raised and the MoT had a right and a duty to give a general Direction. If the BTC have not the discretion to carry out the Direction they have a duty under Sec.85 to make an Application to the Tribunal to enable them to do so". What this was saying that the

BTC, having been given a judicial authority, 13 months after submission, by the Tribunal to implement a modified version of their proposed Fares Scheme, which was subsequently referred to the CTCC, before being reduced by the MoT, the BTC were empowered to go back to the Tribunal for another prolonged hearing, when its finding may again go to the CTCC and .... This was absurd. Sec.85 enabled the BTC to question a Direction if it would interfere with their duty to pay their way taking one year with another. Even, had the MoT negated the whole increase, it could have been argued that the loss could be made up by other means - this year, next year, sometime ....., or even loaded onto freight rates. The BTC had a stark choice to accept the MoT Direction of 'half a loaf', or delay any increases for many more months. Only a fool would have followed that course. Had those who drafted and passed the 1947 Act intended to have the Tribunal making Recommendations to the MoT, instead of legal and binding Decisions, they were perfectly capable of saying so in words of one syllable - they had not done so. The Prime Minister said "it was not in the national interest to impose disproportionate increases on sub standard fares. It was an objective of the Government to be fair". (The Government could, of course, have achieved that objective without further reducing the lower yield permitted by the Tribunal by directing that the percentage increase should be sufficiently over 20% on all fares to achieve the original yield. Furthermore, the CTCC had said the increases were fair). On 19th April, he argued that Government and Parliament needed the power of Sec.4 of the Act "because the policy of the BTC may be wrong and contrary to the national interest" - but they were overriding the Tribunal, not the BTC. Moreover, the Government was doing what they always said cannot be done - interfering with a Judicial Judgement - the Tribunal was a Court of Law. The Government could have appealed to the Court of Appeal - the LCC did so in 1953.

In the debate in the House of Commons on 28th April, the MoT was absent due to illness, [he resigned due to ill health on 7th May]. The resolution was moved by the Home Secretary, [which the Opposition criticised, saying that he had no ministerial responsibility and it should have been the PM whose hand they detected in the policy]. The Home Secretary said that disproportionate increases should not be applied to railway charges outside the London Area and that a means should be sought of applying the same principle [retrospectively] to the London Area. The Government took the view that fares which the BTC were already charging in the London Area and proposed to charge to the rest of the country were likely to cause great and undue hardship and referred to the deprivation of privileges which were granted by the former railway companies for good and sound reasons, (Armies used to form squares on the battlefield for "good and sound reasons", but they don't now. The most compelling "good and sound reasons" were the respective Acts authorising Railway construction - which specified certain fares, the Government's Cheap Trains Act, 1883, and Government refusal to raise fares during six years of wartime control). He stated that the decrease in Ordinary fares by the Tribunal was of little significance because passengers travelled on Monthly Returns. I had worked in 17 different booking offices by 1952 and could have told him that Ordinary Singles were the second largest selling ticket, and represented a significant part of income, and the third largest 'Furlough' (for Service Personnel), were based on Ordinary Fares. Moreover, LT's principal issues were Ordinary fares. In fact the loss was substantial. BTC 1951 Report shows £13.4m in Ordinary fares; the decrease imposed by the Tribunal was 28.3% = £3.8m. The Report shows £48.9m in Monthly Return fares; the decrease imposed on Ordinary fares by the Tribunal reduced the 10% increase implemented in January 1952 to 7.7% = £1.1m. The "insignificant" loss from the Tribunal decision was £4.9m that is 22.8%. The Government argued that as BTC were now saying that the 1951 Deficit would be anywhere below £10m, there was no need for an increase. (The 1951 Accounts being in balance would not affect accumulated deficits, nor provide reserves - see earlier BTC forecast in January 1952). Opposition MP's said the PM had brusquely overridden the MoT. During the Debate, an MP recalled that "ten weeks earlier the Speaker had ruled that fares could not be discussed because there was no Ministerial responsibility". Opposition MP's said that as the MoT had known since January of the increases, he could have acted before the London increases (and all decreases) were introduced. Responding to questions on the statutory requirement for consultation with the BTC, the Government spokesman winding up the debate said "there were conversations with the Chairman of the BTC but no correspondence". Although he was twice asked for the dates on which consultation took place, no dates were given. (The legality of a Direction was considered in 1955 - see page 74).

Government opposed higher increases in sub standard season tickets, workmen's and other concessionary rates by a greater percentage than was to be imposed on standard fares and decided that fares should not be increased disproportionately - all had to be increased by not more than 20%, despite the Tribunal authorisation previously given which would have brought more equality in fare levels. (A restriction to 20% would have been bad enough, but the next step was unbelievable). On 16th June, the MoT said that it was his role "to see that gross anomalies did not persist - but the original Tribunal Decision had done that, the Direction actually perpetuated anomalous fares and disparities. He said that "all passengers are travelling on the backs of the nation's freight charges" - media reports stated that he should, therefore, have been increasing fares not reducing them. (See my comparative summary of passenger and freight charges increases from 1948 to 1955 at the end of this Chapter). He announced modifications to the increased passenger charges introduced in the London Area on 2nd March (which had been implemented before his 15th April Directive), as well as those which, but for his "standstill" order, would have been brought into effect throughout the country on 1st May :-

1. The rate of increase of sub standard fares would be reduced and would not be more than the same increase as standard rates.
2. EMR would be available up to 08.30 hours in all cases where workmen's tickets were available up to that time or later.
3. The issue of shift workers tickets would be resumed in the London Area and would continue outside London where withdrawal [on 1st May], had been authorised by the Tribunal.
4. Fare stages on LT buses would be restored to those prevailing before 2nd March, despite the recommendation of the CTCC.
5. Passengers holding monthly and quarterly seasons purchased before these changes took effect would be given an appropriate refund.

(Fares which the BTC had said were only 6% of the standard fare would by the application of the Tribunal Order have been increased to 11.8% of the New Standard, were held by MoT Direction at 10% of the New Standard fare).

The MoT said the new fares would come into operation in the London Area on 31st August and in the Provinces on 1st September, (17 months overdue).
He said that the sub standard fares affected would be :-
[a] ordinary, EMR and seasons on LT.
[b] workmen's, EMR and seasons on BR. All these would be increased by 20% compared to a maximum increase of 42% under the scheme sanctioned by the Tribunal [BTC asked for 50%].
[c] railway concessionary fares which were on a general basis of 50% of ordinary fare would continue on the basis of 75% of the new reduced ordinary fare; concessionary fares at 66.6% of ordinary fare will be replaced by the new reduced ordinary fare. "In both cases the increase would be less than 10%". (He did himself an injustice - the former would have a 7.4% and the

latter an 8% increase; the margin with other fares widened where the BTC and the Tribunal had sought to narrow them, thus he failed to reduce anomalies).
[d] Discount on bulk travel would cease.
[e] fares for members of the Forces and Merchant Marine and their wives and children would be considered separately, (This was for Duty travel - travel at their own expense would be at 75% of the Ordinary fare, under para [c]).

The MoT said the revenue loss would be £1.9m [London: £1.24m, Provinces: £0.66m], over and above the reduction imposed by the Tribunal. The modified increases were implemented 17 months after the application was made. The Tribunal ruling was bad enough, this further interference was disastrous. The BTC had asked for an increase to combat rapidly escalating prices, [costs had risen 77% faster than fares and rates since prewar], after five years of no increases outside London, and only modest increases in the London Area. Today, people wonder why BR was losing money. Inequalities and anomalies remained unaddressed (a classic example of the Government keeping three dogs and barking itself). The yield was substantially reduced:-

BTC Draft Scheme envisaged a yield of	£17.0m
In October BTC added, due to the long delay	£ 4.5m
Total BTC proposal	£21.5m
The Tribunal reduced the yield by	£ 4.9m
The MoT further reduced the yield by	£ 1.9m
The net yield was then	£14.7m

By 1952, the RPI had risen 20% since 1948 whilst the Fares Index had fallen by 7%. In 1951, the RPI had risen by 19% against the Fares Index falling by 11%. Between 1951 and 1952, the RPI rose 8.6% against 4.4% in Fares. There was absolutely no justification for holding down fares on the grounds that they were too high. Quite obviously they were too low. Opposition MP's said the only possible motive for holding fares down was the impending Local Authority elections. Tories had taken office in late 1951, following four years of nationalisation under Labour in which this adverse trend had been developing. Had the Tories not interfered they could have attributed the increases to Labour policies. Conceding BTC's full application in 1951, immediately it was submitted would still have left fares behind in the inflationary spiral. BTC losses arising from the delay were as follows:

£17m requested 17 months earlier	= £24.1m
£4.5m requested 11 months earlier	= £ 4.14m
Total	= £28.24m

This was compounded by the further loss of £6.8m pa (£21.5m reduced to £14.7m - see above), over each following year. The losses were further inflated by the Minister of Labour who added £12m pa to the wage bill, (see Page 12). Notwithstanding what the Government said about fares for 400,000 in HM Forces being considered separately, they would benefit immediately, as fares (for travel at their own expense) went up by only 7.4% after five static years, whilst many of the general public paid 20% more.

BTC Passenger Charges Scheme, 1953, - 26 pages of "exhibits" - detailed financial data - were submitted in support of the Application on 5th January to raise certain fares - mainly affecting travel to work - Season tickets and Early Morning Returns which were much lower than ordinary fares, but for which services were more costly to provide - yielding £6.1m in the London Area [LT £5m, BR £1.1m] and £0.5m BR outside London. BTC proposed to increase LT and LT&S Ordinary fares and BR [London Area] Day Returns, EMR and seasons by modest flat rate amounts, and similar increases outside London. [BTC 1953 Annual Report: "fares outside London are generally higher than comparable London journeys"]. The BTC would leave ordinary fares untouched and press for season and EMR to be increased throughout the country. The Tribunal hearing began on 17th February when the LCC and eleven others challenged the jurisdiction of the Tribunal to consider the scheme based on a clause in the 1947 Act which required a 12 month period to elapse after authorising a Scheme before considering an alteration to it. (It is doubtful that those who drafted the 1947 Act could have anticipated that ten months could elapse between Application and Authorisation - much less the ensuing delays). When the Tribunal ruled that it had jurisdiction, the LCC took their case to the Court of Appeal. The Appeal hinged on whether the BTC was submitting a new Draft Scheme or an Alteration to the 1952 Scheme. The LCC argued that the new Scheme was not new because it contained no new or innovative concepts, it was simply for increases in fares. The Appeal Court hearing took place on 3rd, 4th and 5th March, and rejected the case, referring it back to the Tribunal on 9th March where up to 40 advocates appeared at the 25 day hearing spread over ten weeks. Proceedings covered 522 pages. 42 Objectors, who tabled 35 pages of exhibits and statements, included the County Borough of Southend Rail Travellers Association, who were again vociferous in protecting the privileged position of the LT&S line on the grounds that it was a dormitory of London and even that some parts should be treated as a separate enclave. Why they should expect this to justify fares lower than those in the Provinces is not evident. Certainly the cost of running, maintaining and replacing their trains would be more costly than those in the Provinces because the effect of the peak was so much more marked in the London Area. Some objectors seemed to believe that freight traffic was subsidising passengers in the provinces, but all revenue went into one pot, hence if freight subsidised passenger it would do so nationally. Moreover, provincial passengers were paying higher fares per mile anyway. The QC for the BTC said that to avoid increases, 6.7m additional passengers would be required each week to provide additional revenue of £5.5m and asked those who were suggesting this option, whence those extra passengers were to be found - there was no reply. He also said that objectors had been given ample opportunity to raise a large number of matters [eg economies], but they had not done so. They could not claim that the BTC was not efficient and economical. The President of the Tribunal said: "The real case was that this Tribunal is not a proper body to examine the efficiency of the LTE". (If they were not able to do so in respect of the LTE, how had its predecessor, the Railway Rates Tribunal been expected to do so for the four main line companies - which were far bigger?). The Tribunal estimated the London Area deficit as £4.8m - £4.9m [£0.7m - £0.8m less than the BTC]. The Tribunal Order of 20th July confirmed the Scheme with modification to EMR fares, arising from the Tribunal estimate of the prospective deficit of London Area services. The Draft Scheme yield of £6.1m in the London Area was reduced by the Tribunal to £5.6m, and from £0.55m to £0.5m outside London, due to the fares reductions they imposed on EMR and seasons. BTC were to implement on 16th August 1953. (The RPI had risen 22% since 1948, fares had fallen 4% in the same period).

BTC Application for Passenger Charges Scheme, 1954, the first under the 1953 Act, was submitted on 1st April, and would replace the 1953 Scheme. A yield of £5-6m was forecast of which £4.25m would be from LT. The hearing, involving 13 advocates, opened 18th May, taking 15 days spread over eight weeks, Proceedings covering 340 pages. There were 19 objectors, of whom 16 appeared, including LCC and 12 other local authorities. BTC said it had been accepted by the Tribunal and most objectors that the London area must pay its way - objectors had fallen from 90 to 19. The BTC had returned to the Tribunal again due to costs rising and the inadequacy of previous decisions. Cheap evening tickets had produced less rather than more revenue in London. The small surplus expected from the 1953 scheme had been eroded by cost increases; just under 80% of receipts of LT derived from ordinary fares. No changes were proposed outside the London Area with regard to maximum scales under the 1953 Scheme. The main proposal was for a small increase in EMR and season tickets on LT with increases on BR London Area by assimilation [fares for similar journeys increased correspondingly]. The Tribunal President said "he did not like the proposed increase of 9d (about 4p) in the weekly season rates and asked for figures showing the proportion of season revenue". LT said 24% of season revenue was on weekly tickets, 30% monthly and 46% quarterly. On 10th June, a Preliminary Decision by the Tribunal decided LT had pitched requirements too high and modified the proposals to reduce their yield to £3.6m. Both the BTC and objectors were asked to submit revised proposals, recasting the original fares to achieve this reduced level. The hearing resumed 5th July. Detailed suggestions were received only from the BTC and LCC, but the latter would not achieve £3.6m. The BTC revised proposals involved dropping proposed increases in LT&S, LT and other London single and day fares, modifying EMR increases, reducing some season rates, but increasing those over eight miles. The modifications reduced the yield by £0.75m after allowing for £0.17m increase from Seasons. South Essex Traffic Advisory Committee objected to a proposed increase in a monthly season from Upminster to Charing Cross (17 miles) from £3.5.3d (£3.26p) to £3.10s (£3.50) under the modified proposals (one return journey per day, five days per week, averages over a year at 736 miles per month; at £3.50 per month = 0.47p per mile - 65% below the average BR fare). The Tribunal rejected the revised proposals and issued a Judgement on 9th July, confirmed by Order 23rd August, effective from 26th September, which revoked the 1953 Scheme as far as the London Area was concerned but did not affect it for BR outside London. The Order confirmed the revised fares except for the seasons which had to remain at the level set out in the original proposal, reducing the yield by £0.92m, about 17% less than BTC had originally requested, despite unquestionable evidence of deficits. BTC were "disappointed by the Decision and services would not be self supporting". (the RPI had risen 26%, fares remained 4% below 1948).

The BTC applied to the Tribunal on 7th March 1955 under Sec.23 [of the 1953 Act] for a temporary increase in fares - mainly in the London area: Seasons, EMR, Day and some ordinary fares, mostly ½d or 1d rises; (1d = less than ½p), which they authorised on 28th April for implementation on 5th June 1955 - three months to deal with an emergency [that delay, which also involved a freight increase cost £8.1m]. It had to be followed within one month by a formal submission, which was therefore the **1955 Application** to alter the **BTC Passenger Charges Scheme 1954,** There were 17 notices of objection - including 13 from local authorities, 12 advocates and 16 objectors appeared during the six day hearing from 13th to 23rd June and produced a 117 page report. It was the first Application for the alteration of a Charges Scheme. The BTC in its submission said that "we are not doing more than seek to offset increases in cost" and that EMR were unduly low and uneconomic and there was no justification to retain them. They pointed out that bus companies not owned by the BTC had been putting in applications to Licensing Authorities "at regular intervals" to increase fares. The yield was forecast at £3.8m [LT £2.6m, BR £1.2m]. One witness, the Chairman of the Federated Ratepayers of Enfield claimed that fares had gone up by 80% since the war - told by the BTC advocate it was 40%, he didn't argue. (Clearly he had not studied publicly available data when he would not have negated his own case by a 100% inaccuracy - fares had been increased in 1946 and 1947 by almost 40%, since when fare levels had declined, but were now back to 1948 levels). He said that the BTC should charge less for people travelling regularly to work (viz peak hour commuters who had forced costs through the ceiling) whilst shoppers (who try to avoid the peak like the plague) should pay more. It was suggested at the hearing that a staggering of hours was needed to alleviate the peak problem. One witness for objectors was the Chairman of numerous organisations, but did not himself travel by rail - he cycled 1½ miles to work. His "evidence" related to others who had changed from rail to cycle because of "high fares". He claimed that "only two things had gone up in price - coal and transport". He didn't say what his employment was, but admitted that his gross pay had increased by 100%, net 95%, so one can only wonder about the effect on prices of his wage increases. (It is surprising that a person who didn't travel by train could be construed as a witness in a Court, especially when his whole "evidence" was based on hearsay). Objectors referred to the second increase in six months - the previous application had been submitted a year earlier but the delay between application and implementation reduced the margin. They ignored Tribunal reductions of fares BTC had sought to increase. The Alteration was confirmed by Order on 11th August for implementation on 4th September. (The RPI had risen 34% since 1948, the average fare was now back to 1948 levels).

On 30th November 1955, the BTC applied for alterations under Sec.23 for temporary amendments to the 1954 Scheme, as altered by the Order of 11th August, affecting London area fares. The Tribunal gave temporary authority on 2nd December for increases on road services on 18th December and rail on 8th January 1956. The BTC then submitted a new **Application to Alter 1954 Charges Scheme** on 30th December to confirm those alterations. This was overlapped by another Submission.
The BTC made an Application under Sec.23 on 20th February, 1956 which the Tribunal considered. On 23rd March before an Order was made, the Application was withdrawn in accordance with the BTC intention to co-operate with Government Policy for six months. On 25th May, two months of the original six month standstill commitment to Government having elapsed, the BTC envisaged seeking approval for implementation at the end of that period. Therefore, they submitted a draft **1956 Passenger Charges Scheme** to revoke the 1954 Scheme and to increase some maximum charges, [EMR, season tickets, Day & Ordinary on BR with similar increases on LT]. On 9th July, 1956, the BTC asked to adjourn the 1956 Application after they had "decided to co-operate with Government to stabilise prices to the end of the year", (the six months had increased to ten). Despite LCC objections to an adjournment, the Tribunal agreed and proceeded to hear the earlier application. (A ten months delay, cost £28m. The Tribunal's Annual Report for 1957 records that "as no steps were taken by the BTC for six months, the adjourned Application was dismissed under Rule 33 of the Tribunal Rules". The BTC was, of course, tied to an end of year moratorium, viz., seven months by the Government).

On 22nd March 1955, the Attorney-General informed the Cabinet that "the MoT does not, in my opinion, have power under Sec.4 [1] of the Transport Act 1947, to give a Direction which will relieve the Commission [BTC] of the duty so to conduct their undertaking as to secure that their income is sufficient to meet expenditure taking one year with another. He has powers to delay or prohibit increased fares if, in his opinion, the national interest would be affected and if such a duty would not necessarily result in breach of the BTC duty under Sec 3 [4]". He explained that a Direction may be in order if the burden of increased costs could be met in other ways such as economies. (The 1952 Direction had been issued "to avoid hardship", no reference was made to potential additional economies. A serious problem would arise if the MoT said the BTC could make more economies, but the BTC disagreed. The MoT would have had grave difficulty in identifying his economies). The submission of this Secret Memorandum to Cabinet suggests that a Direction similar to that given in 1952 was being contemplated, but was avoided by the BTC "agreeing to co-operate on stabilisation of prices".

The hearing of the Application of 30th December 1955 began on 9th July 1956, [after the 1956 Charges Scheme had been adjourned], before 13 advocates and occupied four days, ending on 2nd August. Reference was made to the continued existence of sub standard fares which the BTC had not been allowed to uplift to standard four years earlier. Now, under existing powers these would be increased in the autumn yielding £1.5m, but an element of sub standard anomalies would still remain. Some sub standard fares would be raised in London from 2nd September 1956 - about 13% of all travel on LT [comprising over a half of EMR and one third of seasons] were at sub standard fares. The yield of the 1955 Application would be £3.8m [LT £3.3m, BR £0.5m]. There were nine objections including one from South Essex Traffic Advisory Committee which suggested a weekly season be introduced at a lower cost available for one journey each way per day (how staff would check if tens of thousands of passengers were using a season only once in each direction was not explained. It was an irrelevance, since it was peak travel which created excessive costs whilst the off peak was underutilised). The LCC suggested seasons should be untouched and ordinary fares bear the burden (season holders caused peak costs and were at the root of the deficit). The Post Office Union objected "that increases fail to recognise that the cost of travelling is constantly increasing because of the ever growing distance between the travelling public's place of work and home", (presumably they expected BR to charge the same however far they extended their travelling distance, hence if they moved further away from London to obtain less costly houses, they would gain, BR would lose). At the end of the last day, the President said: "We allow anybody who feels he has something to say, to say it even although he has no rights to be heard, subject only to excluding any reference to subsidies". Proceedings covered 95 pages. (When I read phrases such as "You are, are you not, the Director of Budgets for the BTC?", I could not avoid wondering whether archaic legal customs prolonged hearings). The Order, dated 7th August, 1956, authorised alterations in the manner sought for implementation on 1st September. (The RPI had risen by 38% since 1948, the Fares Index was still trailing behind at 4% above 1948).

On 5th April 1956, the BTC applied under Sec.79 for alterations in the 1954 Scheme, as amended in August and December, 1955, for powers to rename 'Third Class' as 'Second Class'; and for authority to negotiate with European countries on through fares. The Tribunal considered this at a Public Inquiry on 11th May, there were no objections. An Order was issued on that day giving the necessary authority. (It is incredible that the BTC had to ask authority for such changes).

An unusual case which did not affect the general public took place in 1956. The BTC sought to end a practice by which Police Forces enjoyed cheap rail travel. Under the 1842 "Act for the better Regulation of Railways & Conveyance of Troops", the Secretary for War had made provision for "whenever it shall be necessary to move any of the Officers or Soldiers of HM Forces of the line, Ordnance Corps, Marines, Militia and Police Forces" ..... to be carried at rates negotiated with individual railway companies - usually at 75% of the public rate. Police then were a relatively new organisation and ranked with the Army as a means of keeping order. The Cheap Trains Act 1883, provided for the conveyance of the Queen's Forces, including the Police, but no negotiation had taken place with them so far as fares were concerned. The Army and Navy then travelled at 75%, - the Act provided for over 150 personnel, at 50% reduction. In 1932, with "road transport rearing its ugly head" - as BR's advocate said - railways conceded 50% of the ordinary fare. In 1951, BTC negotiated a new agreement with the Armed Forces at 70% for single journeys, and 60% for return journeys, but this was thrown into confusion by the unexpected dramatic reduction in ordinary fares by the Tribunal. Consequently, in 1953, BTC negotiated a revised agreement based on 85% for all journeys which approximated to the same yield. The BTC gave a 15% discount on accounts rendered to the Armed

Forces for duty travel - travel by service personnel on weekend leave was at their own expense and was at 75% of the ordinary fare. There being no agreement with the Police, BR began to charge standard fares in 1952, and the Police Forces objected saying it was unlawful. The Metropolitan Police paid full fares on LT although the Cheap Trains Act applied to LT trains, but not buses. BR had to refund the amount "overpaid" until they could bring a case before the Tribunal to resolve the matter. They wrote to all Police Forces on 17th April 1956, and it was decided that the Dorset Force would appear on behalf of all Forces at a hearing which began on 10th June. They demanded fares at 75% of standard for duty travel, which was better than the Armed Forces enjoyed. The total annual account for Police Forces was under £60,000 pa, therefore the sum in dispute was small. The President said "Surely the question of concessions generally is whether we are the better judges of what will best for railways or whether the BTC are the best judges!" The Tribunal decided that "charges to be made for the Police Forces shall be at the rates which from time to time apply to the general public".

BTC 1957 Passenger Charges Scheme submitted on 11th April, revoking the 1954 Scheme, was to permit some increases in maximum charges authorised in that Scheme, seeking headroom in fares and to gradually phase out EMR. London lines and LT&S Ordinary, EMR and seasons were to be subject to increases, and outside London, EMR and seasons would have similar increases. The Scheme had a forecast yield of LT £4.5m, BR London lines £1.4m, other BR £3.4m. There were 41 objections mostly from local authorities. A seven day hearing began 29th May and spread over seven weeks, with 16 advocates appearing; the Proceedings covered 183 pages. After BTC's advocate had spoken of increases in costs overtaking income as "nibbling away" - converting surplus into deficit, the President of the Court asked: "Why not wait until they have nibbled away a sufficient amount to require remedying", (BR had an Operating deficit of £16m and forecast a deficit of £35m plus £40m to Central Charges - devoured rather than nibbled). The BR advocate answered "because by then it is too late". A QC appearing for the LCC objected to increases as "there is no statutory justification for asking for a surplus" - the Act required the BTC to create reserves and to pay its way taking one year with another, hence a surplus was a prerequisite. Somerset CC pleaded for restraint on seasons because of student travel. (Councils should subsidise student travel not BR, in any case, BTC Accounts showed that fares were below 1938 levels in real terms - how much restraint did they want? I cannot recall any restraint in Council Rates I paid). The Surrey Union of Residents & Ratepayers complained about withdrawal of old coaches because of the expense of replacing them (and thereby putting up fares - in view of later attitudes this was incredible). Rev TA Craggs, Uttoxeter, sent a 28 paragraph letter, saying he couldn't understand the purpose of a time restraint on Cheap Day tickets - after 0930 (which was to fill empty seats off peak), and went on about the post First War problems of people keeping in touch and thought BR should be making it cheap for them to do so after the Second War (acting as a national nanny, instead of paying its way). He also referred to "a Yorkshire village where people were "bus minded - they paid 3/- (15p) for a bus journey of 79 stops taking 72 minutes, rather than 2/- (10p) for a rail journey of 15 stops taking 55 minutes". (How could people be objecting to BR fare increases with this sort of comparison - did they want to travel for nothing?). Despite this he complained about high fares which "had destroyed a fellowship engendered after World War 1. The BTC stated that any increases approved would be implemented selectively; a significant word in view of claims made in later years, that BR did not implement selective pricing until their "arm was twisted by the NBPI in 1968". The Tribunal confirmed the Scheme on 6th August 1957, with some amendments to come into force on 8th August. (The RPI had risen 45% since 1948 compared to average fares by 6%).

BTC Passenger Charges Scheme 1958 submitted 1st September, revoked the 1957 Scheme and set out to provide "true maximum fares" giving headroom between actual and authorised fares in contrast with previous hand to mouth Schemes and "will avoid the procession of annual applications by giving managers flexibility upwards, instead of only downwards - which was used". Hence they had returned regularly for increases. LT&S fares will be the same as LT, but other BR London Area fares will be on same maximum rate as the rest of BR, viz higher levels. Minor amendments to charges included sleeping car and Pullman supplements, Reservations, dogs, PLA and left luggage. The forecast yield was £10.5m, [BR £4.6m, LT Rail £1.9m, Road £4m]. 62 objectors asked to be heard. The hearing began in London on 18th December and occupied 22 days over a period of 27 weeks, being adjourned between 23rd December and 3rd February due to non availability of the Hall. 19 advocates appeared. Although "past schemes had asked for maximum fares, it was generally understood these would be the actual fares". BTC was effectively asking for the present maximum of 2d per mile ordinary fare to be increased to 3d per mile, which would still be below prewar in real terms, with proportionate increases in EMR and seasons. They were repeating their request for EMR to be dropped as a statutory obligation and have them only selectively where commercially justified and possibly to abolish them eventually. In the meantime they wished to narrow the gap between EMR and ordinary fares. BTC pointed out that 44 Municipal and 21 privately owned bus companies had withdrawn workpeoples fares since 1952. Peak travel did not pay because season holders were travelling at ½d per mile which was exceedingly cheap - the average fare was 1½d (just over ½p) per mile. They were seeking new headroom for season tickets of 18-50% - the higher being at 50 miles - to prevent the gap widening further between them and ordinary fares and had proposed a new maximum scale for seasons in the London Area. The present structure tended to encourage peak hour travel because seasons had a lower cost per mile than any other ticket, often less than half the ordinary fare. A season would still have a discount of 27% on a 10 mile journey. [BR managers had advocated seeking authority to end the statutory duty to issue Day Return tickets in the peak, but BTC Minutes show that General Sir Brian Robertson, the Chairman of the BTC, personally decided not to do so]. Some objectors referred to a rate being economic when they meant economical. BTC said the fares were not economic to them. On the subject of the contribution to be made annually by LT to the BTC Central Charges [Overheads, Capital Redemption and Interest Charges on the Fixed Interest Stock], the President of the Court said: "we shall have to get this contribution for LT fixed by Parliament for a period of some years". A QC replied: "That would be a great blow to the Bar, if that were to happen, Sir"; (it would indeed; by reducing argument between lawyers for applicants and objectors and shortening the duration and cost of hearings). The Borough of Hastings "acknowledged a considerable sum spent on re-equipment and improvements", but objected to higher fares to pay for it. The Ratepayers of Kent were unable to see the consequences of peak travel, and seemed to imply that Northeners were not paying enough, (although the average fare per mile in the Provinces was higher than in the London Area). Kent CC "opposed any further increase in fares" - not this increase - by inference in perpetuity. (Did that happen to rates in Kent? There was a prejudice against paying fares which surpassed the reluctance to pay for other goods and services; fares per mile were 115% above 1938, retail prices 165%). In an interim decision on 8th May 1959, the Tribunal rejected the Draft Scheme as a whole because they were not satisfied the season rates would give reasonable flexibility and asked the BTC to supply a new scale of maximum season rates so that the difference between existing and proposed maximum rates was halved, and to give an estimate of additional revenue from such a scale. The BTC did so; there was then a further period of three weeks for objection, before the Inquiry resumed on 23rd June. Proceedings covered 520 pages. The Tribunal authorised the revised scheme on 8th July

1959 and it became the **1959 Passenger Charges Scheme,** having started as the
1958 Scheme, to be implemented 1st August 1959. It introduced season rates
lower than those submitted and empowered BTC to raise ordinary fares on BR
services other than LT&S from 2d to 3d per mile. BTC would be released from
statutory EMR at the end of 1960, meanwhile EMR fares would be increased.
LT wanted £6m for central charges and £5m for reserves; the Tribunal reduced
the latter to £2½m. Before the scheme was approved there was no headroom in
permitted maxima for seasons and EMR. (The RPI had risen 47% from 1948 to
1959, compared to the Fares Index by 8%.)

The BTC applied in March 1960 to increase fares to a level which would
produce £2.5m pa. The Application under Sec.23 of the 1953 Act was
considered on 14th April by the Tribunal who ordered that the increase
sought could take place. In November 1960, the BTC made a further
Application to temporarily amend the 1959 Charges Scheme as amended on 14th
April. The Tribunal gave temporary authority on 21st November 1960 to
increase LT fares from 15th January 1961 to yield £2.75m. To obtain a
working surplus, LT made a further application to add to increases due to
begin on 15th January to produce an extra £2m pa. The fares approved for
introduction on 15th January on a temporary basis had to be confirmed by the
Tribunal. BR sought powers to increase ordinary fares and seasons on LT&S
and day returns and seasons on other BR London lines - to maintain parity
with LT. For seasons outside London, BR sought powers for headroom of 20%
above the existing maxima which would be similar to the headroom already
existing on ordinary fares outside London. These led to two **BTC 1960**
Applications to alter the 1959 Passenger Charges Scheme which was an example
of the inflexibility of the legislation. Hearings took place over 13 days
between 24th January and 6th March 1961 for permanent authorisation of the
increases requested in the preceding March of London Area fares and season
rates. It involved 13 advocates, 42 objectors and Proceedings covered 289
pages. The BTC had submitted the initial **1960 Application** and before this
had been heard came forward with another **1960 Application** for the alteration
of **BTC Passenger Charges Scheme 1959.** The "hearing of the first application
had been delayed by commitments of the Tribunal and ill health".
Applications submitted could not be withdrawn, so they had "to get rid of
the temporary order of the Tribunal under Section 23 of the 1953 Act, before
proceeding with the second application which covers everything in the
first"; "Objections had been received by the Tribunal up to the day before
the hearing began, therefore advocates had to have time to examine and
consider their implications". Long distance season holders would still have
a discount of 60% at 50 miles, 66% at 80miles, on a 5 day week, although the
cost of providing trains was greater for such traffic. Kent CC said that
"fares were as high as people can pay"; (fares were below 1938 in real
terms). The BTC's advocate, to illustrate the distance one could travel on
a season, mentioned that the cost of a monthly season would enable a user to
travel 2244 miles Brighton - London compared to London - Turkey by the
Simplon-Orient train 2178½ miles. The President queried whether this was
via the new Simplon-Orient route! The Order dated 14th June refused a 20%
headroom over the existing maximum cost of seasons allowing only 5% then and
a further 5% on 1st January 1962 together yielding £8m. (The RPI had risen
57% since 1948, compared to fares by 29%).

The BTC made an emergency application on 16th March 1962 for permission to
increase fares, and to increase seasons by 10% - an extra 5% on the increase
of 5% authorised from 1st January 1962 but not used, "before introducing
this present increase of 10%" in order to make one increase instead of two.
On 26th March the Tribunal made an Order to increase London season and
Ordinary fares on 15th April and 2nd June. In accordance with Sec.23 of the
1953 Act, the BTC submitted on 16th April, an **Application to Alter the BTC**
Passenger Charges Scheme 1959. The Inquiry was held on six days between 4th

and 22nd June 1962, to make permanent the temporary fare increases authorised by the Tribunal Order of 26th March in which LT and LT&S ordinary fares were raised to BR levels and increases made in suburban Day Return fares and LT&S concessionary fares, - LT&S was part of BR but had long enjoyed advantageous discrimination. Seasons on LT, LT&S and throughout BR were increased by 10%. The yield was LT £2.6m and BR £1.5m. The 10% season increase was made up of a 5% previously authorised to apply from 1st January 1962 plus a further 5%, temporarily authorised to apply from 2nd June. The BTC said that from 1952, seasons had lagged behind ordinary fares, this increase would bring them back into line. BR had used up the remaining ½d headroom on 3rd June and fares were 3d per mile. Again it was evident that the LT&S line enjoyed fares below the rest of BR - a 30 mile single ticket cost 5/6d (27½p) on the LT&S compared with 7/6d (37½p) elsewhere on BR. It was mentioned that the electrification of the LT&S had cost £18.3m (which must have been financed from sources remote from the LT&S since passengers on that line had been paying sub standard fares and successfully opposing the creation of reserves). The hearing involved 13 advocates and 25 objectors, Proceedings covering 139 pages. This "was expected to be the last Passenger Charges Scheme in consequence of the 1962 Transport Act which terminated the Tribunal's power except in the London area". The Tribunal Order was issued on 9th July authorising the increases to take effect on 16th July. (The RPI had risen by 61% since 1948, the Fares index by 40%). From 1st September 1962, the Tribunal role was restricted to passenger fares in the London Area by the MoT's Transport, London Fares, Order 1962. (On 10th September, the President of the Tribunal, Sir Hubert Hull retired at the age of 75, having been President since 1950).

On 7th June 1963, BR and LT applied for certain maximum charges fixed under the London Fares Schemes to be temporarily increased from 23rd June. Both applied for a confirming Order on 5th July and also sought authority for increases in certain maximum season rates. The **BRB Application for a London Fares Order 1963**, [LT made a similar application] was to confirm the temporary 10% increase authorised by the Tribunal on 23rd June, and to reduce from 10% to 5% the discount on a quarterly season against the cost of a monthly season. LT was seeking £2.6m and BR £2.2m. The hearing began on 11th November and lasted ten days, there were nine advocates and 27 objectors, Proceedings covering 282 pages. The Tribunal mentioned "Assimilation" - the practice of parity between LT and BR, which did not exist prior to 1950, and was adopted and perpetuated by Tribunal decisions. BR ordinary fares were different from LT in the London Area because of the LT practice of tapering fares. If BR followed LT practice, there would be an enormous difference between the BR fare from London to the last station inside the London Area boundary and the first station outside that boundary. Hence, BR worked on a fixed rate per mile for ordinary fares. Whilst BR and LT had been part of "one undertaking" it had been the practice to work out LT costs, which were all related to London travel, whilst BR had no means to split costs precisely between London and the rest of the country. Then the percentage increases approved for LT by the Tribunal were applied to BR London lines. When attempts were made in earlier applications to split BR costs for the Tribunal, objectors tried to swing a heavier share of costs and overheads away from London onto the Provinces and spent days arguing over minutiae. LT said they needed £2.6m, objectors told them they only needed £2m, and still opposed provision to replace assets arguing that reserves were "to cover only bad weather and strikes" (not, I'm sure, a Private Sector principle). The Order, issued on 19th December 1963, confirmed the increases introduced temporarily on 23rd June, but refused to grant additional increases applied for in respect of increased maximum charges for seasons. In announcing the reasons for its Decision - a new Government directive - on 5th February 1964, the Tribunal referred to the "less onerous duty imposed on BRB" - a reference to the Government paper

"Financial & Economic Obligations of Nationalised Industries - Cmnd 1357 - April 1961, which gave BR five years to earn surpluses to cover deficits - as a White Paper it was not binding. (If past experiences were any guide BR would not be allowed to earn a surplus). In view of this "less onerous duty" the Tribunal had formed the opinion that BR could make a proper contribution to discharging its duties without reducing the existing discount of 10% on quarterly seasons. This discount had been applied for 35 years, and there was no record of the reason it had been set at that level. (Such a decision was bound to delay the BTC earning surpluses). The Tribunal set out an eleven paragraph definition of depreciation. They decreed that fares should be equal for different journeys of similar length and argued that a season ticket holder was entitled to discount on various grounds including the possibility of less than full use of the ticket (perhaps there should be discounts on car tax and insurance for those who make "less than full use" of their cars). This decree again refutes later allegations that BR was slow in turning to selective pricing - BR was told not to do so. (The RPI had risen since 1948 by 63%, Fares by 41%).

On 12th March 1964, BRB and LTB applied under Sec.46 of the 1962 Act for an Order to raise the maximum charges for journeys not exceeding one mile from 3d to 4d, leaving other charges unchanged. These increases had been temporarily imposed by the two Boards on 1st March under Sec 48. The hearing of the **BRB 1964 Application to Alter the London Fares Order 1963** took place 1st June 1964, before four advocates and six objectors, producing a 17 page report. In 1963, BR increases were to maintain parity with LT, [LT had made a similar application]. In this hearing BR had noted the intention of LT to apply for an increase and had to follow suit to avoid a transfer of peak passengers. LT's yield would be £2.7m and BR £30,000, - by raising LT&S line fares to the level of LT where LT trains run alongside to the same stations - but BR still had to go before the Tribunal even for this level of increase. Reference was made to the Phelps Brown Committee which showed that fares were effectively costing less. The Harrow Public Transport Association said that higher fares should not be charged in the London Area than elsewhere. These increases were to bring London Area fares up to the level BR were currently charging in the rest of the UK [where BR had freedom on fare levels after 1962]. The Association criticised the proposed increase in fare from 3d to 4d per mile, when the submission showed the general rate of 3d per mile was unchanged but there was to be 4d for a journey of one mile. Objectors also said there were too many staff at stations (other groups say that there are not enough). The Application was approved on 12th July by the London Fares [Variation] Order 1964. (The RPI had risen since 1948, by 71%, Fares by 43%).

On 10th July, 1964, BRB and LTB announced, under Sec.48 of the 1962 Act, that certain charges fixed under the London Fares Orders would be temporarily increased from 19th July. BR applied for the **BRB [London] Fares Orders 1965**: on 7th August 1964 to make the temporary increases permanent and seek new maxima; [LT made a similar application]:
1. Abolish statutory day returns - advocated by the General Managers of the two busiest commuter Regions in 1958 (see page 77), to avoid having to issue them in the peak, but issue cheap off peak and weekend tickets, cutting shoppers' peak travel - a practical way of tackling overcrowding - yield £0.28m. Obligatory day returns were introduced by the 1950 Charges Scheme.
2. Abolish favoured concessions on LT&S which enjoyed the lower LT scales. BR & LT were by then the same up to 10 miles, and over 10 miles LT&S was paying less than rest of BR. Terminate the practice of maximum ordinary fares on LT&S being on the same scale as LT and raise to BR's 3d per mile scale, yield £0.04m.
3. Season fares to be increased by 5% on the LT&S line to bring them up to BR levels with a net yield of £0.66m.

4. End "Assimilation" - BR & LT fares at one level in the London Area - introduced when BR and LT were part of the same organisation.

Objectors were given 2½ months to lodge objections. The six day hearing began on 23rd November 1964 before 12 advocates and 16 objectors, Proceedings being on 153 pages, plus a four page Order giving reasons for the decision. The QC for the Middlesex CC, Surrey CC and LCC challenged the yield which BR forecast it would get from an increase, argued that BR's £32.7m for the cost of London services was too much by £1m, and said that figures in connection with through trains were too high (doubtless if Provincial and Home Counties argued over respective cost allocations at the same time, both would say they were too high leaving no one to pick up the unallocated balance). He contended that London was being "overcharged in movement, track, signalling, terminal, documentation and administration costs" but his witness did not quantify the extent, (BR were evidently guilty until proved innocent). He submitted that as BR were not for the time being under an obligation to establish a general reserve [a Government decision], they ought not to seek to raise from London passengers more revenue than is sufficient to meet their working expenses and interest charges in respect of the carriage of those passengers. "Any excess would not form a reserve for London passengers but will merely reduce to an insignificant extent the deficit in the undertaking as a whole"; (any steps to reduce the deficit should have been welcomed). Objectors who were ruled not to have legal status included the South Nutfield Over 60 Club - "not a body purely representative of passengers"; the South Nutfield Parish Council which was insufficiently large - the 1953 Transport Act set out Objector Status and gives as examples an Urban District Council representing 50,000 residents; and Chelmsford Railway Users who were outside the London Area. The Tribunal criticised BR for not allocating EVERY train's expenses on a basis of **Primary Apportionment** of train miles AND a **Secondary Apportionment** of passenger miles. (The mind boggles at the size of this task and I could not perceive its value as it could only be arbitrary and create more data for objectors to dispute). The Tribunal said that the proposal to raise season rates was "for more revenue" whilst LT&S increases were for "rationalisation". The Tribunal opposed the change in LT&S line fares, because "whilst it may remove an anomaly for BR it creates one for their competitors" (When did that become illegal?). On the proposal to increase seasons by 5% which would raise them above LT fares, the Tribunal "were not satisfied that BR couldn't discharge their financial duties without this increase". Another gain for the LT&S line. The Tribunal agreed only to the Day Return alteration. The Decision was issued on 22nd January 1965. From 1st February fares outside London, which were not controlled by the Tribunal, increased by 8%, and season tickets by 5% in marked contrast to this Decision. (The RPI had risen since 1948, by 79%, Fares by 59%).

On 4th January 1966, BRB and LTB announced temporary increases in maximum charges from 16th January, and then lodged applications to have the increases confirmed. **BRB 1966 Application for London Fares Order** was for changes with a yield of £2.1m - the LT&S line was still below other BR lines, [LT made a similar application]:-
1. Increase maximum ordinary fare from 3d to 3¼d per mile: 3d had applied from June 1962 in the London Area, elsewhere it had been 3¼d since February 1965 = £0.4m
2. Restrictions on young persons' concessions = £0.4m. BR said some bus operators had increased these fares from 50% to 75%.
3. Increases under Sec.48 of the 1962 Act £1.3m - consisting of:-
[a] abolish 1½ and 2½ mile maximum ordinary fare on LT&S line.
[b] increase the maximum ordinary fare at 4-12 miles.
[c] increase the maximum ordinary fare at other distances on LT&S.
[d] increase of 5% in maximum season rate.

Proceedings on BR's case occupied five days from 26th April to 5th May 1966, covered 154 pages; and involved ten advocates and seven objectors. Referring to the Barking residents complaint that they had no cheap fare, BR's advocate pointed out that "in BR's previous application, their spirited representation to the Tribunal to reject BR's proposal for the line to go over to BR's system of ordinary fares with cheap day tickets in the off peak was successful. They now want the best of both worlds having got cheap ordinary fares - in the peak - they want off peak fares cheaper still". The ordinary single on the LT&S at 10 miles was lower than all other BR fares up to January 1966, and a weekly season saved 4% or a monthly season 33%. One objector claimed that the London passenger travelling about the metropolis by BR was subsidising the rest of the UK, (he had a mirror image of the situation - see Page 81, end of paragraph on 1965 Order). The BRB reminded the Tribunal of earlier Decisions - BTC v Dorset Police Authority: "Police enjoyed the right to a concession under the Cheap Trains Act 1883 and that under the Transport Acts the amount of any concession was subject to the jurisdiction of the Transport Tribunal. The Decision had been that there was no case for police being in a different position from the public generally, and the price of transport cannot be regulated as to vary in accordance with the means of those who buy them", (see Page 75; earlier Decisions had appeared to make such provision). BR's advocate said "we have destructive criticism in fair measure, but of constructive suggestions - not a word". The changes were approved by an Order of 18th July effective from 1st August 1966. (The RPI had risen since 1948, by 86%, fares by 65%).

However the **BRB 1967 Report** records "The Government refused, 'because of the freeze' to allow certain increases in fares and charges, including some approved by the Transport Tribunal for the London area, as long ago as July 1966". The Government referred the proposals to the NBPI. No changes in fare levels were made in the London area in 1967. In the spring of 1967 the BRB informed the MoT of a wish to raise fares. These proposals were referred to the NBPI on 3rd October 1967, who approved on 30th May 1968, a 10% increase in ordinary fares, and 7½% in season rates in the London area, "which would raise the RPI by less than 0.04%". Despite this, they were then submitted to the Transport Tribunal, "which considers fares in the London area", which they did at a four day hearing between 9th and 15th July 1968 and were told that the BRB submission was for increases of 10% on ordinary fares, and 7½% on seasons, with a yield of £2.5m. The BRB said that over 63% of all passenger journeys were made at reduced prices. There were eight objectors including the Travellers Associations' Joint Committee (TAJC), which said that "it is our view that a lower level of fares on journeys up to 12 miles will increase travel on lightly used lines and that this will improve the BRB finances and should help to decrease road congestion"; (there were no lightly used lines in the peak in London, and it was not the Tribunal's duty to take account of road congestion, there was no transfer of cash to BR for reducing road congestion). The TAJC said that the decision highlighted the Tribunal's function in protecting the public from excessive increases. (That was not the role of the Tribunal which "must do nothing which will, in their opinion, prevent the BRB from discharging its financial duty". The NBPI had been set up to control price increases, and they had approved what the Tribunal then reduced). The TAJC referred to the White Paper "Transport in London" which would abolish the Tribunal, and said "The BRB is acting in a dictatorial manner concerning return tickets which are going to be made available on a daily basis only"; (the change was dictated by fraudulent travel. I have not yet encountered a single private sector company which implements price increases after democratic consultation with its customers, which, by definition, must be the inferred converse of their criticism). The Tribunal rejected proposals to raise ordinary fares by 10%, although these embraced increases they had approved two years earlier, which were then frozen by the Government and considered by the NBPI who had approved increases of 10% only three months earlier. The Tribunal authorised increases averaging 7½% on seasons and on ordinary fares. The Tribunal agreed to increase fares on the LT&S to the level of those charged by LT "because these fares had been similar for many years". (LT&S favoured again). BRB forecast the yield would be £2.3m. The Tribunal's London Fares 1968 Order was dated 16th August and was implemented 1st September 1968. (The RPI had risen since 1948, by 101%, Fares by 69%).

Freight Charges

The 1949 BTC Report mentions that a Draft Freight Scheme would be submitted first to the Traders' Co-ordinating Committee on Transport before submission to the Tribunal. In 1951, the Tribunal forecast that if the new "Freight Charges Scheme was lodged in August 1951 it would not be in operation before 1954 at the earliest" - three years for them to consider one scheme, whereas the Government had allowed two years for the preparation of Schemes for its rail and road passenger and freight businesses, and its canals and docks. The RRT had taken seven years to implement one freight scheme for rail.

On 28th November 1949, the MoT asked the permanent members of the Tribunal acting as a Consultative Committee for advice on a BTC request for increases in freight charges of 16.66% for merchandise by goods and passenger trains. They held a Public Inquiry which sat for 13 days in January and February, 1950, attended by 17 advocates, and produced a report of 235 pages, listing 2849 Questions. There were 13 objectors including the BISF who were asked what effect an increase in rail charges would have on their costs, but not how a 16% increase in steel prices had affected BR. The SMMT said that the aggregate effect of freight rate increases upon each separate raw material would add £2 to a small car and £4 to a larger model. He was asked "how they coped with the 16% steel price rise in the previous year" and replied that they had managed to cover it. He was told by an advocate that the public were well aware that cars were priced a few pounds below the next £100, because it looked cheaper rather than due to precise costing, so it didn't necessarily follow that the additional freight cost should increase the selling price. The NFU said that passengers should pay more instead of freight customers. The Tribunal reported on BR charges to the MoT on 6th February recommending the increase of 16.66%, which the MoT authorised from 15th May 1950. [The BTC 1950 Report conservatively estimated that the delay in approving the increase cost £11m. The 1951 Report placed it at £15m]. The CTCC 1950 Report said that this BTC application to the MoT to authorise an increase in rates for merchandise was also referred to them by the FBI although the Tribunal Public Inquiry was considering it. The CTCC said "as recently as 1947 (three years earlier - which industry apart from BR had not increased charges for three years?), increases in charges were authorised by the MoT - at that time it was estimated this increase would provide adequate revenue for the requirements of the BTC" (for ever?). It is not clear why two public bodies considered the same issue. The increase produced £30m.

On 20th March 1951 the MoT asked the Tribunal acting as a Consultative Committee for advice on a BTC request for 10% increase in BR freight and parcel rates, and docks and canals charges - the total estimated yield of £20m would leave a gap of £25m plus accumulated deficits of £40m. There was no Public Inquiry and they recommended a 10% flat increase on 6th April, which the MoT approved from 16th April. The FBI protested that the BTC had not linked pay to productivity. (British industry was the last to criticise pay deals without strings as industrial demarcation was a national disgrace).

Due to a further steep increase in costs, the BTC asked on 17th November 1951 for a further 10% - subject to a maximum of 10/- per ton (50p) - with 20% on smalls and 50% on returned empties (the latter were not wanted by road haulage as being unprofitable) with a net yield of £22m. The MoT wrote to the Tribunal on 23rd November, who recommended 10% only - with certain exceptions - on 3rd December, which he authorised from 31st December on all traffic, rejecting the request for higher increases on the costly smalls and returned empties, reducing the yield by £1m. The MoT told the House of Commons that BTC costs had risen by £40m in 1951, comprising £26m wages, (the Government had told BR to pay higher wages than they could afford - see Page 12), and £14m other price rises. He was aware that even if the Tribunal approved the BTC 1951 Passenger Charges Application and he approved the current Freight Application, they would be left with a deficit of £16-17m pa. Despite this, decisions by the Tribunal and himself reduced the BTC yield by £7.8m pa, (£6.8m fares; £1m freight), and would thereby increase the deficit by £24-25m in contravention of the provisions of the 1947 Transport Act.

In late 1952, the BTC asked the MoT to authorise 5% on freight rates. He wrote to the Tribunal on 29th October. They replied on 13th November that they had concluded that an increase of $7\frac{1}{2}$% was desirable to avoid financial difficulties. The MoT decided to authorise, from 1st December, only what the BTC had requested, with a net yield of £12m. The MoT said that the BTC had the power to increase rates by 5% for its own road haulage fleet, and that it was doing so. (This emphasised the absurdity of the concept of Charges Schemes - the BTC had to apply to the Tribunal or the MoT for permission to raise rail freight rates but needed no external authority to do so for its road fleet). One MP suggested to the MoT that freight should be at a flat rate throughout UK on the same lines as the Post Office but the MoT said it would only serve to transfer large volumes of traffic to road over shorter distances.

The BTC asked for a 10% increase in freight charges on 30th December 1953. On 10th February 1954 the MoT accepted the advice of the Tribunal acting as a Consultative Committee to authorise an increase of 10% on merchandise rates. The Tribunal saw the application as a stop gap, and that the BTC may need more. It was approved by the MoT from 1st March, "rather later than the BTC had hoped when the application had been lodged", (The delay cost £6.8m).

The BTC asked for emergency powers on 7th March 1955 to raise freight rates by $7\frac{1}{2}$% and smalls by 15% which were well below the index of wholesale prices, to yield £17m. The BTC said it would benefit BR if they had liberty to adjust charges. The MoT asked the Tribunal acting as a Consultative Committee for advice on 12th April. In that letter, he said that "he was impressed with the importance of taking steps to prevent the financial position of the Commission from becoming unmanageable". The Tribunal reported on 26th April that the BTC "request should be granted as soon as possible". The MoT authorised increases to be introduced 5th June 1955, which contrasted with the urgency both he and the Tribunal had voiced. BTC said that the delay which also involved a fares increase cost £8.1m.

The BTC Merchandise Charges Scheme 1955 was submitted on 21st March following months of consultation with representatives of rail users and other interested parties, despite which 28 objections were lodged with the Tribunal. It proposed to set maximum charges and Terms & Conditions of Carriage and would cover 85% of merchandise traffic - the Scheme excluded coal and coke. Four objectors claimed that the Scheme was ultra vires, so the Tribunal held an Inquiry on 12th July to consider points of law, handing down a decision on 7th September that all contentions or preliminary points of law were unfounded except as regards Terms & Conditions. (How could it be claimed that a scheme to alter rates, based on an Act of Parliament was beyond the powers of the BTC? - that alone delayed BR from regaining

traffic by three months. The concept of Charges Schemes was like a Ruritanian farce). The Public Inquiry opened 10th October 1955 and ended on 7th March 1956 after 44 days of hearings. There were 26 advocates. The volume of 'exhibits' and documentation which BR had to prepare was mountainous. Objectors included the Dustbin Manufacturers Association, the National Association of Sack Merchants, Cable Makers, the Globe Tank Foundry, Galvanised Tank Manufacturers Association, Cement Makers Federation, Brewers, NCB, Central Electricity Authority, Agricultural Engineers Association, British Coking Association, Joint Iron Council, National Galvanisers Association, National Federation of Scrap Iron & Steel, BISF, UK Chamber of Shipping, Hull Chamber of Commerce & Shipping, Association of British Chambers of Commerce, Gas Council, and the Traders Co-ordinating Committee on Transport. (The latter was one whom the BTC had already consulted - perhaps they shouldn't have bothered). The British Chambers of Commerce said long distance rail users should not be called upon to subsidise freight traffic in other areas, e.g. senders in remote parts of Scotland shouldn't subsidise others (with so many unprofitable lines in Scotland, the boot would be on the other foot). Their advocate stated that the BTC should be forced as a matter of law to carry goods at charges which were less than their costs. The Traders Coordinating Committee said maximum charges were too high (by inference in perpetuity), but agreed that charges should cover the cost of carriage. They opposed the concept of loadability, and urged perpetuation of standard charges, albeit increased (this was contrary to the 1953 Act, and therefore irrelevant). They advocated goods being broadly classified (retaining the disadvantages to BR which did not apply to road haulage). BISF said there should be no maximum charges and that the cost of transport was a high proportion of the manufacturing cost, (The table on Page 21 disproves that claim, but materials were a significant factor in BR cost increases). Among the witnesses was Mr.Tait, Director of Costings for the BTC, who without doubt knew more about BR costs than the whole of the rest of those present put together, and since they included BTC's briefed legal advocates that didn't leave much knowledge for anyone else. Among remarks passed was one by the President of the Tribunal: "In our opinion some of the figures in Mr Tait's tables were too high". How could they arrive at that? He was the leading expert on railway costing. The cost to the nation of this, indeed all, hearings must have been phenomenal. The cost to BR in delay was worse, not merely in respect of revenue lost from traffic on which rates should have been increased, but more significantly from traffic lost to denationalised road haulage since 1953, because the two industries had reverted to their 1930's relationship. At the conclusion of the Hearing, the Tribunal President said any of 28 objectors could ask for resumption if any new information became available - but made no similar offer to the BTC. The Proceedings were recorded on a mammoth 948 pages. The Tribunal published an Interim Decision on 23rd July stating conclusions and the manner in which they proposed to alter the Draft Scheme. It set out amendments to the original scheme and the main area of difference in costs between BR's costing expert and the Tribunal for:
* wagon provision and maintenance,
* terminal shunting costs,
* track and signalling costs.

Outside BR, experience of shunting must be rare, and the data BR had on wagons, track and signalling could only be unarguable. BR still had to have statutory maximum charges - road didn't, (this was how the Government defined freedom for BR). The Tribunal confirmed the Scheme as amended by Order dated 31st December 1956, and directed that it should come into force on 1st July 1957. Due to the incredible length of time this case took, the Draft 1955 Scheme had become the **1957 Freight Charges Scheme**. The Tribunal imposed a lower level of maxima than BTC sought and said it was undesirable to fix maximum rates for consignments over 100 tons in owners wagons. BTC said "the authorised maximum rates were lower than charges being levied for an appreciable quantity of good loading traffic passing over medium distances". The rates for these traffics had to be reduced. Road haulage had no reduction made in its charges, nor any maxima imposed. Until 1st July 1957 Rate Books remained open to inspection, by traders and competitors - four years after road denationalisation. Chargeable distances by the shortest route had to be calculated, there being 7000 stations it required 50m distances to be calculated, even with a new computer that task took one year. BTC's Chief Commercial Officer said that unfavourable consequences would arise following from some of the Tribunal's decisions on the New Freight Charges Scheme.

In December 1956 a deputation of shipowners saw the MoT fearing cut throat competition by BR following the introduction of the 1957 BR Freight Charges Scheme which was supposed to give BR the commercial freedom they had sought for 30 years. Shipowners reminded the MoT of the good work of their industry in the war (but not of rail having to carry wartime freight diverted from coastwise shipping, - see Page 6. They were unduly concerned - the Tribunal had already inserted a clause to protect them. How that could be justified in view of their remit is difficult to comprehend).

Early in 1956, due to the delay in progressing the 1955 Freight Charges Scheme, the BTC applied to increase rates: 25% on returned empties, 15% on smalls and 10% on all other freight. The MoT, having asked the Tribunal on 20th March for advice on the application, rejected the advice when they recommended authorisation. He reduced the proposals by 50%. The Tribunal, in a memorandum to the MoT, did not agree with him and said "other considerations may have caused him to disregard the [statutory financial] objectives of the BTC" - inferring stabilisation of prices - "but this policy had not been applied to other Nationalised Industries or the Post Office, who put up their prices a week earlier". (The Gas Council increased their prices a few weeks later). The Tribunal stated that the increases were "urgently necessary", and recalled a statement by the MoT to the House of Commons that "it was expedient that regulations should be framed to reduce the amount sought from £24.8m to £14.1m for freight and from £5.7m to £1m for passenger". The Tribunal pointed out that "the MoT decision would prevent the BTC from, obtaining as much as they had hoped for Post Office traffic, and that the total yield would fall from £37m to £20.2m, with the deficit increasing by £35m to £104m by the end of 1956. The Tribunal are unable to agree with your decision". The BTC implemented the reduced scale on 23rd April 1956: 12½% on returned empties, 7½% smalls, 5% other freight. When this was discussed in Cabinet, on 6th March 1956, the MoT said "the balance of advantage would lie in increasing freight charges by 5%, and not the 10% as I had earlier proposed". On 13th March the Cabinet was told "a reduction in BTC proposals for freight increases from 10% to 5% might not generally affect the net increase in revenue since with higher increases in freight charges there would have been a greater loss of traffic". This rule of thumb judgement has no place in business. BTC already included in its submissions to the Tribunal an assessment of sales resistance, and the Tribunal took account of the BTC forecast and, on occasions, amended it.

On 12th July, 1957, the BTC announced in the press that it was increasing freight charges by 10% from 1st August. It then had to apply to the Tribunal for confirmation, which it did on 30th July, and was given approval by the Tribunal on 6th August for an increase of 10% in maximum freight charges. A Tribunal Public Inquiry was held on 20th November 1957, to amend the 1957 Freight Charges Scheme - the retitled 1955 Scheme delayed by tortuous procedures - which confirmed a 10% increase - there were no objections. The BTC advocate was asked why they had rounded up a Depreciation figure of £525.5m to £526m (about 0.1%), and the President of the Tribunal said because BR always round up! (Did he know a company which rounded down such figures - which is the inference I drew from the comment? It was standard commercial practice).

On 21st December 1959, an Application was made under the Road & Rail Traffic Act 1933, by the Chamber of Shipping for an Order that charges made by the BTC for the carriage of coal for the Gas Board be cancelled or varied or that such other relief be given which the Tribunal may order. The Tribunal Annual Report for 1960 states that "as a result of negotiation between the BTC and the Chamber of Shipping the application was withdrawn.

Administration

Each Application was preceded by the preparation of "exhibits and statements" to prove BR's need to increase prices, to anticipate the line of argument of objectors and prepare counter arguments. The standard procedure was for the BTC to lodge its application, which was then published in the London and Edinburgh Gazettes and selected newspapers. Objectors were then given 6-8 weeks to lodge an objection, after which the Tribunal would arrange a date for the hearing to commence. The first two or three days were allocated to the BTC to present its case, after which the hearing would be adjourned for about two weeks for objectors to consider their responses. If a private sector company had been faced with this procedure and had to place top executives at the disposal of this "Court of Law" annually for weeks or months and then to wait months or years for a Decision they would have been bankrupted. Before a ruling was issued, rising costs would have already overtaken the value of an increase, even had it not been reduced from the level at which the BTC had originally decided was essential. On receipt of a Decision, there may be a period of weeks in which to make adjustments to reflect what BR were now permitted to do. Despite this the public and media are unable to comprehend how BR losses arose. Whilst the Tribunal was engaged on a Freight Charges Application, an Application for a Passenger increase would be delayed, and, of course, vice versa, since there was only one Tribunal.

Reports of the hearings ("Proceedings") were on foolscap size pages and were a verbatim record. All the cases involved barristers (including KC's/QC's) being briefed by the BTC, and objectors. Witnesses for the applicants - BTC, (after 1962, BRB and LTB), and the objectors would be examined and cross examined and recalled. The number of advocates shown in the preceding pages was on a random day, some days may have had more, some less. Hearings were sometimes delayed due to non availability of accommodation or advocates due to holidays or sickness - all of which added to deficits.

Decisions Compared

The contrast in the authorisation of increases in passenger and freight rates is marked, as is the way in which they were pursued. All increases in fares, but not freight charges, were subject to a Public Inquiry. Had proposals for both been authorised to the same degree, increases in freight rates would have been less, and fares higher. The BTC had a duty to pay its way - as a whole, not separately by passenger and freight. The same Tribunal which usually accepted BR proposals for freight increases, tended to reject proposals for passenger - when neither was an exact science. When freight costs where first worked out on a more precise basis, and BR were establishing maximum instead of actual rates, the Tribunal reduced BR's proposed freight rates.

In the fourteen years in which the Tribunal had powers in respect of freight rates, there were nine applications, of these, only two were subject to an Inquiry. Of these, the Tribunal supported one application, but reduced the other. Of the seven cases which did not go to an Inquiry, the Tribunal reduced one, and in one case proposed a higher increase than the BTC had requested. The MoT rejected the latter recommendation, and on another occasion reduced a Tribunal recommendation to approve a proposed increase. Applications made to the MoT for authority to increase freight charges up to 1956 inclusive were made under Sec.82 of the Transport Act 1947. The MoT could only give such authority for charges to be changed in respect of services and facilities for which a Charges Scheme was not in force, but it did not preclude a Public Inquiry.

In the twenty years in which the Tribunal had powers in respect of fares, there were seventeen applications, all of which were subject to a Public Inquiry. They reduced BTC proposals in nine cases. The MoT rejected their Decision once (after the Tribunal had already made reductions), and the BTC twice withdrew submissions to the Tribunal "at the request of the MoT".

To summarise the details in the preceding pages: the Tribunal reduced proposed freight rates on 22% occasions, and passenger fares on 53% occasions, whilst the MoT reduced proposed increases in freight in 11% cases and held down fares on 17½% occasions. The MoT also asked the CTCC for recommendations on fares in 1952 and rejected their advice. BR fares were continually held down due to the concept of assimilation, (keeping LT and BR fares in line), to which the Tribunal clung long after BR and LT became separate legal entities. Because BR fares in the London area were kept broadly in line with LT fares (which had been lower from prewar days), this had a reaction on BR fares elsewhere.

The following table shows how freight rates were being allowed by the Government to increase faster than fares, whereas both should have been increasing at a broadly similar rate, in view of the BTC remit. Indeed average fares were actually reduced, whilst freight rates were increased. These charges are shown alongside comparable external indices to prove that BR charges were anti inflationary:-

	RPI	Fares	Freight Rates	Wholesale Prices
1948	100.0	100.0	100.0	100.0
1949	103.8	93.5	97.5	104.9
1950	106.7	91.4	107.5	119.6
1951	119.4	89.2	119.5	145.6
1952	120.2	93.5	134.5	149.4
1953	122.1	95.7	138.5	149.6
1954	126.3	96.4	148.0	150.5
1955	134.1	100.0	154.0	155.2

The Wholesale Price Index was not available after 1955.

An anonymous office wag paraphrased a slogan BR had on the theme of care for animals in transit - from "Customers can complain, cattle can't" to read "Voters can complain, vagons can't".

Believing that, if you are criticised on statistical grounds you must first check the source data, I decided in 1985 to analyse BR complaints. In 1983, BRHQ directed the statistics should be based on complaints not complainants. Thus if a letter referred to a train being late and full, that became two complaints instead of one. It was my understanding that the change arose from an external suggestion. In my view, it was counter productive, not least because it made comparisons impractical. BR's 63,000 complaints in 1983 sounded damning, especially as the Private Sector published no statistics, falsely inferring perfection. Relate the total to the number of passengers and the ratio of complaints to journeys was 0.01% which meant that 99.99% did not complain. Can the Private Sector claim such a standard, much less prove it? Is it reasonable to expect 100%? I think not. Nevertheless, those working in centrally heated offices expect it of BR whilst being unable to achieve it themselves. It occurred to me that some complainants must have been given redress and would not be regarded as dissatisfied if BR adopted Private Sector practice. If you return a defective product which is replaced, the Private Sector regard you as a satisfied customer; even if you make a 30 mile round trip to obtain satisfaction. They should deliver a replacement at once, and give compensation for inconvenience, but none offer to do so. In November 1986, the Restaurants Manager at Birmingham Airport told our visiting BR Quality of Service group that staff "endeavour to resolve things before there is a complaint, by replacing an unsatisfactory item". I had always thought that I was complaining when I asked for an unsatisfactory meal or dirty cutlery to be replaced or demanded a refund. BR statistics included such "complaints". My analysis revealed that 9% of letters included praise or thanks for some particular act, and revealed cases which were not complaints about Quality of Service or even about travel, as these examples show:

Incorrectly Classified - by Overzealous staff   5%
Suggestions on fares; Possible fraud; Requested information regarding cycles on trains; Unfounded rumours of station closures.
Unreasonable Complaints   6%
Unable to hear tannoy in privately owned on-station shops. Passenger travelling 89 miles allowed 9 minutes from arrival at Birmingham to the starting time of a speech he was to make in the city - the train was delayed by an accident - by road he would probably allow an extra hour. Passengers asked for a train to Castleton, and complained after arriving at Castleton, Lancs - our staff hadn't realised they referred to a minor Derbyshire village with no station. Had no ticket from an open station, "didn't have time to get a ticket" charged £2 on train supplement - imagine running from a shop saying I'll pay later, but BR customers believe that alone among other buyers they should be allowed to take the "goods" now and pay later.
Dubious complaints   3%
Wrong information given by staff two months earlier, complainant gave no details of train or date but claimed for a taxi. Dirty train four months earlier but gave no details of train or date. (No company will refund on such sparse information). Claim for sleeper berth refund after alighting for refreshments en route and missing train which departed on time - journey was paid for by a sponsor "because BR refused to sponsor the journey in aid of charity" - BR offered to refund the sponsor or charity if given their name and address, there was no reply. Train late, missed concert, demanded refund of fares, tickets had been handed in; BR asked for unused Concert tickets as proof of travel, but no reply was received.
Passenger's errors and misconduct   3%
Alleged reservations not available but passenger had looked at return instead of outward reservation ticket. Reserved seats occupied by others - hadn't complained to guards who had collected fares.

Fares   5%

Fare levels are not an element of quality of service. I wish to pay less for cars, suits, holidays, or anything else, but pricing policy is a matter for the commercial judgement of a company, overcharge and they may lose business. Overcrowded trains are symptomatic of underpricing.

Complaints from non travellers or not about travel   11%

Potato thrown from a train by a passenger at the conservatory of a house – complained twice; Repositioned signals "enabled drivers to look into windows of houses". No BT phones at small stations. Vandalism to cars in a car park over 200 yards away – no car park authority accepts responsibility for damage or loss in carparks, but motorists who accept that situation, take a completely different (usually sarcastic) stance where BR is concerned.

I concluded 33% of the complaints should not have been categorised as Quality of Service complaints and would not have been by any Private Sector company which dared to publish such statistics.

Net Level of Complaints

Next I ascertained whether genuine complaints had been given redress or accepted an apology – which the Private Sector regard as giving satisfaction. 55% had been given a voucher or cheque and others an apology or explanation. Only 2% wrote again still expressing dissatisfaction with BR's reply. It seemed to me that the picture being painted of BR was much worse than the facts revealed.

I examined the role of Quangos set up before the population adopted motoring as their primary means of travel. The Central Transport Consultative Committee (CTCC) and the nine Area Transport Users Consultative Committees (TUCC) were focussing on the wrong statistics. Their publicity invites complaints by passengers dissatisified with a reply from BR. The complaints they received was the true measure of public dissatisfaction and that was, I found, approximately 3% of BR's gross total – (see Page 92). In an internal report, I set out my findings using analogy of the way the Private Sector respond to complaints and pointed out that the Office of Fair Trading Reports exclude cases in which the company has "given satisfaction". OFT statistics were usually expressed in financial terms rather than actual numbers making comparisons with BR difficult. By relating the average price of a car to the total value of motoring complaints I produced a figure of 74,000 complaints in the 1984 OFT statistics, which was 5% of motorists i.e. 50 times as high as rail complaints and the latter was gross, – including those given satisfaction and non-travel complaints – whereas the former is net. I drew up an instruction to exclude from our complaints statistics, suggestions and unreasonable or irrelevant complaints, and to deduct those given satisfaction. After further thought, I concluded that it would be seen as trying to doctor the figures. Instead, I recommended to BRB's Joint Managing Director that BR should cease to supply statistics to the CTCC/TUCC's since complaints made to the TUCC's were the true scale of dissatisfaction with BR and analagous with Private Sector practice. To my surprise, he did so at once – Board Officers and colleagues to whom I had earlier voiced my revolutionary views had not been supportive. I advised compensation be given when dissatisfaction is detected before, in private sector parlance, "it became a complaint". I also suggested that we should have a target level for complaints received, arguing that since we, quite sensibly, had a target for punctuality which was below 100% we must expect complaints about delays. Similar comments apply to cancellations. Any company subjected to the scrutiny of a complaints body for 44 years, and to a discriminatory Citizens Charter would expect to find that it received complaints which progressively increased in number. Few who complain to private sector companies are aware that others have also complained about the same point, hence the scale of public dissatisfaction is not known.

When Railways were nationalised, the Government set up the Central Transport Consultative Committee (CTCC) and Area Committees for Scotland and Wales. The CTCC role under the 1947 Act was: "to consider and recommend any matter, including charges, affecting services and facilities of the BTC which has been the subject of representation made to the CTCC by users of these services, or appears to be a matter to which consideration should be given, or which MoT or BTC may refer to them for consideration". The 'BTC' included BR, BRS, BTC bus companies, inland waterways, docks and also hotels and ships owned by BR. The CTCC had no mandate on ships or buses owned by other companies, even if operating on the same routes as the BTC. The CTCC 1950 Report stated that the Association of British Chambers of Commerce and local Chambers of Commerce urged the setting up of Area Consultative Committees (TUCC's) mentioned in the 1947 Act. (The Chambers of Commerce did not set up watchdogs for their own customers). Under the 1962 Act, the duties of TUCC's were reduced to embrace only proposals for closure and Quality of Service, and the CTCC and TUCC's ceased to have an involvement in fares. In 1948, BR was seen as having a virtual monopoly. Perhaps, then there was a need for a body to represent passengers. But BR was not a monopoly then, having 20-25% of the market, and it certainly is not today, with about 9%; (MoT 1956 paper "Proposals for Railways", stated: the BTC "have not and never have had a complete monopoly"). Nevertheless, these bodies still exist in an age of cars, express buses and airlines. They claim to be the Rail Users' watchdog - a role in which many others participate: County, District, Borough, Community & Parish Councillors, Trading Standards Officers, MP's, Monopolies & Mergers Commission, Commuter Associations, Enthusiasts, Radio, TV, Newspapers and consumer associations. The independent Inspectorate of Railways, the best watchdogs, have been effectively monitoring Railway construction, safety, operations and vehicle design, since 1840, and have made the only major external contribution to safety, operations and design.

CTCC 1980 **Report** refers to a "De Facto monopoly enjoyed by BR". (In their 1987-88 Report, the CTCC criticised BR for using "an obscure legal term", viz 'lien' in the Conditions of Carriage, which Carriers had used since time immemorial. I was familiar with the meaning of lien, but found this obscure word in a in a small pocket dictionary, which did not contain the term "De Facto". The CTCC were saying that BR had, "in fact" a monopoly, which the average motorist would know was incorrect, and which the MoT had confirmed in 1956. As the South East is the only part approaching the definition of a monopoly, the Government should direct BR to sell off part of Network South East to the private sector - if they can find an entrepreneur with an inexhaustible money supply, an overpowering desire to lose it, and who is willing to tolerate external interference).

CTCC 1981 **Report:** "BR prevaricated with questions of finance and productivity .... the rail customer who alone is at the receiving end of all these problems". (The MoT decided that BR would be free to operate commercially. As that is still statutory policy, the CTCC should not be entitled to such data, no other industry would supply it. To say that "the passenger alone" is at the receiving end, is to overlook the taxpayer).

CTCC 1982 **Report** refers to new electric stock standing idle on the Bedford - St.Pancras line which "may jeopardise the future investment programme". It had exactly the opposite effect as BR management foresaw, when they decided it would not be brought into use until Unions agreed to new economical manning arrangements. It was placed where crews would see it every day.

Complaints

The TUCC role on complaints is in cases in which a complainant is dissatisfied with BR's reply - CTCC 1958 Report: "will investigate any reasonable complaint in which the complainant has failed [in the opinion of TUCC] to obtain a satisfactory reply from the department primarily concerned with the complaint"; 1959 Report: "do not investigate grievances unless they have first been put to the BTC"; TUCC Notices, at stations, inform passengers to send a complaint to BR in the first instance. The 1963 TUCC Handbook, [on sale to the public], reiterates this principle: "Only if the user is dissatisfied with the way in which they [BRB] have dealt with his complaint should he make use of the Consultative Committee to try to obtain redress". TUCC's are, uniquely, in a position to advertise themselves on every station, and to have their brochures handed out by BR staff. (Imagine the Private Sector being required to do likewise on behalf of Trading Standards Officers or Office of Fair Trading). Having publicised this role, I noted, in 1985, that the CTCC did not publish the number of complaints which TUCC's received. Thus, the CTCC's own objective - 1982 Report: "The CTCC attach great importance to keeping the public informed of the Committees' work" had not been implemented in this important particular. In some years not even all TUCC's published the number of complaints which they received. In their 1982 & 1983 Annual Reports, the most recently available when I carried out my investigation, a third of the TUCC's did not publish these important statistics in their own Annual Reports. Writing to those Committees, I obtained the missing figures and summarised the total received by TUCC's. These statistics, which I included in my internal report, appeared to be the first nationally aggregated TUCC statistics published, which considering the importance attributed to complaints was remarkable. I revealed that the TUCC's, in aggregate, were dealing with an average of 1800 complaints pa (2.8% of BR's gross figure). This was equivalent to three complaints per week for each Area TUCC which had a full time Secretary (and usually an Assistant Secretary) plus several part time members.

The CTCC published the gross number of complaints which BR received, instead of the net number which TUCC's received, giving a vastly different picture of dissastisfaction. If BR has given a complainant satisfaction, that complaint has been redressed - it would be so regarded in the Private Sector, if they published such data. In my view, the CTCC should have published, since 1949, in their Annual Reports, TUCC net statistics, which are the true measure of public dissatisfaction. In contrast with the absence of these statistics in its Reports, the CTCC included statistics of closures dealt with by each Area TUCC. When I was preparing this book, I based my claim that I was the first to publicise the aggregate total of complaints to TUCC's on my examination of CTCC Annual Reports. Therefore, I was surprised to find, that in evidence to the Select Committee in 1971, CTCC/TUCC representatives stated that "In 1970 the various area committees and the CTCC dealt with 4,000 complaints". The 1983 total represented a dramatic decline in the level of complaints, contrary to the impression the public were then gaining.

When, on my recommendation, BR ceased to supply the CTCC and TUCC's with gross complaints statistics in 1986, the CTCC began to quote TUCC net data in CTCC Annual Reports. Their statistics relate to the number of complaints not the number of complainants. The subtle distinction is illustrated by an analogous example. If you had taken your car to a garage and it was not ready at the promised time, they had failed to remedy one fault and did not replace a part which was out of stock and you wrote to complain - that would be three complaints to be registered by the TUCC for motorists - if there was such a body!

In the **CTCC 1986-7 Report**, there was no total number of complaints, it was

"3% above the previous year"; in **1987-8**, "over 4800, an increase of 3% over 1986-7"; in **1988-9** "almost 5000; 4% above the previous year"; in **1989-90** "over 5200, 4.6% higher"; and in **1990-1** it was 8053, 54% higher". Complaints are categorised by the CTCC :-

* "Suitability of Service". (I found that changing schedules to meet the aspirations of one person or group created new complainants from those then inconvenienced by earlier departures or later arrivals. When I complained that the BBC's service was unsuitable because they dropped without prior warning a TV programme on Bridge which I had set my video to record, they told me they were catering for the majority - a Private Sector practice - by continuing to broadcast a tennis match from Europe when it overran).

* "Overcrowding". (Arises because of a belief that one should be able to go to any station and get on the next train - which some passengers must assume is elasticated. It is a problem which is especially noticeable in commuter areas where it will be solved by pricing to create a balance between impossible demand and practical supply).

* "Fares Policy". (The CTCC has no remit on fares. There is no company which would not be besieged with complaints on prices if they gave the slightest hint of being willing to consider reductions).

* "Refunds & Claims". (My personal research into complaints revealed some unsubstantiated claims, see Page 89).

* "Station Facilities". (Complaints made to BR included vandalised stations and toilets, also litter, by inference, not swept up immediately it was thrown down by passengers and trespassers).

* "Staff Conduct". (These complaints, often uncorroborated, were accepted by BR at face value. During my journeys, I sometimes gave my name as a witness to a member of staff who was courteous to an abusive passenger who refused to pay excess which was due and threatened to report him).

CTCC **1991 Report** stated that 2033 complaints on Suitability of Service "to a certain extent reflects a unique campaign urging users to write to the TUCC which resulted in over 1000 complaints". My inquiries revealed that 1181 complaints (58% of that category), were from a newspaper campaign to change a train service, and should not have been included until BR had responded to the complainants, in accordance with the principle espoused by the CTCC. CTCC **1989-90 Report** says 1988-9 complaints at 5228 was a record. 5228 was 0.0007% of the 746.4 million passenger journeys, or one complaint to every 142,769 journeys. (How many places must the decimal point move before there is acceptance that complaints are not at an excessive level? Most firms would take full page advertisements to boast of such a low level of complaint to an independent Government funded body).

CTCC **1991 Report** expresses concern on delay in replying to letters. (Delay in replies to my complaints by Supermarkets, Banks, Building Societies, Insurance Companies, Stockbrokers, the Media, I tolerate. I only become intolerant when they do not reply to several letters which they later admit having received, or when they give cause for further complaint in their eventual reply. In complaining to private sector organisations, I have discovered an unusual phenomenon. The Post Office selectively loses some of my complaints, but no other correspondence. Cheques I send are never lost, they are paid in the very next day, albeit goods may be a long time in arriving. My experience may not be unique).

A complaint to a TUCC relates to an "unsatisfactory reply from BR", irrespective of the original nature of the complaint. Categorisation is, therefore, an irrelevancy - one total of alleged unsatisfactory replies from BR, with an indication of the extent to which the TUCC did not accept that a complainant had a case and the extent of a revised response from BR following TUCC intervention is relevant. If someone complains of an unsatisfactory reply from BR regarding a delay for which he had asked for a refund, it would be misleading to treat them as two complaints. I would expect to find that some complaints about refunds relate to delays or cancellations. To enable me to put complaints to TUCC's into perspective alongside my own earlier research, I asked the Midlands Area TUCC for permission to analyse their complaints - guaranteeing, of course, to respect confidentiality of individuals - not that I feared that any genuine complainant would have any qualms on that score. They declined my repeated request, offering only a discussion, which would not serve the same objective.

Generalisations are unhelpful in pursuing improvement :
CTCC 1981 Report: "a considerable number of complaints have been received by TUCC's about the great difficulty in contacting these locations" [Telephone Enquiries] there were no statistics to put that into perspective alongside the millions of calls made. (In 1985, my investigation into TEB standards revealed that the LMR were dealing with about 200,000 calls per week that is 10.4m calls pa for one of the five Regions. I estimated that BR as a whole were dealing with around 45m. If all complaints received by the CTCC & TUCC's were in connection with TEB's that would mean that 0.004% of callers were complaining - however, complaints they received covered all aspects. It is probable that some of them misdialled or picked up a wrong number).

CTCC 1983 Report: "there are too many instances of rudeness and unhelpfulness particularly at London Terminals"; "Too often staff are unhelpful or even rude"; (see my comments on Staff Conduct - Page 93).
CTCC 1984/85 Report: "We often hear of staff treating passengers as if they were an interference with the job". I wrote, on behalf of the LM Region, in 1985, to the CTCC who were unable to supply specific cases for me to investigate and neither could TUCC's to whom the CTCC referred me.
CTCC 1985/86 Report: "still too many complaints of bad manners and unhelpfulness". (Rudeness, unhelpfulness, bad manners or discourtesy by staff is inexcusable. They should pay heed to the principles inherent in notices which can be seen on Public view in Private Sector establishments : "The Customer is always right - sometimes confused, misinformed, rude, stubborn, changeable and even downright stupid - but never wrong").

CTCC 1982 Report refers to a lack of a code of practice in procedure for complaints as inhibiting complaints (the total lack of a code in the Private Sector doesn't inhibit me, or I guess tens of thousands of others - Charters and Codes of Practice are overrated). The CTCC "feel strongly that in answering complaints BR should follow the example of other Nationalised Industries in drawing attention to a right to consult a Consultative Committee if still aggrieved". (When they are privatised the practice must cease because when I wrote three letters on the same complaint, BT did not give me such advice).

CTCC 1986/87 Report refers to the Code of Practice on Customer Service and that "in fifteen months, eight passengers have filed claims under the arbitration scheme" and the CTCC expressed disappointment that only a small number of passengers are prepared to take grievances to arbitration which "may indicate BR and TUCC need to draw attention of aggrieved passengers to the scheme". It may alternatively indicate that there is only a small number of complainants with a sound case.

Fares
The Association of British Chambers of Commerce asked the CTCC in June 1952 to press the BTC to reconsider the withdrawal of Traders Season, Bulk Travel and Commercial Travellers tickets, which the Tribunal had approved in January, the CTCC accepted in April and the Government in May as being fair. The ABCC said that Commercial Travellers tickets were "an assured and

important source of revenue, second only to season tickets". The relative scale of BTC revenue was - Monthly Returns £48m, Ordinary £22m, Seasons £14m, EMR £8m, followed by HM Forces travel. Commercial Travellers paying one sixth less than the 1928 standard fare accounted for £0.2m - way down the league, and from my personal Booking Office experience, probably the lowest revenue earner of all ticket categories.

CTCC 1958 Report opposed withdrawing some through bookings which BR said had become too expensive to provide with a mechanised booking system, saying that they should be provided despite the implications of additional costs.

The 1962 Transport Act ended the statutory involvement of the CTCC and TUCC's on fares since BR had been directed to manage its affairs like any other business. This was a bit tongue in cheek by the Government, because the Tribunal still had powers over London Area fares and the MoT retained statutory authority to give directions. The CTCC continued to comment on fares - to which I drew the attention of BRB in my 1985 report, pointing out that BR cannot operate as a business given external interference in pricing. I argued that anyone who purchased a product after being told the price cannot reasonably claim dissatisfaction with the price; there was an option not to buy (BR has under 10% of the market). I will receive a dusty answer if I complain after paying £10,000 for a car that the price was too high, especially after using it. Even having found a defect, requiring it to be back with suppliers for weeks, I obtained no compensation. Why should a customer expect from BR what he cannot get from other companies? If I could prove that someone else had paid less for the same car I would still get no refund. If uncommercial refunds are given, the taxpayer will foot the bill.

CTCC 1972 Report records the MoT response to requests to increase their terms of reference by reintroducing their role on fares: "Government believe BRB should be free to operate commercially; generally fares and charges should thus be a matter of management for BRB to decide, it is therefore Government policy that BRB should exercise commercial judgement in their pricing policy". Despite this the **CTCC 1976 Report** states that they had set up a sub committee to consider BR's policy on reduced fares in March 1976 and it published its views in a report "Fares Fair" December 1977.

CTCC 1978 Report: "a basic principle is that those excluded from reduced fare offers were entitled to be shown that those included were generating a genuine commercial benefit to BR" (the MoT 1972 decision does not require that. Had the whole of the Private Sector suddenly decided so to do?); "the CTCC are continuing to monitor BRB thinking on reduced fare structures". **1980 Report:** "In the face of steep increases in fares" (fares had not caught up in real terms on prewar prices) "TUCC for London said passengers should have right of access to BR fare lists to guard against misinformation by BR staff" (Are we to be given right of access to retail computers, enabling us to check prices, and see whether, the item which is not on the shelf, is in the stockroom contrary to the invariable denial customers receive? Perhaps steps could also be taken to ensure that Building Societies always tell every customer when a change of account would bring increased interest).

CTCC 1981 Report - the Government had not changed their remit but the CTCC continued to air its views - "present fares structure is complex and requires simplifying". They referred to a "statutory inability to consider fares and charges - a drawback from which none of the other Consumer Councils of Nationalised Industries suffers" (overlooking the fact that those industries were making profits, having been allowed to decide their own prices mangerially since 1948, thus if their Consumer bodies can influence lower prices, the taxpayer does not suffer, as they would by interference in BR prices).

CTCC 1983 Report: "the whole fare structure is in need of simplification"; and "on first class day return fares - complaints received - CTCC will continue to give close attention"; "BRB continually being urged to increase geographical spread of inter city savers so that passengers who do not qualify for a railcard will benefit from reduced fares"; (the objective was not to offer the cheapest fares to all, but to maximise net revenue). "BR criticised because the South East sector offered £2 anywhere in November to senior citizens, other areas didn't" (it is not BR's remit to provide social equality. BR is not required to act as a branch of the DHSS; when BR tried to treat everyone equally, they received objections - see Chapter 2 - when BR price to maximise net revenue - a basic private sector practice - they are criticised - heads they lose, tails they lose).

CTCC 1985/86 Report (having no statutory role on fares) has a Passenger Marketing sub committee commenting on fares; "passengers should not be expected to pay over the rate of inflation" (why not - they were doing so with much of their non BR expenditure, and where were the pressures for BR fares to keep pace with inflation from 1948 to 1982?). Restrictions on London Savers are questioned, (imposed to reduce overcrowding or protect revenue). The CTCC took up with BR the unevenness of the January 1986 fares increase which varied from 5% to 14%. BRB said they were charging what the market would bear. They stated it is their role to guard against erosion of opportunity for off peak travel (a responsibility not mentioned in the statutes). The Report confirms that the CTCC still had no statutory right to consider or comment on fares or charges, but refers to "an impending relaxation of its role as indicated by the MoT in the House of Commons on 13th December 1983". During a debate on the **London** Regional Transport Bill, Mrs.Chalker said "industries must work to the financial objectives and determine fares without being subject to specific directions. Within that framework, there is a role for Consumer bodies in relation to the structure and relationship of fares, which will be dealt with when a suitable legislative opportunity arises. On the same day, in a written answer, another Minister, Mr.Mitchell said "It is for the BRB to determine fares. In October 1987, he said "it is for BR to set fares to take account of costs", and that "he did not intend to issue any objective to BR on fares").

CTCC 1987/88 Report criticised BR for a policy of pricing business off trains as a solution to worsening overcrowding problems. (History reveals industries which continually expanded capacity to meet increasing demand, eventually found they had passed the saturation point and went bankrupt - and they were not buying trains at £1-2m each). "BR adjust prices upwards where demand is strong", (a common private sector practice - see Page 152).

CTCC 1988/89 Report: "Government and BR have agreed CTCC will be consulted about and may consider structures and relativity of fares". (Government might as well transfer all BR's powers to the CTCC and transpose BRB management with the CTCC - some BR managers would enjoy the opportunity to criticise someone else trying to achieve the impossible). CTCC "does not support inflation beating increases (which reduce taxpayers support), and are dismayed by increases in long distance season tickets". BR explained that "revenue per mile from Inter City seasons was considerably less than from Savers and seasons elsewhere, [the Saver being for off peak travel whilst seasons are used in the peak], revenue from Inter City seasons being far below the cost of providing services with no subsidy for Inter City". The MoT agreed with BR. Despite the statutory restriction, CTCC said it "will continue to speak out against fare increases which are well above the level of inflation". They stated that they were still debarred from Fares issues but reserved the right to comment in general terms, in advance of a change in the law which has been promised by the Government (will this follow statutes on inflation beating car insurance premiums which will benefit ten times as many people?). The CTCC advocated keeping fare increases low on routes where objectives are not met, (but does not say who will make up the difference - the taxpayer or passengers on routes which are meeting objectives).

CTCC 1990/1991 Report: Local fare rises are "more difficult to monitor", (as the CTCC had no role in fares it is not apparent why they should be trying to monitor them); "CTCC is debarred by statute from considering fares", - thirteen years after the Fares Fair Report.

The 1977 "Fares Fair" 33 page Report mentions that BR "should now seek to divorce itself completely from the notion that its market pricing exists to help some social groupings at the expense of others". (From the inception of market pricing, I never met a single manager who held that view, and I personally knew hundreds); "BR should be invited to state what proportion of total journeys it **ultimately** seeks to sell at a reduced fare"; (Why? Will Travel Agents and Hoteliers be stating what proportion of holidays they intend to sell at reduced rates - in **perpetuity**, and will they now publicise them so that no one need pay full price?). They referred to the risk of undermining the fairness of the standard fare; (Market forces are not based on fairness). They said that passengers should be able to buy a number of tickets in bulk at a discount rate - like postage stamps; (I always buy in bulk, but cannot get stamps at discount and neither have I found anyone else who can). "BR should eliminate attempts to fiddle with the rush hour problem in the South East by half hearted re-pricing"; (I agree re-pricing should not be half hearted. If the Government grasp the nettle and privatise the South East, there will be no half heartedness about Private Sector re-pricing). "Information supplied by BR indicates, that over the past 40 years or so, the average of fare levels has lagged behind the general cost of living. This conclusion may surprise many and if borne out by closer investigation deserves wider prominence"; (The task of confirming it was not difficult - see Page 34). I could find no reference to this being investigated and either confirmed or rejected in CTCC Reports.

In its 1951 **Annual Report**, the then CTCC stated that they were "not able to make recommendations on this highly technical subject" [the fares structure]. The Chairmen of the CTCC, and Scottish and Welsh TUCC's told the top secret 1961 **Special Advisory Group**, that BR should be given freedom to decide its own fares. Finally, the CTCC 1989/90 **Report** states that in 1988/89 BR had the highest number of passengers for 20 years - this does not sit easily with claims that fares are too high.

Closures

The Transport Act 1962: TUCC's [not CTCC] deal with rail closures, of which BR will give six weeks notice; TUCC functions are confined to passenger services and they are to report - not recommend - on hardship to the MoT. Hitherto, the TUCC conducted hearings, making recommendations to the CTCC, which considered and made recommendations to the MoT, or referred back to the TUCC, (perhaps the most convuluted procedure any bureaucrat could have dreamed up - but they did manage to make it worse - see Page 47). The lines for which BR receive financial support were mostly proposed for closure as irretrievable loss makers. The public must pay the price to keep them open. To those who believe that Rail managers were not trying to make lines profitable, I reply: "you must be more naive than you look" or "why don't you put your money where your mouth is?" Managers made every endeavour to eliminate losses to avoid closures. If they were not motivated by business, altruistic or operational reasons, they would ere long become redundant. For some reason which I cannot fathom, the public seem to believe that BR managers, including those recruited from the Private Sector, preferred redundancy.

Before the War, main line railways closed uneconomic lines and stations, and they were facing a road haulage industry and private car market far weaker than those post war. Sir William Wood, Vice President of the LMSR, told the Railway Rates Tribunal on 14th June 1939, "since 1928, 235 miles of track and 223 stations have been closed to all traffic and 951 miles and 412 stations to passenger traffic only".

TUCC's acquired a role in closures which was not set out in the 1947 Transport Act. The closure of a Private Sector establishment serving the public is not subject to this procedure. When a supermarket chain or other company decides to close a branch, they do not have to submit to a Public Inquiry. If they did and were told to keep a loss making branch open to avoid real hardship, it would be considered reasonable if the Government made up the loss. The media and the public would not continually carp about that subsidy or the company's pricing policy. Hundreds of villagers could lose their only shop because it "doesn't pay". There is no redress against Joe Bloggs, Grocer, or national companies. Neither will they supply financial data to justify their action. On the contrary BR are more likely to be expected to open a station for a few non motorists to travel to the nearest town once weekly. A company may give two weeks notice that it is to close, leaving employees with no prospect of finding another job in a high unemployment area. But let one person be inconvenienced by a rail closure and the country is up in arms. You do not have to live near a line to object to closure, merely be thinking of travelling on it. These "maybe" customers are not ones bank managers and auditors would see as creating a financial line of entry in a private sector company's books.

Among some of the "hardship" objections submitted to a TUCC was that of the village of Thurgoland near Sheffield. The poorly used station was about a mile away. Unable to reduce costs and increase revenue sufficiently to eliminate losses, BR had to go for closure. The objection was that when there was a bad winter, rail was the only line of communication. We should have been grateful for this rare confirmation that BR keep moving even in blizzards, although the first word from the public is to complain of delays! Years later, a director in the solid fuel business told me that their records showed that bad winters occurred about every seven years. Were there villages which never having had a station, did not survive a bad winter after the only grocer closes when his customers were drawn to the hypermarket? BR are expected to be profit motivated and a Social Service. Thurgoland, in comparison with my second anecdote, had a strong case! It was said that when the line at Ilkley was proposed for closure, one lady objected because when her bitch was taken to be serviced at some distant location it was sick if it travelled by car! It may be apochryphal, but sounds feasible. In 1939, when the SR announced the closure of the Brighton - Dyke (Devil's Dyke) line - there were no public hearings involved then, but there were complaints that when it snowed people used the line! As usual on the last day, hundreds who never travelled on the line, made a special "nostalgic" journey.

CTCC 1950 Report: "among suggestions received was one that lines should not be closed until after every possible means of making them remunerative at an acceptable level of fares has been tried". Acceptable to whom was not defined nor for how many years trials should continue, nor who was to cover losses during the trials, presumably they would be subsidised by those whose services were making profits, since then there was no Government "subsidy".

CTCC 1956 Report said the Hooton-West Kirby was a typical rural non paying line which couldn't be recovered from losses of £20,000 pa by diesels which would cost £60,000 pa, so that the 60,000 passenger journeys in 1955 would need to increase by 400,000 to pay for diesels.

CTCC 1977 **Report** refers to the "part played by seemingly uneconomic branch lines in feeding traffic into main lines" - this is a popular myth. A line which does not cover its own costs, by a factor of 5:1 cannot make any contribution to a main line. Investigation shows that the main centres of production and consumption lie, as one would expect, on the main lines.

CTCC 1986/87 **Report:** representations were made to BR and DoT for "basic financial information to enable them to balance the cost of possible alternative services against expected savings from closure" and to judge hardship arguing that objectors are not given details of savings to establish BR's case. (This is absurd, it would effectively return to the pre 1962 situation - either there is hardship or there is not - the amount BR will save does not remotely affect that issue).

CTCC 1988/89 **Report:** "all past bus replacement services ceased after a short time due to the level of patronage", (confirming that the volume had not justified a train service); "the bus is inherently less reliable than train services, slower and more susceptible to adverse weather conditions" - (not the impression one gets from BR's critics); "The policy of destaffing left passengers with fewer facilities e.g., a lack of serviceable seats" (mostly due to vandalism, which is also a problem at staffed stations, even when staff are on duty, and at night when stations are closed; Shelters, toilets and staff are deemed essential on stations with fewer passengers than at many bus-stops. When the CTCC had a road passenger role, it stated in its 1955 Report that the provision of bus shelters, at exposed sites, because of cost and usage factors was "primarily one for Local Authorities to decide". Why should it be different for BR? In 1963, the CTCC were reported as praising BR for destaffing 11 stations on the Hastings line as an alternative to closure - see also Page 46).

CTCC 1991 **Report:** concerned "at the sale by BR of land which might well be required for future use to reopen closed stations or to provide new stations". (Land is not released for sale until declared "non operational" by managers who consider future options; BR cannot afford to hang onto land in perpetuity. BR has been criticised for "hanging onto land which could be put to better use" - albeit, sometimes, after land was sold it stood derelict for a long time).

Reduced Role
CTCC 1985/86 **Report:** "never before has it been more important for the CTCC/TUCC to represent passengers interests". Forty years ago, no other body pursued complaints against BR, now there are many who do so whilst ignoring analogous private sector complaints. That apart, it is difficult to justify this claim in view of alternatives now available - cars, airlines and motorway coaches. Moreover, in the past they were engaged in hundreds of Public Hearings in connection with closure proposals. In 1961, for example, they dealt with schemes involving 36 branch lines and 566 route miles - a not insubstantial task which has virtually disappeared. It is worth noting the following comparisons:-

	Totals		Ratio	
	1948	1991	1948	1991
TUCC Areas	11	9	100	82
Passenger stations	6686	2470	100	37
Passenger journeys	1024m	746m	100	73
Market Share	20%	9%	100	45
Route miles	19630	10307*	100	53

* only 8897 route miles have passenger services = 45

This reveals a disproportionate decline in the number of TUCC's, even before taking account of their lost role for other activities - buses, freight, parcels, shipping, hotels, canals, docks, and rail fares.

Vehicle Design

The CTCC wish to be involved before the production stage, (but have no funds to back their ideas, does this apply with the production of all consumer goods?). CTCC 1987/88 Report refers to "the airline type face-to back seating which it is felt would break up family and social groups", and is concerned about leg room. (Why is face-to-back acceptable in coaches, cars, aircraft and ferries but not on trains? It is a practical way of reducing standing, curtails the practice of 'feet-on-seats' and increases leg room by avoiding a tangling of legs. The most common passenger groups today are one and two - nice cosy groups of four to "occupy a table" are the rarity. Threes and fives are as common as fours. In carriages with face-to-back and face-to-face seats, the former, offering more privacy, are more quickly filled than the latter). The CTCC is "looking forward to a positive involvement in the design of rolling stock to be operated by BR on services via the Channel Tunnel". (These will be the minority of trains, because SNCF and the Channel Tunnel company's own trains will outnumber BR's).

Carriage Cleaning

TUCC's asked for statistics on the frequency of cleaning carriages as if knowing that coaches had a daily clean was synonomous with them being cleaned well. As LMR Operations Officer - responsible for all day to day operations - I decided that this statistic had no real value and was no substitute for visual quality checks, and directed the LMR not to produce them, and, hence, refused to provide them for TUCC's associated with the LMR. Later, as Divisional Manager at Stoke on Trent, and consequently, the BR Liaison Officer with the Wales TUCC I refused to supply this data for North Wales pointing out that quantatitive statistics are ineffective in judging qualitative subjects. I also pointed out that half of the trains departing from Welsh stations had their overnight clean at Depots in England. Conversely, some trains departing from stations in England were cleaned in Scotland or Wales so it was doubly valueless to have data for Welsh depots as requested. To my delight, one member of the Wales TUCC, a statistician, openly agreed with me.

Timetables

CTCC 1967 Report: "reductions in passenger service should be considered by TUCC's". (The Private Sector is constantly redeploying assets to increase profit, without consulting outsiders. Why should BR, unlike Airways or Ferries which waste no time consulting with Quangos, but simply pull out of unprofitable routes to transfer resources to better paying routes, have to hold up timetable changes whilst the TUCC considered them).

CTCC 1972 Report: "the MoT opposed allowing TUCC's considering reductions of commercial services which would lead to unacceptable delay in adjusting services to meet the competitive position".

CTCC 1983 Report: "passengers are entitled to expect trains to run on time", we "believe that a target of five minutes late is inadequate for the discipline of the service". In 1983, the Scottish TUCC said BR should work to a 100% punctuality target. (With no industry achieving perfection, even cocooned in centrally heated premises, compared with BR exposed to the elements, this is absurd. Manufacturers do not work to a 100% standard, but to "tolerances" which are less than a perfect finish, despite which, defective products reach customers as frequent advertisements recalling potentially harmful products prove. Shoppers are told that shoe and clothing sizes "are generous". Anyone with a basic knowledge of motivating staff, knows that one sets targets above present levels, but not so far out of reach as to be demotivating, and progressively raises them as each target is achieved. Even then, no one should ever set a target of 100% which is completely unattainable by humans in any walk of life).

CTCC 1984/85 Report referred to "the reduction of through trains". (Through from where to where?. Every train is through to somewhere. The only comparison is to aggregate the number of stops for every train, amounting to millions, and compare it with a preceding year - a formidable task). "There is an increased number of journeys relying on connections". (Analysing all journeys to establish that would be a phenomenal task - BRB 1970 Report, para 3.13: "there are 6m different point to point journeys possible on BR"; BRB 1969 Report: "798 million separate journeys by passengers").

CTCC 1986/87 Report: the MoT refused to tell BR to install a passing loop at Beccles; (It is incredible that they asked the MoT to overrule BR management on such an issue).

CTCC 1987/88 Report: endeavoured to "maintain some kind of sleeper service between Newcastle and London, with the strong backing of users"; (The Report did not mention if this included financial guarantees to cover losses).
* "The withdrawal of a sleeper would affect the economic viability of the North East" (is difficult to visualise - a sleeping car service for a three hour journey must be of very limited attraction. Its higher cost, lower capacity, and platform occupation time - three hours travelling means five hours occupying expensive platform space, since eight hours sleep is the norm - shout out loss maker. Any investor would rank sleepers between English cities as yesterday's business. It focusses attention on BR's dilemma. If they adopt advice against their own better judgement and it fails, wasting taxpayers' money they are blamed; if they reject advice they are "not prepared to listen").
* The CTCC are "concerned at a planned reduction in Inter City and Provincial Sector rolling stock fleets - when passenger demand was forecast to increase rapidly". (BRB Accounts show that passenger journeys increased by 5% in 1988-89 but fell by 2.2% in 1989-90, demonstrating the risks of using forecasts to buy expensive rolling stock. Many years ago, BR managers discovered that in a recession, an early economy is leisure travel. It is, therefore, prudent to exercise extreme caution when considering external forecasts unsupported by cash or guarantees).
* The CTCC "adversely compared City institutions' forecasts of high employment in Central London and Docklands with BR low forecasts of growth in passenger demand" - commuters. (That external forecast bit the dust with the recession. Sound investment policy must consider the possible down side prospects. There are two trends in company administration which will have a major effect upon commuter travel - neither is the staggering of hours. Far more likely are the transfer of offices out of London and other cities, and an expansion of home based work using computers and modern communication links to offices. Anyone considering investment in rolling stock for commuters must consider losses which would arise in this down side scenario. BR has no contract to which it can hold commuters - they can cease to travel at a second's notice, leaving BR with incalculable losses. Monthly or three monthly seasons are a blip in the life of rolling stock. Most companies left with surplus assets have a secondhand market to explore - there is, for all practical purposes, no viable market for redundant BR rolling stock).

CTCC 1991 Report:
* criticises BR for consulting local user groups on timetable changes rather than the TUCC's. (No law requires BR to consult with TUCC's on timetable changes. What would happen if the TUCC said one thing and the users another? If BR, unlike the Private Sector, consults customers, it is better directly, rather than post officing through a TUCC. **CTCC 1950 Report:** "it

is all to the good that the BTC & Executives should meet their customers directly and without an intermediary wherever possible");

* CTCC had "long pressed for punctuality to be monitored at intermediate points rather than just at their final destination". (Timetables have recovery time towards the end of a journey to allow for track maintenance speed limits - which, unlike those on road, are observed. To maintain punctuality at every intermediate point requires recovery time in advance of each point, thereby extending schedules, increasing costs through poorer utilisation of locomotives, rolling stock and crews, and extending station times to the point where some stations may require additional platforms. For example Crewe to London had a recovery allowance. If a train made four en route calls, it would require four extra recovery allowances - extending overall journey times by 14 minutes or so - to make proper provision for a speed restriction which may fall between any pair of points).
* "Members were astonished to hear that Inter City did not consider it had a prescribed quality target in respect of punctuality and that as a commercial non supported sector it was no longer obliged to publish such a target". (CTCC are right, Inter City are jumping the gun, they must wait until they are privatised to take that attitude).

Signalling & Peaks
NBPI Report 1969 Appdx I - CTCC Memo: with the 'Block System', one train cannot enter a section which is occupied - "this system leads to delays since a train cannot enter a section which is occupied" (The system was designed that way to prevent collisions); "in the medium term reliability could be improved by reducing trains booked through bottlenecks - unless the carrying capacity of each train could be increased, such changes would either lead to more overcrowding or encourage passengers to move away from the peak", (Obviously so. If a survey is made of peak passengers, they will applaud the theory provided it applies to others, none will offer to travel off peak. See Page 133 for Peak problems).

Safety
CTCC 1986/87 Report had a section on rail safety, an area of technical expertise which many BR managers had assumed was to remain in the capable hands of the independent Railway Inspectorate, whose reputation is world wide. Had the MoT wanted the CTCC to undertake the highly technical subject of rail safety, he should have included unambiguous words in an Act.
CTCC 1987/88 Report quotes a report on Automatic Level Crossings, which concluded that 74 of 250 such crossings would exceed a "probable fatality rate of one [person] in a hundred years", and ought to be converted to half barrier crossings, (how many road junctions have similar prospects and ought to have half barriers?)
CTCC 1990/91 Report: The CTCC, alarmed that the cost of the Railway Inspectorate's new safety standards for platforms, due to come into effect October 1991, may cause stations to be closed, approached the Inspectorate who will "adopt a flexible attitude". (Those of us who were responsible for safety would have been amazed by this, and would have asked "who will be responsible if a passenger is injured because a station has had its safety improvements deferred?" - see Page 51).

Self Appraisal
In evidence to the 1971 Select Committee on Nationalised Industries on "Relations with the Public", the CTCC said:

* "It is possible to argue for or against the Consultative Committee system, but since such Committees are an established fact, we do not see good purpose is served by placing restrictions upon them in what they may consider". (If there is no value-for-money role, keeping them "because they

are there" is a waste of funds which the MoT gives them, and that expended by BR in responding to them and attending their meetings. Moreover, I would question their expertise in safety, technical matters and vehicle design, and earlier CTCC's admitted a lack of expertise on fares and advocated BR being free to decide fares - so there must be some restrictions on their remit. There is a danger of giving them power without accountability).

* They referred to the "original responsibilities of CTCC & TUCC's" (but not to changes which have reduced the dominance of BR in transport from 24/25% to less than 10% of the market, and the hiving off of former parts of the BTC and hence reducing their task).

* "Railway users ..... stand alone as users of public services without any redress on charges". (Any company which sells to the public is a public service, many are more essential than BR. Why should rail users expect 'redress' on charges - by which they simply mean lower prices, whatever the original price - which no other consumer has? I tried for over two years to obtain redress on a car insurance premium, which was increased three times the rate of inflation, below which BR, not for the first time, was then held. It took most of that time to get one unsatisfactory reply to my four letters of complaint. I secured no refund).

* "Road service passengers have no one to represent them" - Having said that "rail users stand alone .... " (see above).

* "BR operate a selective pricing system - guided by their own market research"; (If this is a crime, the entire private sector is guilty).

* The CTCC and TUCC's sought to have themselves publicised in BR timetables at BR expense - another hidden cost boosting deficits. (When there were such references on our leaflets I called for them to be replaced by commercial advertising - to increase our income. Why they sought this means when most passengers get information from staff and when, according to their answers, they had an unrestricted budget for publicity I cannot comprehend). "The Committees were funded by the MoT", "we do not have a budget in the sense of a hard or fast grant in aid - we got the money we wanted for this particular project" [publicity]. "We have never been restricted by funds. We have never been told by the Ministry that we are restricted to an annual amount". (Lucky them). Having said they had no budget, they refer to "our annual budget of approximately £70,000 of which £40,000 goes in direct salaries. We have roughly 300 members in the 12 committees, all of whom give their time voluntarily. There are no paid positions".

* "They [the public] do know of us, but not to the degree we would like them to know us"; (the CTCC 1954 Report stated "it is evident that this statutory consultative machinery [TUCC's] is becoming well known to bodies interested in transport problems associated with the BTC - Chambers of Commerce, Area Boards for Industry, Local Authorities, TUC, local trades councils, residents & ratepayers; but not indivduals". It is inconceivable that these organisations were not keeping members informed, and all of them consist of and represent individuals).

* On Closures, they bemoaned their loss of power under the 1962 Act. Before that, after a public hearing, they recommended whether closure should be rejected, but only the MoT made the decision. Now, they report on hardship, and the MoT decides. The MoT overrode some recommendations before 1962.

* On complaints: "the public, having failed to get a satisfactory response from the Board, may then decide not to approach the TUCC" - due to their limited remit. (It is difficult to comprehend what evidence there could be

103

that people who did not write to TUCC's, had an unsatisfactory response).
They protested that BR do not refer "unsatisfied complainants" to the TUCC.
(If a complainant does not write again after BR have replied, how can he be
deemed dissatisfied? Why should BR be expected to do what the Private
Sector does not do? Only one of scores of companies to which I complained
"suggested" I contact an Ombudsman, but that was after I had said in my
fourth letter of complaint to them that I had already done so. Hardly
gratuitous information, and the phraseology smacked of a brush off).

* "BR appear to be preoccupied with the need to make a profit at the expense
of quality of service"; (These objectives are not incompatible - they are
interlinked. BR's remit is to pay its way, and in so doing quality cannot
be ignored). CTCC "appreciate that the Board must have regard to financial
targets" (The Act does not mention "having regard to" - meaning 'to
consider' or "think about", which would allow them to ignore their statutory
duty - only to fulfilling the financial target: 1962 Act, section 18 [1]
"conduct their business as to secure that their revenue is not less than
sufficient for making provision for the meeting of all charges").

* "BR do not have to justify price increases"; (BR has a financial remit -
that, their Accounts and the outcome of decisions - which the MoT can
reverse - is the justification. The Private Sector does not justify prices
to customers, and invariably do not even publicly announce price increases).

* If they had powers to deal with charges and BR "were considering an
increase which might affect single fares and season tickets, they would wish
to give advice"; (BR have the market research - on what would the CTCC base
their advice? If they advocated reversing proposed percentage increases on
singles and seasons, what would the "losers" say having learned that BR had,
on the advice of the CTCC, transposed the higher and lower percentages
respectively envisaged for those categories of passengers?)

* Mr.Milligan, Chairman, South Eastern Area TUCC: "I am the only person [on
my committee of 23], who holds a season ticket. However, the people
nominated by the Societies [to be members of the committee] are wrong in
that they ought to produce someone who sometimes travels on the railways".
Mr.Hunt, Deputy Chairman, North West Area TUCC: "I have one or two more
railway users on my committee than Mr.Milligan". (These answers indicate
that of approximately 45 or so members of two of the TUCC's, only three or
four travelled by rail. On what did the others base their views?).

* Asked for a third time to explain how public interests would suffer if the
Committees were abolished, they said "We regard ourselves as the watchdogs
of the travelling public - who use trains. To whom would they apply if the
TUCC's were not in existence?" (One assumes "the Office of Fair Trading").

Unlike State owned BR, no Private Sector company debates or justifies
prices, fares, closures or timetable changes. Nor do they provide financial
or productivity data to an external body. It would be discriminatory for
the Government to maintain the role of the CTCC and TUCC in respect of BR
operated services, but not those of Private Sector trains on the same
routes. That ought to influence Government to wind up the CTCC and TUCC's
and release their funds and resources for other purposes. The CTCC and
TUCC's should be wound up - before, not after, privatisation. Their
Statutory duties of "Quality of Service" - largely manifested in complaints,
and the infrequent "Closures" should be respectively transferred to the
Office of Fair Trading and a Government Inspector on an "as-required" basis.
There are many other "Watchdogs" who will keep an eye on BR and Private
Operators at no cost to the taxpayers, most of whom do not use rail anyway.

The image which most people gain of BR, (under 10% of travel is by rail), is from the media. Reading reports on undeniably rare railway accidents, one may be forgiven for not knowing that the carnage on roads is about 500 times as great, and is rarely subject to the formal independent Public Inquiries which follow rail accidents, despite the comment in November 1988, by the Secretary of State for Transport, that there are "three Clapham accidents on the roads every week". When BR published complaints statistics whilst no other industry admitted to, much less published any, one may be forgiven for believing that the private sector was perfect, and BR alone was not. To the open mind, this must be transparently wrong, even if the reports are not contested by a published response from BR or any informed person.

Risks to Children

BR are often criticised unjustly in connection with "children wandering onto railway lines because of inadequate fencing". As Area Manager at Leicester in 1969, I was asked to meet Radio Leicester's reporter to answer such a complaint, and arranged to meet him on site. A quarter of a mile away, beyond a private field and across a road, was a row of houses. When he arrived at the site at the foot of an embankment, I called for him to come up. He scrambled through the fence and struggled to the top. I asked, how with a slope like that children can wander onto the line. He asked "will BR improve the fencing if a child is killed?" I asked why small unaccompanied children were crossing a road and an intervening field before they could get to the railway? I told him that as a parent my greatest fear had been of my children wandering onto the road in front of our house, so I had enclosed our rear garden by a six foot fence. Finding that the curiosity of a child knows no bounds and that our three year old was standing on his tricycle to open the gate latch with a stick, I had to fix a lock on the gate, and then had to take care as he followed us to see where the key was kept! I said that the parents' fear should be the road at the front of their houses not a railway a quarter of a mile away. I have responded to similar complaints elsewhere, including a tragedy at Colwyn Bay in 1976 in which we proved to the coroner that on the day preceding a dual fatality, the fence concerned had been repaired, to be vandalised yet again.

Answering Back

I had no Public Relations role until my last few years with BR, but had gained an impression that BR's media policy was not positive enough. BR did not appear to be responding to comment and criticism. I made one attempt to correct an unfair article in the National media without success. Since retiring I have made over 30 vain attempts, which indicate that BRHQ had a tough nut to crack. BR cannot compel the media to publish replies to criticism, but it can respond directly to passengers, and even to some non passengers, by using its billboards, TV screens, its own magazines and public address facilities. The problem illustrates the need for a "right to reply" to criticism. From 1982, as Divisional Manager, Stoke on Trent and later as Assistant Divisional General Manager, Manchester, I put my theories into practice with Provincial newspapers, countering readers' letters. Only once did an editor not immediately print my letter, who when telephoned, requested that it be abbreviated. I refused, pointing out that it did no more than reply to each point made by their reader, and introduced nothing new. I said that if they did not print, no press releases would come from BR. My letter was printed in full and the issues were not pursued further.

Only three of my many replies produced a further letter in a newspaper. I replied to a letter in the Stoke Evening Sentinel from a lady whose 60 year old sister had travelled from Newcastle upon Tyne to Stoke on Trent for Christmas 1982 without a seat. She criticised BR for not putting on enough coaches. I said that we did not know how many would travel on a given day, much less a specific train, as many would have return tickets, tickets booked in advance or from points beyond Newcastle. Furthermore every coach fit for traffic was in service at Christmas. I pointed the finger of criticism at other passengers, some of whom must have been younger, but none had had the courtesy to offer a seat - a sad reflection of this day and age. The lady wrote again thanking me for my explanation and agreeing with my views on social attitudes. The other two cases involved impractical and financially ruinous advice from amateurs (see Pages 145 & 152).

Unanswered, these and other letters would have sown more criticism, not least among those who did not travel by rail. The ending of a line of correspondence to the media by a firm reply created a more informed public. Internally, many did not agree with this approach. In 1984, I attended a dinner in Liverpool at which the speaker was a Director of Unilever, who spoke about public relations. His company had been ignoring media criticism and found that it did not pay. I was pleased to have my views confirmed by such an auspicious source.

Since retiring, excluding repeats or complaints, I have written 17 unpublished letters to the national press, and written or telephoned the BBC 15 times, having had only one comment broadcast. The public would have a different view of BR if each criticism was balanced by a contradictory view or analogous comparison with the Private Sector, as is invariably confirmed when I answer verbal criticism. The space (on paper or on the air) for letters is, I am told, limited. However, I did think that my views came nearer to the "man bites dog" principle than reports on BR, which are closer to "dog bites man". (Readers may have heard the old journalistic advice "when man bites dog, that's news but ..."). BR should use the media's "lack of space" to demonstrate that BR's lack of space problem is far more difficult to resolve, and that BR's publicised failings are mirrored, albeit unpublicised, in the Private Sector. That regarded as good private sector practice is condemned when adopted by BR: avoiding excess capacity, pricing to maximise net income, dropping unprofitable 'lines', (see Page 22).

Customer Relations
In May 1991, I complained to The Sunday Times that there was no evidence in an article to support the claim that BR "flagrantly hates its customers". It also said that "mass transit systems have to be able to compete for every journey mile undertaken" which I said is "quite impractical since so many journeys originate from isolated houses, farms and villages and for which mass transit systems must be an obvious non runner". I said that if a private sector company can be found which doesn't make mistakes and persuaded to run railways, it will solve problems by the application of standard private sector practice - price rises above RPI, closures, (which will reduce connections which can cause delays), and asset stripping.

In November 1991 I wrote to the Daily Telegraph, referring to a letter from a reader who could not see the wood for the trees even in the Autumn, (he had written about leaves on the line). I wrote that "he should be advising BR to adopt Private Sector terminology. The Private Sector do not make excuses, but give reasons. They, unlike the Public Sector, suffer from 'circumstances beyond our control' with matters such as price rises, late deliveries, defective products and broken promises. They are blighted by 'gremlins' - extra terrestrial alien microbes which selectively attack Private Sector computers and equipment. (A Royal Commission should ascertain the objectives of an alien power which ignores public sector equipment purchased from the Private Sector). An unwillingness to cater for every Peak Demand is sound Private Sector practice, unlike the Public Sector where it is due to incompetence. Staff shortages are an insurmountable problem in the Private Sector, but due to managerial incompetence in the Public Sector. Unless the Government remove unique constraints and responsibilities, Privatised railways will have the same problems but they will be able to use Privatesectorspeak in Public Relations".

In March 1992, BBC's Today Team remarked that BR Drivers, who will drive through the Chunnel, ought to be taught to apologise in French for leaves on the line, I telephoned to say that, whilst BR are teaching their Drivers to give apologies in French - the BBC must continue with apologies in English - 'Sorry, I got the time (or date) wrong'; 'Sorry, I got the guest's name wrong'; 'Sorry for mixing up tapes or disc tracks'; 'Sorry for not providing enough people to answer telephones having invited listeners to phone'; 'Sorry for repeating old films, and making unadvertised changes'.

Infrastructure
In November, 1991, I wrote to the Financial Times about an article which said that, from 1948, the purpose of BR was to provide a social service; that the cost of assets was written off, interest and depreciation charges being met from taxation, and that references to assets in BR Accounts was limited to maintenance charges. I said that the 1947 Act required the BTC "to pay its way taking one year with another" - that could not be construed as a social service. Regarding asset valuation, capital expenditure on assets was recorded in BR Accounts after 1948 and comprised 18 pages of Depreciation & Capital Account Expenditure and Capital Account Movements. The format of Accounts was abbreviated in 1962. I contend that depreciation only became a charge on the taxpayer, because Government enforced a policy of deficit financing (see Chapter 1, Part II). The form of the accounts is directed by the MoT under statutory powers. Any change could only be made with his/her authority. Current BR management told the Financial Times they were delighted with the article, which BR said was accurate. That changed nothing, and did not explain away the Financial Tables devoted to Depreciation and Capital expenditure in the BTC Accounts from 1948 onwards. I complained to the Press Complaints Commission, who supported the Editor. BR managers took steps to economise and avoid replacing assets, whilst reusable assets were deployed elsewhere to avoid expenditure. BR were overruled on line closures which were kept in use for years, wastefully using assets, (Chapter 1, Part IV); Councils opposed economies, (Chapter 6). Schemes to improve asset utilisation, which I initiated, developed and implemented - which were not part of the Modernisation Plan nor directed by higher authority, included: Yard closures at Penistone, Rotherham, Ickles, Warsop, Langwith, Wath and Crewe; Signalbox closures in the Rugby District and Stoke Division; Rolling Stock schemes at Doncaster, Sunderland, Rugby, Stoke and Sheffield. Locomotives at Rugby, Leicester and Crewe. These were in addition to my own schemes for staff economy, quality improvements and safety. I implemented schemes developed by others, and developed plans for other to progress. Other managers initiated similar projects throughout BR.

MoT Paper "Railway Policy" 1967 [Cmnd 3439], Appendix E: "depreciation should continue to be assessed on a replacement cost basis". SAG files (released 1991): "it was the policy of the former railway companies and continued by the BTC not to depreciate certain assets, but to charge to revenue as and when it occurred". "Many fixed assets, following former railway practice, have never been depreciated". The SAG advocated changes, but listed "assets which should continue not to be subject to depreciation".

In January, 1992 a Sunday Times article attributed the origin of the concept of a separate track owning authority to the Adam Smith Institute, which I understand was set up in 1977. I pointed out that the BRB 1974 Report had put the concept to Government (see Page 52). It was advocated by the LNER in 1946 in "The State and the Railways".

Punctuality

In April 1989 I wrote to the Daily Telegraph, commenting on an article about commuters making compensation claims from BR. I said that those in the South East made enormous gains as a result of improvements to rail services, without which many houses would never have been built. Without rail services, most houses would be worth a fraction of present prices. It is notable how swiftly householders alongside lines being electrified pushed up house prices because of the benefits arising from faster and more frequent train services. I suggested that those claiming from BR for delays caused by further modernisation to their routes, should deduct their claim from the increased value of their houses, add the difference between city and rural salaries, (obtained by virtue of the rail service), and add further gains by selling houses at high prices in London and buying cheap in the country. These amounts should then be paid to BR which created that wealth. BR will not then need support from the taxpayer. Recently I have noted that, in contrast with those who pocket gains made from electrification, those whose property is affected by developments such as the Chunnel demand a blight payment. A case of heads the householder wins, tails he mustn't lose. If BR is required to make blight payments it should first receive past gains.

In December 1990 I protested to the BBC at an announcer's remark about a single snowflake bringing BR to a stand, saying that "she ought to be the one condemned to turn out to work a train or signal box at 2.0am or 6.0am. Critics seem incapable of comprehending that 140,000 BR staff do not live on the premises. When others leave cars at home because road conditions are difficult and may damage their precious cars, descending as a hypercritical deluge on BR, not one considers the dedication of BR staff who braved the worst, many hours earlier, to get to work.

In February, 1991 I phoned BBC's "Any Answers", to explain the enormity of the task of clearing blowing snow and drifts. Contrary to popular belief, point heaters do not resolve all problems and an infinite number would still leave services subject to disruption in snowstorms, in the same way other forms of transport and industry are affected. Had I been called to speak, I would have suggested that the panel don their arctic clothing and get out on the track at 2.0am in a snowstorm, exchanging perspiration for perspicacity.

One does grow weary of those who keep playing the same old record over and over and over again. My response to those who make remarks about the wrong kind of snow, is to request that they cease using the wrong kind of ink, because it stains hands and clothes and transfers from one page to another, making it difficult to read an article. To those on the air, I ask that they avoid playing the wrong tape or playing it at the wrong speed.

In December 1991 the Daily Telegraph lamented the lack of seasonal goodwill towards BR. I wrote that the reason was the tendency to rake over past issues, such as the Clapham Jcn collision, without the same coverage of the 500 "Road Claphams" in that period. I referred to a newspaper photograph of cars in a flooded road - less than 25% of the related report referred to rail, yet the headline was "Rail travellers face delays after flood damage".

In February 1992 I wrote to the Sunday Times about an article on punctuality and service which mentioned a security alert, a body on the line, a line obstructed by vandals, a collision with a lorry on a level crossing without conceding that the delays these cause are not the fault of BR. They referred to punctuality currently being based on the terminus arrival, when it has applied since time immemorial, and to recovery time in timetables - a practice as old as the hills and not done to "cook the books", which I explained thus. The road user provides for inevitable delays by exceeding the speed limit, by up to 50%. Were BR's drivers to do this, they would face suspension from driving, trial by media and perhaps, manslaughter (a charge which rarely applies in road accidents). So poor old BR adopts the safe practice making calculated allowances to cover planned "roadworks" to add to schedules based on trains travelling at the maximum permitted speed. The article mentioned schedules of 33 minutes on some Inter City trains from Watford to Euston compared to some with 17 minutes. The former were overnight trains, the latter were daytime trains. I pointed out that this was to allow for track diversions during night time "roadworks". For practical reasons, allowances are inserted towards the end of a journey and aim to give an arrival time which is achievable and ensure that rolling stock is available for a return trip. Since businesses in centrally heated buildings cannot achieve perfection, how can it be reasonably demanded from those subjected to so many external influences.

Some ask if BR would guarantee not to inconvenience customers in future. When that question was put to me, I asked to be pointed in the direction of any company prepared to make such a guarantee. I have been looking, without success, for one for 40 years. A company which guarantees to replace a defective item eventually, or even immediately, does not qualify.

Standing
In January 1991, on BBC an MP asked whether it was beyond the wit of BR to devise a fares system where standing passengers pay less. I telephoned that it was not, but they may find it difficult to stop people who pay such a fare from cheating by using a variation of the First Class fiddle - paying Standard fare but sitting in the First Class "willing to pay if caught". A "standing only" fare may end standing if passengers, who now force their way onto obviously full trains, decide to wait for the next train with their "Standing only" ticket, taking a seat secure in the knowledge that ticket inspection on commuter trains is rare. If a ticket check occurs they will with a straight face explain that they hadn't noticed that the ticket carried in large block capitals the words "STANDING ONLY", and take the name of the poor ticket collector threatening to write to the Media, TUCC, or an MP criticising BR for "having complex fares".

In June 1991 I telephoned BBC to ask why they expected rail tickets to guarantee a seat when each is valid for hundreds or thousands of trains and the buyer doesn't specify the train? I suggested they try paying for a room in an unspecified hotel within a Group during the peak season without specifying arrival or departure dates, and ask for a refund after a change of mind at short notice. (A recent experience would have caused me to use the analogy of a theatre ticket, where you must give 24 hours notice to change the date of use, even if the theatre is half empty, and they cannot have lost a sale. One presumes that BR's critics do not wish to have a seat guaranteed on these terms. They may also be unenthusiatic about a seat guaranteed on an aircraft - where you find your travelling companion has been seated 15 rows further back - because you booked in only two hours early, whilst others booked in three hours early).

Accidents
In January 1991 the Daily Telegraph devoted 578 column cms to the Cannon Street rail crash, in which one fatality was reported, whilst allocating 5½ column cms to an M4 crash which killed five people. This was a ratio of 500 times as much coverage per fatality. The M4 disaster should, by comparison, have warranted 2980 column cms. They included a list of rail accidents going back to 1952, totalling 294 fatalities. That represented eight pa compared to 5000 being killed each year on roads. The age of rail coaches was highlighted along with their frequency of examinations as 'being twice per week'. In road accidents neither the frequency of examinations (once pa after the first three years for most cars) nor the age of the

vehicles, nor the adequacy of car maintenance (found seriously wanting by Consumer surveys) are mentioned. As my letter was not printed I complained to the Press Complaints Commission. They informed the paper, who wrote to me saying they did not think their coverage excessive given the particularly public circumstances and the very great number of commuters involved, although fortunately the death toll was very small. I asked if there was no public interest in road deaths and stated that whilst many rail commuters were injured, doubtless they were happier being injured in a rail accident than killed in a road accident and that the death toll was very small because of the strength of rail vehicles, as is invariably the case. Some time ago two trains collided at 100mph, resulting in one fatality. A similar collision on roads would leave scores dead. Many commuters would be delayed by the rail accident, but no one establishes the scale of delay to road travellers, which is many times greater. (The BBC reported a lorry overturned - a not uncommon occurrence - on 15th September 1991, in a contraflow on the M6, blocking the M6 for nine hours, diversions were set up between Junctions 14 & 15 - the scale of the delay was not published).

Prices
In January 1991 the Daily Telegraph quoted the £3225 paid for an annual season ticket from Diss to London. It would have impressed readers less if it had been expressed as 4.6p per mile, about one seventh the cost of an average sized car. Travelling the 69,350 miles pa by car would cost over £20,000 pa, and after two years the net value of the car could be expressed in peanuts, the driver's life expectancy would be sharply reduced by tension and carbon monoxide, and every minute of the journeys would be time wasted - equivalent to 60 days pa to a conscientious businessman. The less industrious do not work on the train but play the game in which they pretend they all work for complaint free businesses, criticising BR, safe in the knowledge that no one will venture that delays may be caused by private sector equipment, other passengers or vandals, as some quick tempered passenger may take such criticisms to heart. Neither will they attack the track record of stockbrokers, insurers, manufacturers, retailers, hoteliers, or restauranteurs who may be fellow passengers. All can gloat over profits made by selling dear in London and moving to cheaper pastures, yet retaining inflated City salaries, and agreeing that wages must be kept down. That they gain these benefits by virtue of rail travel will escape biased minds. Quoting BR fares in annual terms imparts minimum information and maximum emotion. I spent £3500 pa on a car which reveals nothing. Convert it to the common denominator of cost per mile, and my 10,000 miles pa costs 35p per mile, about average for a car, but several times as expensive as rail.

In June 1991 I wrote to the Daily Telegraph, noting a report that car insurance is "set to rise by 25%". It was not greeted with the hysteria which greets BR increases substantially below this outrageous level. Two years earlier, when the MoT vetoed proposed rail increases slightly above the rate of inflation, the country was in hysterics. I drew attention to the car insurance premium increase I faced, with maximum No Claims Bonus, of three times the rate of inflation, and that as ten times as many people travel by car as train, the Minister and the media were looking the wrong way. I mentioned my inability to get the insurance company to reply to three letters over four months when I demanded an explanation and I could prove they had received the letters. The Insurance Ombudsman said I must write to the company Chief Executive, who refused to divulge evidence of "an increase in claims in this area", which was at variance with my local knowledge, but sought to comfort me by telling me that at the time the general level of increase of other companies was an "across the board 50%". For the industry to top that with 25% this year will give BR formidable latitude for the next five years or so; (Less than 12 months later, a report covering 8 column cms said that car insurance was to rise 30% more. Now, as the media headlines BR's fare increases of double the rate of inflation, I have been asked to pay an insurance premium which is 25 times the rate of inflation, despite no claims and no improvement in quality).

In February 1992 I wrote to the Daily Telegraph, protesting that BR is be the trail blazer on practices in which the private sector should take a lead. BR are expected to keep price rises below the inflation rate, whilst others are not. BR were expected to attain a 100% safety standard for 10% of travellers, whilst road carnage continues unabated. The Government praised privatised water, which it said, was 95% safe. Now BR is to be the sole organisation to have its statistics subject to independent verification. Travellers are suspicious, it is said, of BR data. I am suspicious of private sector statistics - but when I asked an insurance company to prove its claim that my area had become more risky to justify increasing car premiums by thrice the inflation rate, I was unable to check their data. Will this schizophrenia ever end? If those raising doubts knew the first thing about BR, they would know that punctuality statistics are produced by members of the staff, who if they weren't so honest, might be more inclined to doctor figures to prove standards were worse - not better - to justify more staff. Far more would benefit if independent checks were made on companies who have "paid overdue accounts", "despatched an order", "not received a thrice repeated complaint" or "fully carried out repairs".

Other Industry
In December 1990 I wrote to the Daily Telegraph referring to a TV statement by a CBI representative that all that was now needed was for the public sector to treat customers as the private sector does. In the light of my experiences with the private sector, I prayed that did not happen. It seemed to me, that in the Public Sector, the customer must always be believed to be right - if not always by BR staff (who may doubt complaints with no details or "proof of purchase", from four months earlier), certainly by all others, who have an implicit faith that not one BR complainant could possibly be wrong or dishonest. Likewise, the Post Office must be at fault for losing mail because a customer swears that he posted your cheque last Michaelmas. The person who coined the phrase "your cheque is in the post" is owed a debt of gratitude by many businesses. Contrast these with the treatment one receives from much of the private sector: "No one else complained" (why that invalidates mine I fail to comprehend), or "You must have misused it", or "It hasn't been properly maintained" (without any evidence). Even those who replace defective goods or give a refund expect you to inconvenience yourself by making an extra journey to get satisfaction. Industry put up prices whilst everyone believed that BR alone should keep increases at or below the rate of inflation. Price rises I faced, when inflation was in single figures, included 23% increase in car insurance, 280% over two years in members fees of a Leisure Club (PLC), and 1119% increase over $4\frac{1}{2}$ years in the price of a part for a domestic appliance from the sole national supplier. These put the Public Sector very firmly in the shade. The CBI should look at companies which keep you hanging on the phone listening to unending jingles, are constantly "out of stock" or "not made/stocked now - it's not viable" (an excuse not accepted from the public sector), or "there's no demand" - when I have asked for it. Critics should prepare a plan as to whom they will blame for the country's ills when all the Public Sector has been privatised. (My files bulge with complaints to Private Sector companies, from most of whom, I received no satisfaction).

In February 1992 I wrote to the Daily Telegraph, that there is little wonder that car theft is increasing. Manufacturers make cars which children can, without a key, open and drive off in seconds, and insurance companies do not encourage prevention. Installing a £200 alarm, which renders a car immobile if someone breaks-in, did not reduce the car insurance premium by so much as a penny. Why are they not taking positive action to encourage crime prevention, particularly when they will be beneficiaries? Their sole course of action at the moment is to increase premiums on a standard car by up to 38% and considerably more on a "performance car" - putting BR increases in the shade. What we need is a Citizens' Charter for motorists, who are ten times greater in number than rail passengers.

Citizens Charter

In July 1990, a BBC announcer said "fat chance of BR offering refunds for late or cancelled trains". I telephoned to say there is as much chance as there is of the Private Sector and others doing so. If companies supplied free of charge, goods for which I have had to wait or were 'temporarily out of stock' I would be a rich man. Perhaps we could start with a refund on the TV licence when programmes are running late or are cancelled, or when we hear those familiar words "loss of vision", or "played the wrong tape".

In March 1991 I wrote to the Sunday Times that the Government was ill advised on the need for protection of BR's customers. The plethora of those acting as rail passengers watchdog (see page 91) is legendary. Where is the protection for the 90% using other transport and for other consumers? It doesn't exist because the Private Sector has the good sense not to publish self critical data. I quoted insurance premiums raised by three times the inflation rate, two year old cars which could not be converted to lead free petrol, garages who would not refund money when one complains of poor work, manufacturers who say a less costly part is not available when it is. I have had poor service in hotels, bad meals in restaurants, and complained, with no redress. "Guarantees" which are the basis of so much misplaced faith in the private sector, are overrated. Most consumer products are "guaranteed" for 10%, or less, of the life you reasonably expect. By analogy, if BR gave corresponding guarantees on punctuality, they should guarantee the first 10% of a journey. If a money back guarantee was to be introduced, a start should be made in the Private Sector which the Public Sector is supposed to emulate. They may then improve products enough to end the balance of payments deficit. Other transport might also set an example.

In December 1991, I telephoned the BBC referring to an item on refunds to commuters asking how can the CTCC and the BBC presenter be surprised if BR refunds are paid at the expense of other customers. Surely they cannot believe that when customers of the private sector complain, and after several repeats EVENTUALLY get a reply, which may EVEN contain a refund (instead of the cheaper "very sincere apologies"), that it is made at the expense of a manager or employee, although that would explain a reluctance to give refunds. The broadcast postulated a commuter delayed by rail en route to negotiate a multi million pound deal. I said that any doing so without a margin for contingencies or delays, by whatever form of transport, is a fool and ought not to be in charge of such important matters. If this practice exists there is no wonder the UK has a balance of payments problem.

I telephoned the BBC in March 1992 when the Chairman of the CTCC criticised BR for setting compensation targets too high. They are low in comparison with most of the Private Sector who do not offer ANY compensation for late deliveries. It often takes several letters to get a reply - obtaining compensation seems as difficult as drawing blood from a stone. Only a minority travel by BR - the majority who travel by road, suffer horrendous delays. Where is the compensation for travellers using all other transport?

Documentaries

In 1989, a TV Railwatch team spent a week with part of BR. Quotes by members of the BBC Team which the viewer may have missed, include:
* "A driver should get a medal for exceeding the speed limit". (If he did,

and derailed a train, there would no medal, and no sympathy from the media).
* "This telephone panel looks out of the dark ages", (It looked less reminiscent of the dark ages than many films on TV).
* "Why doesn't BR give the customer what it wants", (They were leading with their chins. What this customer wanted from the BBC was fewer repeats, no schedule changes, prompt response to phone calls and no breakdowns).
* They criticised facilities for disabled. (Changes in the past 20 years have given disabled people more mobility, but BR has made provision, unlike some other forms of transport. BR have a "minor" problem in that their rolling stock has a life span which is twice the length of this development - buses and motor coaches do not. By now, all should have lifts, but don't. Some hotels make no provision. In 1983, when arranging accommodation for a party including someone in a wheelchair, I was amazed to find that a new four star hotel had no lift. In 1992, we were dismayed to find the lift out of order at a hotel at which a wedding reception was held, at which guests, including one in a wheelchair, were staying. Learning that it had been out of order for months, we complained to the receptionist, who said they didn't know one of the guests was in a wheelchair. We pointed out that they didn't need to know, their brochure which was accepted at face value, boasted of the ease with which they could cope with disabled visitors. I asked why they had not amended the brochure, as they admitted, that due to some legal argument it may be several more months before the fault was remedied?

Railways & Road Transport
A Daily Telegraph article in June 1993, said that a **rail lobby campaign** led to the requirement for a man to walk ahead of road vehicles, carrying a red flag under an 1865 Act and "held back road transport until it was repealed in 1878". As its' title defines, the 1865 Locomotives on Highways Act was aimed at the only form of mechanical road transport - steam powered, which had boiler explosions on public roads and was passed 20 years before the car was invented and 55 years before lorries were capable of competing with rail. Had the internal combustion engine not been invented, steam powered vehicles would have made no inroads into rail traffic. The first motor car appeared here in 1894, the first was made in the UK in 1895, the red flag requirement being repealed in 1896, not 1878. Railways had no cause to fear ponderously slow traction engines, nor the puny motor car when it appeared. Not even the most ardent advocate of the early motor car could have foreseen its future. If a lobby was responsible for the red flag, it must have been landowners or the 'horse lobby'. The "rail lobby" was so ineffective that it couldn't persuade Government to concede equality with road haulage.

Journalists criticise BR managers for using cars. I have pointed out to the media, that there is no legislation to prevent greengrocers eating meat, butchers eating fish, BBC staff reading newspapers, newspaper staff watching TV. I have not heard a bus manager criticised for using a car. As trains are not allowed down Suburbia's 'Acacia Avenues' - many residents complain about trains on nearby lines which existed 100 years before their house was built - then it seems not unreasonable for BR managers or staff to use cars.

Surveys
In June 1986, The "WHICH?" magazine published a report about BR. Among its comments, criticisms and suggestions were the following :
* **"Not enough car parking space at Inter City stations".** (Most Councils can be criticised for insufficient parking. It is, for them, as for BR, due to the cost and availability of urban land. Few bus stations have carparks. The price of airport carparks in greenfield areas is horrendous. There would be a riot if BR charged similar rates for short & long term parking).
* **About 200 members of 'WHICH' were asked whether they had complained".** (Had any written to praise? The first phone call I received as Divisional Manager at Stoke was from a man who thanked BR, after taking his elderly

mother by train and ship to France - her first outting for 20 years).
* **Legislation covering Railwaymen under the influence of alcohol and drugs should be brought into line with road.** (It is not against the law to drive a car after drinking. On BR, the limit for a train driver is zero - those contravening it often lose their jobs. Road should adopt BR's zero limit).
* **"Technology is becoming available to brake a train automatically if a driver fails to respond to a signal warning".** (Such equipment had long been in use. Consideration was being given to further advances, but road transport should be pressured to catch up on yesterday's technology).
* **"WHICH" wants more public announcements on trains.** (In 1980, I called for more equipment, and radio on trains. BR couldn't finance it. Even then, information was given on many trains. In contrast, there is, even now, none for the 90% who travel by road. Do passengers require more? On November 7th 1991, I joined the 06.19 Blackpool to Euston train at Crewe. Both there and again at Stafford, the Conductor made the usual announcement regarding the train's calling points. Two passengers sitting across the gangway from me moaned audibly, on both occasions, that they had heard it all before. Despite travelling first class, they obviously lacked first class brains, or it would have been obvious that the announcements were intended for those who had just joined. They also lacked first class manners, because they were rather noticeably 'hogging' four seats, before reluctantly admitting to passengers joining at Stafford that two seats were unoccupied).
* **BR should experiment with common queueing system used by banks, to reduce delays at ticket offices.** (The system is only as good as the number of cashiers and the alacrity of customers in moving to a cashier who becomes available. The frequency of closing positions in banks negates the benefits of the system. Rail passengers expect to be allowed to travel and pay later, rather than wait. If bank customers cannot wait, fearful of missing a train or bus, or finding a ticket on a car, will a bank waive charges for paying later (being overdrawn) ? Recent reports show BR is well down the league of slowest queues, and better than a dozen Private Sector groups. This did not surprise me, since most of the private sector have no target queueing times. A few minutes at a station contrasts sharply with two hours before scheduled airport departures even if flights are delayed by hours or days).
* **Train catering at all times of the day.** (There should be a campaign for the private sector, much of which has a fixation for closing at 2pm sharp, to lead the way. As only 10% travel by rail, we need a campaign for the 90% who travel by car - not all on motorways. Even on motorways, service is not perfect. In January 1988, I complained to Trust House Forte that we had to queue in a cold doorway at an M1 service station, although there were empty tables which were out of use due to staff shortage. They tendered sincere apologies and said it was difficult to ensure a 100% staff turnout. As a former BR manager, I recognise their dilemma, although it did not explain why we were not allowed to sit inside until someone was available to serve us. Those who are tolerant of staff absence in private sector companies, and accept similar problems in their own companies, are almost certainly intolerant of the same problem on BR - attributing it to incompetence).
* **Longer trains for commuters - the obvious solution to overcrowding would seem to be to add another coach.** (One extra coach per train adds about 10% to the suburban fleet to cater for existing revenue, thus increasing losses. More vehicles will stand idle off-peak. The solution is to limit the number of season ticket holders to nominated trains, and to charge the higher fares then required to cover all costs. Anyone believing otherwise should back their ideas with their own money - when they will most assuredly lose it).
* **Copy your letter of complaint to BR to the TUCC.** (A pointless exercise which will benefit only the Post Office. The TUCC duty is to consider a complaint only where a person is dissatisfied with BR's reply. How can they be dissatisfied with a reply they haven't received? Those dissatisfied with BR's reply, will have to send a copy to the TUCC. Those satisfied with BR's reply have sent the TUCC an unnecessary copy, and both have wasted postage).

Some councils are understanding of problems facing BR, and some give
practical help to improve services or facilities. Many became antipathetic
towards BR, due to route closures which were implicit in the 1947 Act and
the 1955 Modernisation Plan. A Privatised railway would have closed loss
making routes, as they did before the war. Some councils believed that
branch lines were the roots of freight traffic. They were not, most traffic
was to and from major industrial or urban areas, and hence, on main lines;
(BRB 1963 Report, para 4: "one third of the system carries 1% of rail
traffic" - after 2700 miles of the most unremunerative routes: 13.5%, had
been closed). BR were seen as the villains for proposing closures, whereas
after protracted public inquiries the MoT may refuse or delay closure,
further increasing losses. Motorways and road improvements exacerbated the
problem, not least because roads, unlike railways are justified solely on
the basis of social benefit, calculated on the basis of time which may be
saved by road users. Many invested in "a little car" to be like the
'Joneses'. Car ownership was taking off by the 1950's. Giving friends a
lift to work for a share of the petrol cost, although illegal, became
commonplace. Many saw closures as the thin end of a wedge which would drain
communities away. No one foresaw that an explosion in car ownership would
protect communities more than branch lines could. Anyone travelling non
stop by car from or to a rural area would always be quicker than rail.

Naturally, Councils saw only the issue concerning them - their branch line -
"this one is a special case", fearing that those without a car, may be
disadvantaged by a closure, if only for one annual journey. They wanted to
will the end but not the means. Branch lines are for the benefit of local
residents, both directly and indirectly through visitors or tourists who
spend money in the area. Loss making lines should be funded by someone
other than passengers on profitable lines. Until 1968, it was left to BR to
subsidise such lines from revenue elsewhere. Thereafter, by Government
decision, they were to be funded by taxpayers, some of whom have never had a
branch line and others who have lost their own line, which is iniquitous.
Loss making train services should be funded by Councils who subsidise buses
and who would take a different view on economies or closures if they
subsidised local trains. In 1982, within my Division, a typical County
Council and four District Councils within its boundaries, gave a total
subsidy of £1.5m pa to the Crosville Bus Co. Some councils believed that
there was an alternative, to legislate freight onto rail, but few directed
suppliers to send their own substantial purchases by rail. Few branch lines
have sufficient freight potential to support a line. With opposition from
unions in other industries, there was no prospect that legislative action
would take place. Any Party promising to legislate traffic onto rail was in
for a long spell in Opposition.

Some councils opposed action to reduce costs - modern level crossings,
remote operation of signals from main line signal boxes, singling of lines,
all incurring investment - and unstaffed stations, to secure the future of a
line. Many BR managers were perplexed by this attitude which could only
hasten a line's demise. Often, there were suggestions to reduce fares or
run more trains, which would only widen the gap. Sometimes, there were
demands for more staff, perhaps prompted by a desire for a "nice station
garden" (councils do less in this context, for the same financial reasons,
than they did when most stations had gardens), or on grounds of safety.
(CTCC 1963 Report: "The danger to passengers at an unstaffed halt is
negligible compared to that at any bus stop on a main road").

My "Civic Round"
In 1982 the Mayor of Colwyn Bay "declared the improved station open" by

unveiling their attractive plaque, and hoped that BR would attract more business to the town. Expressing thanks for the plaque, I proposed a meeting to discuss how we could work together to increase business, and arranged to meet the Chief Executive and his officers "to inform them of the implications and problems of BR finances and to discuss ways of taking action of mutual benefit". At the meeting, I explained the constraints within which BR had to work, and the legislative background to our present situation. Under the Government's PSO, for each £1 by which we increased net revenue, we lost a £1 of the PSO and for each additional £1 we lost, we received nothing - a heads we lose, tails we lose situation. However, it was our duty to reduce the cost to the taxpayer, coining the phrase "Narrowing the Net Revenue Gap" as the title of this activity. I suggested how the council could increase BR revenue on the line, whilst providing a social service for residents. BR's Senior Citizen Railcards gave reduced rates of travel, and research showed each railcard produced an average of £50 pa in ticket sales. A few councils bought cards in bulk, which we could, therefore supply at a discount. Some gave Railcards to Senior Citizens as an alternative to bus passes, others resold them at a discount. Colwyn Bay Council placed their first order quickly, following it by several repeat orders, and responded to a request to issue our brochures through various outlets. I set up meetings with all 22 District and Borough councils in my Division, and within a year, had increased sales to councils by 600% - 19 Authorities purchasing cards compared with 10 before the campaign began. This campaign increased sales, including those through Ticket Offices in my Division by an overall 40%, (compared with other Divisions having reductions, except one with a 2% increase), and increased revenue by an estimated £1.4m pa. So unique was this development that I asked Sir Peter Parker, BR's Chairman, to sign a document jointly with Stafford Borough Council who had agreed to buy 8000 railcards - the largest single purchase. We made the signing a public event for publicity purposes. All District and Borough Councils in my Division, including the three which did not support my initiative, subsidised Senior Citizens' bus travel.

County, District and Borough Councils responded to my request to join us in enviromental schemes to smarten up stations, particularly, but not exclusively those which were unstaffed, and also some lineside locations. Most Councils were exceedingly helpful - providing plants and sharing material costs, whilst the Manpower Services Commission provided the labour.

Advice & Criticism
One councillor of Ceredigion District Council, said that BR ought to run an excursion from Aberystwyth to Edinburgh. I said that "in my professional judgement that would lose money increasing the line's perilous deficit" and explained the "heads we lose, tails we lose" principle. "There would be no risk to BR finances if a Council, Councillor or anyone chartered a train - the train costs being paid by the promoter who would pocket the profits, if there were any". (There was no charter train in this instance, but other Councils had responded to this approach).

A Clwyd Councillor criticised BR for not electrifying the North Wales coast line. Having had wide experience of electrification - planning, finance, construction and operations, and being experienced in each type of system operated by BR, I explained that under prevailing investment criteria the traffic volume required to pay for it did not exist on or near that line. Clwyd CC opposed BRHQ's 1984 plan to partially single the Wrexham to Bidston line. I refuted their fear that "Nissan's possible new factory at Shotton would be at risk because we would be unable to move car trains on the single line". A factory siding would be alongside and connected to the unaffected double track. So far as potential passenger growth was concerned, I proved that volume could increase by 1600% on the existing trains. Above that the service could then be doubled and still run on a single line. The proposed single line could be re-doubled should traffic ever require it.

Discussing **passenger** matters with Montgomery District Council, a Councillor related a case of a man who wouldn't have **goods** by rail because of a split delivery of a consignment. Intending to make inquiries, I asked "did it happen last week or last month" - it was 20 years earlier. (It may have been due to a sender's error or failure, but it was impossible to check).

Some Councils opposed an HQ scheme to reduce assets, viz. passenger coaches, without reducing the number of trains: linking North Wales - Manchester and Manchester - Scarborough trains, creating through West to East Coast trains. The object was economy, but I promoted it as an improved service, which was soon confirmed by increased loadings. Some complained of losing an interval service - which the line had not had - the new service was closer to an interval pattern. Councils also opposed withdrawal of the Holyhead - London sleeping car which was hopelessly uneconomic, with an average load of 44%. No private company would have funded one in 1982.

Some councillors said BR ignored suggested service changes, if their ideas were not adopted, overlooking the prospect that they would increase losses. All ideas were considered. It would be foolhardy to do otherwise, only to find that one's successor had implemented them without loss. If there were risks, I was prepared to introduce timetable changes if proposers covered any losses. This must be the acid test which anyone should be prepared to accept. If BR implemented unsuccessful changes, losses would have to be recouped from service cuts, fare rises or changes disliked by councils.

Some councils criticised BR for not preserving old buildings. To Barlaston Parish Council I explained that it was impossible to obtain authentic materials for repairs to the 19th Century North Staffordshire Railway station building at Barlaston, and it was wasteful to maintain a building we did not need, and which, due to its proximity to the electrified line, could not be sold. We planned to dismantle it to provide materials to keep three other buildings of the same architectural period in a good state of repair. In other cases, I offered to sell redundant vandalised buildings on unstaffed stations to local authorities for as little as £1, but without success. Attempts to find occupants usually failed because buildings were at unsupervised locations, which were, or could be, subject to vandalism.

Unusual Problems
In 1983-4, I represented BR at meetings of the Merseyside County Council Passenger Transport Committee. Delays had been occurring on the fairly modern Liverpool "Loop" tunnel line, due to water on the track affecting signalling. Remedial steps had been taken by installing additional pumps, but the problem had recurred. The tunnel had been designed to be above the Water Table with weep holes in the walls to provide for fluctuations. Water seeping in would run down the gradient and be pumped into the Mersey. This reduced construction costs, which would fall directly or indirectly on the PTA, compared with a tunnel designed to keep all water out. To demonstrate the cause of delays to the Council, I asked BR civil engineering staff to draw, for me, a cross section of the rail tunnel showing the original and current levels of the Water Table. This revealed that when the tunnel originally opened, the track was already below the Water Table, whilst seven years later it had risen a further two metres and was then well up the tunnel walls. It was not dangerous, and would not delay trains if pumping capacity was in excess of flows. I contacted the Water Board who said that the cause was a decline in consumption of water from industrial wells. Until it occurred to me to have the drawing prepared, delays were attributed to BR incompetence rather than local industrial decline as firms closed or

moved from the area. Approval was then given by the PTA for more pumps. The Committee discussed rail performance data supplied by the PTE, which obtained all rail statistics from BR. Those being discussed differed from BR data - some punctuality statistics were lower and some higher, whilst some cancellation statistics were noticeably worse. I noted that their four-weekly statistical periods were not the same as BR's. Discussions with the PTE revealed the cause (see Chapter 7).

Costs
Having listened to some Councils telling BR to keep prices down, it came as a cultural shock to find they had replaced the Motor industry as the wage pace setter in 1969, creating the wage explosion which is the father and mother of inflation. Through Pay & Efficiency deals in the preceeding two years, BR had linked pay successfully to productivity and a third stage was in hand. Unlike some private sector pay deals which have been investigated by the media, these were subject to monitored savings. BRB 1970 Report, para 9.3: "BRB had planned P&E Stage III but it was upset by a wages explosion caused by the local authorities pay settlement in October 1969 of 20-25%. Other industries made substantial offers. BR staff could not be expected to settle for pay increases linked to productivity when others had got pay without strings. BR staff settled for 8% in May and 3% in August".

NBPI Report, 1969, [London commuter lines], Para 15: "BR consults Local Authorities to assess the implications of new housing and thus maintains a reasonable base for forecasting travel trends on specific lines. But information on rail capacity is not always taken into account by planning authorities although it is available to them". Para 13: "BR would have to spend £8.8m to create 4600 seats in the peak on SR, but only £1.4m on the Euston line. Commuters could have enjoyed better travelling conditions at lower cost had Council Planners consulted BR before making plans".

Safety
The phobia about modern level crossings is impossible to comprehend since independent reports show they are safer than manned crossings. Some fear "automatic signals" on railways, when they have been used on roads since 1930. No one can deny that the safety of railway crossings is light years ahead of road crossings. I concluded that critics must believe that you will be dead longer if you are hit by a train than by a car. Some may have hoped that level crossings would be replaced by bridges at BR expense, totally ignoring that the mass of road traffic arose after railways were built - by about 100 years or so. Any logical person would concede that those who created the problem (road users) should pay for the solution.

Monopoly Powers
Those councillors who believe that BR has a monopoly, have a mirror image. Railways lost their monopoly in the 1920's. On the other hand, residents cannot opt out of the council tax, wholly or partially, by obtaining some or all requirements from elsewhere. Council powers are awesome.

Councils blocked BR viability plans - **BRB 1968 Report**, para 12: "It is only regrettable that the original concept, including a large office block, which would not merely have made the [Euston] station scheme virtually self financing but would have helped to reduce cross London travel should have been ruled out after many months of argument by those authorities [Camden Borough] who sanctioned the huge Euston Centre office development scheme a stone's throw away". **Select Committee Report 1977**: Councils delayed or rejected schemes to transfer freight from road to rail, (see page 41).

Government's plan to privatise BR because it expects the Private Sector to make better use of stations and land is based on the wrong premise.

In 1983, I suggested to the PTE's Rail Director that we should meet prior to Merseyside County Council Passenger Transport Committee meetings, to discuss problems and complaints. This would pre-empt complaints being raised by the Committee which were not on the Agenda since some were unaswerable without investigation. This created a bad media image which may be unjustified. Experience of private sector handling of complaints, where answers are not immediately available, confirms this was not unreasonable. It was also an opportunity for a two way exchange with a forward thinking PTE which pursued integration of public transport. It proved to be useful and effective.

At the first meeting, I pointed out that statistics on punctuality presented to the Transport Committee by the PTE did not correspond to BR's, and yet BR was the sole source. BR statistics supplied to the PTE, showed percentages of punctuality and of cancelled trains on the PTE network, and were in BR's standard four weekly periods for accounts and statistics. PTE statements were on a cycle varying by one week from ours. He called in the person responsible for compilation, who was "converting BR statistical periods to theirs by adding 75% of one BR period to 25% of another period". In effect, they were averaging averages which can lead to statistical inaccuracy. BR staff said that the PTE had never mentioned that they worked to different periods. BR could have supplied what they needed because each BR Area office prepared weekly records from which four weekly reports were aggregated. Thereafter, we supplied them with weekly statistics enabling them to calculate accurately for their four weekly periods.

In some periods, percentages of trains cancelled in PTE statistics were greater than those in BR statistics. The person compiling PTE statistics explained that they had added to BR figures, trains cancelled - with the prior agreement of the PTE - for engineering work. These related to closure of lines agreed with them for track maintenance, renewals and resignalling. Major engineering work started after the last train on Saturday and, by substituting PTE buses for trains on some Sunday mornings, work could continue to 14.00 hours, thereby keeping costs down. These changes were advertised in the media by the PTE. Work could have been confined to the Saturday night shift, when there were no trains, but this would prolong work over more weekends, increase the total number of hours of work, and hence, the cost. This arises because at the start of work there is a period of disconnection and of getting works trains and machines on the track before work can commence. Likewise there is a period at the end required for removal of trains and machines before track can be reopened for traffic. If one hour is required for this purpose at both ends of the job, there will be, in broad terms, 6 hours work in an 8 hour blockage and 14 hours work in a 16 hour blockage. I said that we could keep cancellations within the PTE target by restricting the work to the unoccupied night shift, but this would increase costs which they paid. The method of recording cancellations reverted to the original basis, which related to unadvertised cancellations.

My research revealed that statistics supplied to the PTE did not include all trains for which they had a financial interest. BR statistics are based on arrival at destination. Whereas most services were wholly within the PTE area at both ends, one group was not. Trains from - but not to - Manchester and Wigan were included and as these travelled some distance before reaching the PTE boundary they were more likely to be delayed than outbound trains to stations within the PTE boundary, covering a much shorter distance. An unbalanced picture arose from including trains which may be more susceptible to delay, but excluding those which were less susceptible. So I introduced a system of special reports at PTE boundary stations for the punctuality of outbound trains. Contractually they should have been in from Day 1.

Government's 1930's plan to help Industry by siphoning revenue from railways under the Railway Freight Rebates Act (see Page 60), was unsuccessful. When war came, industry could not meet UK needs, despite severe rationing and control of materials. The "cradle of the Industrial Revolution" had fallen so far behind foreign competitors that for part of the War, steel was the biggest single commodity shipped from the USA, which also supplied ships and aircraft. UK industry couldn't meet postwar demand for steel and other materials required by BR to repair war damaged infrastructure and replace ageing rolling stock, (see pages 35-41) but pushed up prices (see pages 17-34), whilst Government expected BR to "contain those price increases" (see Page 24). For fourteen consecutive years, the BTC protested about unrestrained cost increases, which, with Government's unique restraint on BR prices, created the deficits which Government, media and public criticise.

Few realise how much BR spends in the Private Sector, and hence, do not comprehend that some reliability problems must stem therefrom. In 1982, BR purchases cost £1254m, of which 80% was from the Private Sector. In 1979, I initiated a major investigation into passenger and freight train punctuality and reliability which revealed that technical defects caused most delays and cancellations, contrary to prevailing opinion that it was largely a matter of sharpening up traincrew, signalmen and station staff, to cut out operating delays. I argued that a proportion of complaints should be laid at the door of the private sector, not attributed to BR - an injured party.

In some years, passengers complained of a lack of information in the period preceding a timetable change, when station departure sheets, or brochures were not available. Sometimes, this was due to overruns in train planning, due to pressures to make short notice changes to reduce costs. At other times, it was due to printers. On occasions, we sent a member of staff to the printers to collect proofs or a supply of finished publications to save a day in transit. We even had to resort to laboriously amending old station departure sheets in ink to display these rather than nothing. Among post sale date errors were timetables with pages missing and others with loose pages. All complaints were levelled at BR.

BR experienced problems with recently purchased diesel and electric locos, units and equipment as the following examples from **BTC Minutes** reveal:
* April 1956 "poor availability levels of diesel locomotives - with an average of 55% availability for traffic, compared to 80% with steam. Waiting for spare parts was identified as the major cause, followed by manufacturing faults".
* March 1958: "time out of service of some main line diesels noted - unreliable and may have to be scrapped".
* November 1959: "certain diesel locomotive types whose performance was unsatisfactory and unlikely to improve, which were causing poor timekeeping and incurring excessive maintenance, will have to be prematurely scrapped".
* December 1960, the Scottish Region suspended the Glasgow electric service "and had taken up with Associated Electrical Industries regarding technical difficulties which they [AEI] would resolve". [An MoT Inquiry was held into defects on trains and consequential service breakdowns. An independent expert said transformers supplied did not have secondary winding assembly strong enough to support the conditions to which they have been subjected in service. "No evidence had been submitted to indicate that the failure was due to any special conditions arising from the dual voltage AC system"].
* January 1961: Withdrawing electric locos from service in Crewe Area. Type 3 Diesels withdrawn after 10,000 miles due to lubricating pump failures.
* September 1961: Discussed recommendations for claims against contractors for delay in delivery of locomotives and rolling stock.

* 1961, BR withdrew 50% of diesel trains operating between Nottingham, Leicester and Birmingham due to axle faults, and re-introduced steam trains.
* 1961-2, Scottish Region had to replace diesel by steam due to breakdowns.
BTC Minutes, November 1956 refer to late deliveries by contractors causing underspending on new coaches, thereby delaying replacement of old coaches.

February 1963, media reported "a lot of teething troubles with diesels in the winter - oil freezing and mechanical difficulties". In November 1963, they reported that the most powerful Western Region diesel hydraulics - 2700hp - were out of service to repair transmission faults which developed after 75,000 miles, and that less powerful diesels - 1700hp and 2200hp - had to be substituted with consequential effect on punctuality. Transmission equipment had to be returned to the manufacturers for urgent modification. **CTCC Report 1983:** "poor performance on Eastern & Western Regions due to problems of HST ... over past 4 years resulting in severe unpunctuality and cancellation". HST problems led to a £7m penalty on suppliers in 1985.

Eastern Region Area Board minutes reveal a prolonged series of defects on Electric Multiple Unit trains (EMU's) and associated equipment supplied by GEC, AEI, English Electric, and Westinghouse in 1961 and 1962, which resulted in reduced services being operated on the LT&S, NE London lines, GN Suburban and Clacton Main line. Even when manufacturers carried out modifications, further defects sometimes arose. In one case, 71 EMU's were given Modification "A", then Modification "B", then Modification "C", followed by unclassified modifications after they failed in very hot weather. (The media missed the classic line "the wrong kind of sunshine" - but in this case BR would not have been the focus). Some EMU's failed immediately they were brought into service. The defect rate of some EMU's was 5-6 times as bad as the Eastern Region average, which itself was not impressive. Delivery dates for converted or modified EMU's were unreliable. On the Shenfield line, only 80% were available by the promised date. In one case a revised delivery date was just two weeks before the service was due to start - a recipe for chaos. Such delays caused wholesale recasting of services, serious unpunctuality and cancellation, increased staff costs and considerable loss of revenue. Cannibalisation of parts from some EMU's to keep others in service was costly, but necessary to minimise cancellations. EMU's had to be borrowed from other routes to provide a minimal service, causing consequential cancellations elsewhere. The introduction of new electric services had to be postponed on some routes, notably the LT&S. Minutes record that in June 1961, 37% of EMU's were out of service. Due to the "30 year rule" being exercised on even the most mundane public records, it is not yet possible to reveal what problems arose after 1962.

Cabinet Minutes, July 1960: debated assisting the ailing North British Locomotive Company, by telling them to reduce their tender by 8-10% to match lower tenders so they may get the contract; or to give BR more capital (it would almost certainly have been an interest bearing loan), to buy their more expensive locomotives. They decided not to do so, but it is revealing that they considered measures which could only increase BR losses.

In 1981, the APT's gearboxes seized up on the main line, south of Rugby, requiring all Up trains to be diverted for several hours via the longer Northampton route, causing 20 minutes delay to each train. To reach a depot with an inspection pit, it had to be skidded along with locked wheels. This did not warm the hearts of staff who had to inspect 16 miles of track and replace damaged rails. Rolling Stock Engineers were not pleased either. To minimise damage it was moved at 20 mph on a 100 mph line.

Delays in supply, and ill-fitting uniforms caused staff complaints, and some public criticism of staff appearance. It was suggested that a cause of ill-fitting uniforms was inaccuracy of measurements which staff themselves had to provide - garments may be tight if staff indulged in wishful thinking about waist lines, but independent research showed baggy garments caused more concern. In 1985, I initiated an investigation into the ordering and supply of uniform clothing, then costing £8m pa, and learned that one supplier was 35 weeks in arrears with issues to new or promoted staff and 13 weeks with replacements to other staff. The Preston Area Manager reported that of 438 uniforms due to be supplied in one month, 50 were of the wrong size, (20 too large, 30 too small), 5 were incomplete and 53 had not been despatched. I made 27 recommendations to improve reliability of supply, staff appearance, and financial control data. In 1986, BRHQ commissioned an investigation by independent consultants, who found that "the majority of staff experienced delay when returning uniforms for replacement - the time range for replacements was between 1-2 months for a shirt and 7-12 months for a full uniform; 18 months was an average wait for replacement of misfits; 32% said trousers were too baggy; Women prefer to buy their own trousers ... uniform ones are too baggy and masculine". Of interest were views gleaned from passengers who said that staff were "usually courteous and helpful, Barrier staff are usually helpful, Travel Centre staff are very helpful", which contrasted sharply with the image being portrayed.

In June 1963, the media reported that SR drivers were wearing their own clothing in protest against the poor quality of uniforms. Drivers said that some of the uniforms had come from Poland. BRHQ told the media that they could not confirm this, as the uniforms were supplied by a UK company.

Many of these problems and failures are to be expected in real life, because both men and machines are fallible. Certainly almost everyone must have experienced similar problems in their domestic purchases. Hence it seems reasonable to accept that "it is due to circumstances beyond our control" or "it was only human error". What I cannot comprehend is why, alone among industry, only BR should not experience "circumstances beyond our control" or "human error", but have every failing attributed to incompetence.

Among BTC papers released by the Public Record Office in 1987, was a memorandum, written in 1951, by David Blee, then the Railway Executive member for Commercial matters. He had been invited as Guest of Honour at the luncheon of the Transport Committee of the Association of British Chambers of Commerce in May 1951, where "the words of welcome by the Chairman turned out to be wholly critical". His revised response, which he developed on the spot, [on the back of his menu card, which was included with the papers], began by telling them that he had resigned from one of their Councils because they did not support measures he took to increase membership, reduce its costs and make it more effective. He then went on to say that "the BTC was not a monopoly, and was not in the same street as many Trades and Industries where price rings were abundantly apparent whenever we went out to tender. What BR bought from industry in 1939 per £100 now cost £259, whilst our charges at 90% of 1939 levels represented the efficiency and economy of the past three years. Everything I buy has gone up". Answering criticisms of delays, he pointed out that with expanding demand for transport, BR had difficulty in expanding resources fast enough. He drew attention to the national manpower shortage by the example of the Birmingham area where 33,000 vacancies were chased by 6000 unemployed, (to which UK industry responded by increasing wages instead of improving productivity). Demonstrating that the Private Sector had also not been able to meet expanding demand without delays, he added that "if I wanted to buy a car, I would put my name on a waiting list and hope to get it in two years time, whilst the wait for a refrigerator was only one year". (Little wonder UK industry lost a world lead in so many fields).

I began to wonder why BR was wrongly blamed for delay when I worked as a young clerk in a Parcels Office in the late 1940's and early 1950's. Asked by a manufacturer for proof of delivery of a package they had despatched, we would contact the destination and often receive a reply "delivered on ..... (date) 'J.Bloggs' signs". We would inform the sender and hear no more. Asked by a trader to trace a parcel despatched to them from another town but not received, we would contact the forwarding station and often back would come the message "not forwarded from here", which we passed on to the trader and heard no more. Had there been a loss in transit there would be a claim, requiring both stations to certify on a claims form (compiled by BR, not the customer), that a package had been despatched but not received. When no claim was made there was no cause for complaint. It was many years before I learned that these were normal commercial practices. A manufacturer (promising delivery dates they could not maintain) said a package had been despatched, when it hadn't, to keep the customer quiet. Those who said they had not received an item which had been delivered were trying to delay payment. Having admitted that the package had been received they would say that "the cheque is in the post". On the seller's market at that time most traders tolerated delay, assuming it was BR's fault without inquiring. In 1969, I met an executive who said he had blamed Liverpool Docks for delay to goods which he knew had not left the USA. He justified this immoral conduct on the grounds that otherwise they would lose the order! Companies using BR now find that transits are monitored by computer, so any looking for a 'whipping boy' have to look elsewhere. Those using their own transport have no handy scapegoat. When you chase them regarding a delivery promised weeks or months ago, they will 'explain' it was "due to heavy orders", or "waiting materials". They will be snookered if you ask why they didn't have the courtesy to inform you, allowing you to place an order elsewhere.

In my personal life, I found that BR was used as a scapegoat by the Private Sector to cover up their problems. When we went to order carpets in 1965 for a house into which we were about to move, (having suffered delay at the hands of solicitors), I told the Sheffield retailer that we required a guarantee that the carpets would be laid within three weeks enabling us to move furniture in, onto carpets already in position. I said that if they gave a guarantee and the carpets arrived after we had moved in, the order would be cancelled. He could give a guarantee "up to a point, but the unforeseen may arise". "Like what?", I asked, and was told: "The carpets come from Kilmarnock and may be delayed on rail". Outlining my job, I said, "There you will have no problem, I will have the transit monitored door to door". "There may be other problems", was his next line. Heading for the door, I said, "I dare say there may be". Another retailer accepted my terms, despite my having told him that I had overheard a customer complaining of non delivery of curtains. Two days later he phoned to say one of our selections was not now being made by the manufacturer. He couldn't explain why our time had been wasted viewing an outdated sample. We had then to make another visit to select an alternative.

Discrimination
Some companies were adept at dumping uneconomic consignments onto BR, including empty crates and boxes sent as "returned empties" when the outward journey had been by road. To do so they would sign a consignment note which declared that they were really "returned empties", being charged at a very cheap rate to reflect a principle that BR had gained from a loaded journey. No one wanted a lorry load of air. The volume of packages at medium and large stations was so great that it was impossible to check every "returned empty" crate against past deliveries. Occasionally, we could carry out a retrospective check which identified that no corresponding delivery had been

made to the company concerned. Sometimes a BR delivery driver would recall that the crate concerned had not been delivered by him. Many companies would use BR to deliver to the far reaches of Scotland and Cornwall whilst reserving main flows for road haulage and their own vehicles. When BR tried to increase rates to reflect that the profitable flows had been creamed off leaving BR with the unprofitable flows, manufacturers and traders objected.

Investigating Transit Delays

In 1966, BR's Eastern Region introduced ATI to enable staff to plan local train services before trunk trains arrived. Hitherto, there was no record of wagons on trains or in Marshalling Yards. The only record of 460,000 wagons was made when wagons arrived at or were despatched from BR depots or private sidings. Under ATI, trains from Sheffield's Tinsley Marshalling Yard would have each wagon's details listed, and telexed to the destination Yard - Train ID, Wagon number, Destination, Contents, Point of origin and Despatch date. ATI had a mixed reception but I had no doubt that it would improve reliability. As Freight Movements Assistant, I had to implement ATI in the Sheffield Division. It occurred to me that there were unplanned benefits in the form of Management Information. I directed the Head of my Freight Transit Section, to obtain and analyse each day's records for evidence of misrouting, delays, poor wagon utilisation and unsafe train loads. Examples of his findings included two wagons - one from Parkgate Iron & Steel Co., (ten miles from Tinsley), with a label despatch date three days prior to departure from Tinsley. Inquiries revealed that the company labelled wagons at the point of loading within their complex and that some wagons were not placed in BR sidings by their locomotives on the same day. BR sidings records showed that this wagon was handed to BR three days after the label date, and moved to Tinsley on the same day. The other was a wagon from Hadfield's, a mile from Tinsley, with a label date a week before despatch from Tinsley. Inquiries revealed that, it was handed to BR on the label date, and recalled by the firm to load an item which had been overlooked. Sidings records showed it was returned to us one week later. There was no intention of these reputable companies to give an impression that BR was delaying wagons but consignees would assume from label dates that we had done so. BR staff at exchange sidings were told to endorse wagon labels with the date handed to BR and to inform senders accordingly.

As Area Manager, Leicester, I investigated coal merchants' complaints about "bunching" - wagons arriving on the same day, and presumed to have been delayed. If bunching occurred, wagon detention charges were reduced. I found that they were mostly due to simultaneous despatches by different collieries. I refused a rebate and suggested that they complain to the NCB.

In 1975, BR completed the implementation of TOPS a real time computer to monitor its wagon fleet, and successor to the less extensive ATI. To publicise this development, BRHQ asked Divisions to invite industrial managers to TOPS offices on 25th October to learn what the system would provide. Hitherto if a customer asked us to trace a wagon we would take details and undertake to phone back. With TOPS, we would say hang on, and in seconds give the required information. BRHQ knew that customers would treat this with some scepticism, hence the demonstration. I directed my six Area Managers to make arrangements, and went myself to the Stoke Area TOPS Office. Among those invited, was the Transport Manager from Shelton Steel Works, whom I asked for details of wagons for which they were waiting. He phoned his office and gave us details of six wagons, which the computer revealed had been consigned by the sender to Shotton Steel Works, and had arrived there. The sender had failed to inform Shelton that the wagons had been reconsigned after an initial advice to Shelton.

Some companies which despatched traffic in train loads from private sidings, failed, from time to time, to assemble a train fully loaded by the appointed departure time. Late arrivals at destination were usually attributed to BR.

"Putting the Block on"

Periodically, companies with private sidings restricted the number of wagons they would accept into the sidings, thereby lengthening transits. This worsened wagon utilisation, caused traffic loss elsewhere - due to non availability of wagons - and congested marshalling yards which created a ripple effect on transits of other traffic. If a firm restricted acceptance into their sidings, they should be debitted with every wagon in BR sidings and en route to them because they were avoiding charges which would arise if all wagons were placed in their sidings. BR staff were not always sharp enough on this issue, and were often afraid that we would lose traffic. Most did not see that the poor utilisation which arose from restricted acceptance was increasing our costs and losing revenue elsewhere. Before TOPS, ascertaining the total number of wagons in the pipeline was difficult, obtaining individual numbers and details of hundreds of wagons en route was virtually impossible. The real time TOPS computer (from 1975) made the task a piece of cake. If the pipeline was congested, and the consignee unable or unwilling to reduce it, in addition to levying detention charges, our options were to stop the loading of specific commodities, or of wagons for that consignee from all senders or from selected points of origin. Often, senders diverted traffic to road, worsening the pipeline delay, because consignees would unload lorries in preference to wagons. That was not an argument against placing stops on traffic, but for industry to get its act together and organise their materials flow. If BR had not been in the freight business, Haulier 'A' with hundreds of lorries standing in a pipeline would not have sat quietly while the consignee started to accept traffic via Haulier 'B'. No haulier would put up with what industry expected of BR. Major industry was production rather than marketing led which probably explains why so many UK industries managed to lose a world lead for so many products. Consequently, most of the works with this particular failing, have been closed down or drastically reduced, and therefore, the road haulage industry was not put to the pipeline test.

In 1966, we experienced problems of restricted acceptance of wagons by Steel, Peech & Tozer, a steel company at Sheffield. BR's Ickles sidings adjoining their works were sometimes congested with wagons awaiting acceptance into their works. BR staff at Ickles were then obliged to put the "block" on acceptances from the major marshalling yard at Tinsley to ease congestion. I directed that charges be raised on all wagons consigned to them which were held back at Tinsley and at as many locations on BR for which figures could be obtained. The firm disputed the figures. To prove the facts, I arranged to clear BR Ickles sidings of every possible wagon, and filled it with wagons for the company. Thereafter until they cleared the backlog, they were debitted with the costs of detention. Six months later, I initiated and developed a plan to transfer BR shunting from Ickles yard, and sell it to the company as an extension of their own sidings and to function as exchange sidings between us. This would reduce BR asset and staff costs, gain capital, reduce pipeline delays and raise detention charges more quickly, whilst giving the company increased space.

Wagon Utilisation

It was a common industrial practice to over order their needs for empty wagons and keep the excess handy "in case they were needed". Some staff subscribed to this, seeing only local rather than national implications, and creating an average utilisation of wagons of one load per wagon per 10 days. Many firms claimed that they had to over order to ensure that they received the number of wagons they needed. The practice started during the war, when traffic increased by 50% or more, with virtually the same wagon fleet. It continued after the war whilst BR operated an old fleet, depleted by bombing and not replaced by modern wagons, because Government and industry failed to ensure enough materials for new wagons. Over ordering continued long after wagon supplies improved and created false shortages. The pre TOPS system for wagon ordering looked good on paper, but was easy to manipulate. TOPS was introduced in 1975 to tighten wagon control. Unlike some colleagues, I was a strong advocate for the early introduction of computer generated wagon supply, and from the date of implementation, displaced wagon distribution controllers, and relied on TOPS. Some companies which owned wagons complained that we were not returning their empty wagons promptly from destinations, but were often contradicted, when a TOPS check revealed that the wagons were still under load and had not been released by the consignee.

In 1967, the NCB, which was noted for slow turnround of wagons, (Beeching said that they were underpaying BR by £10m pa for wagon detention), proposed a joint investigation into "Maldistribution and Misuse of BR High Capacity Wagons". Our HQ agreed and nominated a member of my staff to represent BR instead of asking the Division for a nomination. I would have appointed myself, since the NCB's representative on the investigation, served with me on the CEGB/NCB/BR Liaison Meeting. My first knowledge of the investigation was when I was given the NCB/BR report which was on the agenda of the next Liaison Meeting. The Report showed BR failed to supply the NCB with the number of high capacity wagons ordered at some collieries, albeit, they were supplied with sufficient lower capacity wagons to compensate. (As a result of changes I had made in summertime wagon stabling arrangements, no coal had been grounded due to wagon shortage). After reading the Report, I asked our representative: "Where is the data on misuse?" - pointing out that, whilst "Maldistribution" was a BR failing, "Misuse" must be an NCB failing. He was under the impression that the remit related to BR failings. I knew that there was evidence that the NCB loaded high capacity wagons, (intended only for industrial coal) to domestic coal merchants. That was misuse, not least because many domestic coal merchants took as much as two weeks to unload a standard 16 ton wagon. Industries could unload high capacity wagons in days or hours. At the meeting when the item came up, I opposed discussion until the investigation was complete. The NCB representative seemed puzzled, so I explained that this was a report of maldistribution, the misuse aspect had been overlooked. The NCB representative responded that "Misuse is due to geological problems". This was an example of the apparent belief in other industry, that only they, and not BR, could have "circumstances beyond their control". I replied: "Maldistribution is due to geographical problems", and proposed that we should complete the remit and then each could give reasons for our respective failures. We did so, and pinpointed the NCB misuse. We found cases of high capacity wagons irregularly loaded with domestic coal from collieries which had been correctly supplied and should have loaded these wagons to industrial consumers such as CEGB or BSC. Some collieries had been incorrectly supplied with high capacity wagons, which had loaded them to domestic coal merchants instead of turning them out empty as they should have done, for us to transfer to collieries which needed them. We accepted our respective failings at the next Liaison Meeting and undertook to try to improve arrangements. Had the original report been discussed, the whole responsibility for not meeting CEGB requirements would have been laid on BR, in front of CEGB managers whose complaint about the use of the standard 16 ton wagons had given rise to the investigation. Due to the phraseology of the remit, that did not happen. The reason for BR incorrectly supplying high capacity wagons to collieries was that trains ran direct from industrial sidings to collieries. What went outbound from collieries to their customers, was sent back to collieries in trains of mixed empty wagons. Had we routed empty wagon trains from power stations and steel works via marshalling yards to separate wagons of varying capacities, delay would have been caused to urgent supplies for the collieries. We asked industry to separate wagon types after unloading, which was possible without delay or cost to themselves, so as to break the vicious circle which was, otherwise, costly to break. Over the next few years, Merry-Go-Round trains composed entirely of 32 ton wagons eased CEGB's problem, whilst TOPS improved the distribution of all other types of wagons.

In 1971, I found that BSC at Shotton sent BR a weekly analysis of wagon types received, requesting that their traffic be conveyed in high capacity wagons only. BR staff had accepted the implied criticism of BR. Following my practice of checking the facts, before accepting criticism, I initiated an investigation which revealed that the NCB was not ordering enough high capacity wagons to equate to the tonnage ordered. So when BR fulfilled the wagon order, there would be insufficient for the ordered tonnage and the NCB would have to load some standard wagons. Any short notice provision by BR were likely to be standard wagons. Some high capacity wagons loaded to domestic customers against agreed policy would not have surprised me, but under ordering did. Tabling my findings at an NCB/BR liaison meeting produced an explanation of "geological problems", which may have accounted for poor utilisation, but did not explain under ordering. To my surprise the NCB representative explained that they were under ordering in case they didn't mine as much coal as they had forecast. This was a new concept and had arisen following BR's tougher line on wagon detention charges.

It is tragic that the private sector Coal Trade refused to replace their own 19th Century 12-13 ton wagons, which conveyed almost all coal traffic, with modern high capacity wagons before the War. This was typical of the reluctance of UK industry to modernise. It would certainly have helped with prewar, wartime and post war rail movement and would have reduced losses of other traffic to road as a consequence of better train loads. The 1925 Coal Commission recommended establishing a Standing Committee to review and improve methods of transport to reduce costs of coal and improve wagon utilisation. They said that 20 ton wagons should be gradually introduced over a term of years and that district pools of private owner wagons should be formed by owners. The Standing Committee was set up in 1927, but failed to persuade the coal trade to show any enthusiasm either for larger wagons or district pools. Before 1948, railways were unable to prevent the use of these slow, small capacity wagons. The Government had the powers, but not the will. BTC Minutes record in February 1956 that they were "trying to move to a 35 ton mineral wagon if the NCB and the coal trade would improve their terminals". The pre 1948 standard was 13 tons, BR new standard was 16 tons, with 24½ ton wagons on selected flows - but by the late 1950's only 9% of collieries could load 24½ ton wagons. The BTC was unsuccessful because no progress was made until MGR wagons were introduced in 1965. The NCB took several years to modernise terminal facilities at selected collieries - only 27 collieries having loading bunkers by 1977, leaving a similar number to be converted. In November 1958, BTC Minutes record that they were pressing the coal trade to cooperate to establish more coal concentration depots to follow the one which was opened in that year, but progress was very slow.

Some steelworks over ordered wagons to be "on the safe side", until BR tightened up the basis of detention charges. They did not restrict the use of the longest steel carrying wagons for the longest steel, therefore they would run out of long wagons, having used them for short length loads. They had "production" rather than "geological" problems. Steel, we were told, was "cut by computer" and placed on the nearest rail wagon. To make matters worse, they used BR wagons for "Internal Use", to move steel within the works, for which they should have paid a special hire rate, when there was no rail journey to follow immediately, but the user was not known unless they reported it to BR, because it took place within their premises. The practice of using BR wagons for internal use in industrial private sidings was commonplace. Some industries used BR wagons internally to hold goods awaiting orders or shipment release, creating artificial shortages which lost BR more traffic and created more complaints. Ports held thousands of wagons to await the arrival of ships, because of outdated cargo handling methods. BR was seriously hampered in modernising its freight business by the 19th Century premises which comprised so much of industry. Thus BR had to hang onto small inefficient uneconomic wagons to serve sidings with tight curves and buildings suitable only for the horse drawn era because newer wagons were too large for them. For many years, new wagon design was constrained by the limits imposed by industrial premises.

BR managers developed the concept of "Merry Go Round" (MGR) wagons - new higher capacity wagons, running in permanently coupled trains, loading and unloading without stopping, which the CEGB and NCB agreed to use. These wagons had the best load/tare ratio possible on a two axled automatic discharge hopper wagon with a net load of 32 tons. BR initiated the wagon design and built 5000 wagons to start the concept by 1965. The CEGB began to build new coal fired Power Stations to a design incorporating terminals to unload such trains. The effective implementation of the concept was delayed by constructional problems including the collapse of six cooling towers at the new Ferrybridge Power station and faults in new generators. Whilst the NCB had invested in modern underground equipment, their surface installations had changed little since the collieries were opened, and they were slow to provide the loading bunkers upon which the new concept depended. This delay may have made coal less competitive, and it adversely affected BR finances. BR had to begin using the new wagons because new Power Stations had no facilities to unload any other wagons. BR had to keep staff at locations at which they would not have been required had the NCB accepted the MGR wagons permanently coupled together. NCB staff would not uncouple automatic brakes on the wagons to enable them to be loaded singly, in the traditional way at collieries which did not have new loading bunkers. BR staff had to uncouple the brake pipes on wagons before placing them in such collieries and then recouple them after they were loaded, undermining the whole concept of keeping them permanently coupled. Wagons should have achieved three loads per day, but due to the lack of NCB bunkers, were achieving 2-3 loads per week. There was a strong case for a Minister issuing a Direction to the NCB - instead of to BR on fares - to provide modern facilities in the National Interest, since it would lower the cost of electricity. The CEGB were not as helpful in maximising the utilisation of the new wagons as they could have been. New power stations were equipped with dual discharge tracks for unloading coal trains. However, it was the usual practice to use only one track, when alternate use of both tracks would have improved the utilisation of manpower, locomotives and wagons.

Peak Delays

An example of "doublethink" in the private sector arose when I was Area Manager at Leicester. The owner of a printing company telephoned me, just before Christmas 1969 to complain that a parcel sent to Newcastle Upon Tyne hadn't been delivered. After confirming the delay with my Parcel Office, I explained that the pre-Christmas period was our heaviest peak in the year, with heavy flows from manufacturers, traders, mail order companies and the GPO. Congestion in towns caused by shoppers delayed delivery vehicles and most consignees would not extend their hours for extra deliveries, hence, some delay was unavoidable. He replied it was nothing short of incompetence to fail to deliver currently even at Christmas. I listened patiently, and when he paused, said that the seasonal peak was a problem for all. For instance, I wished to order Christmas cards printed with our new address but had been told it was too late; he said "This is a very .... er .... busy er.... time.... for.... printers". I could almost hear the penny dropping. He became quite affable and said that no one had ever put our problems into

128

that perspective, and asked that I do my best. Few can see "the beam in their own eye" - they are too busy trying to point out "the mote in yours".

Private Sector Performance

Private Sector companies created a bad image by unsightly rubbish tips and piles of rusting cars on their side of our fence, giving passengers a bad visual impression, for which many criticised BR, not realising that there was an unseen boundary fence - they couldn't see the (fence) 'wires for the scrap'. The Dickensian appearance of lineside industry emitting filthy and malodorous smoke, did nothing to make rail travel attractive, particularly as coaches were made very dirty thereby. When industry lost markets to foreign competition, and closed ancient premises, consequential dereliction created even greater eyesores. Industry caused delays and cancellations arising from fires on their lineside premises and leakage of poisonous gases leading to lines being blocked by the Fire Brigade.

In November 1984, an Engineering Council advertisement detailed the decline of UK industry, "because our competitors learned too well" :-

Steel Making	- Post war: 3rd in the world;	1984: 10th
Shipbuilding	- 1900 - 60% built in UK;	1984: 3%
Motor cycles	- exported to 100 countries;	1984: importer
Cars in UK	- Prewar almost all British;	1984: Over 50% foreign
Machine tools	- Pioneered by Britain;	1984: 3.1% world production
Radio	- Discovered in Britain;	1984: import 96%
Computer	- Britain made the first one;	1984: 5% of the market
Textile machines	- Once made all World supplies;	1984: 8% of the market

These industries had not been subjected to the legislative interference which BR had faced. A failure to modernise premises, methods or products, and a failure to overcome demarcation problems and hold down prices led to their decline and demise, causing BR unforecast revenue losses which exacerbated financial and investment problems created by Government.

BR is urged to emulate the Private Sector. Some companies seem unable to admit a fault, but wrap it up in euphemisms. "We are sorry you **MAY** have been inconvenienced", when your letter spells out in words of one syllable that you have been. "Our computer made an error", totally ignoring that most of us know the adage - 'rubbish in, rubbish out'. There is an illusion that a profitable company is efficient, ignoring the prospect that it could, by more effort from managers and workforce, have become more profitable. The performance of some companies is unimpressive. Some closed down when demand was not falling. Some make obscene increases in top salaries and set up share options enabling executives to buy shares below prevailing market prices (much cheaper than other shareholders can buy them), and to resell, making untaxed profits. One company, whose share price had plunged to the floor said its new share option scheme was to motivate managers! It is a common theory that private sector managers are motivated by being paid for a job they would lose if they were ineffective. Industry was slow to use capacity created by the recession to regain a major share of the UK market. The balance of payments is not helped by imported goods bearing historic British manufacturing names. Decreasing top salaries and removing perks would reduce prices and increase demand. Consequential increased employment would create buying power. Current congratulations to industry on **reducing** the trade deficit are premature. When they have recovered their former world lead will be the time for rejoicing. Instead of blaming Government and the Public Sector, UK companies should make an effective effort to sell UK manufactured goods to UK retailers. More employment would enable retailers to sell more UK goods and deter them from asking, as local traders did, for BR to bail them out by offering ultra cheap fares to bring to them, shoppers whom, otherwise, they seemed unable to attract by car or bus.

Members of the public cause poor service and add to folklore by jumping to false conclusions and recounting distorted stories. Many pursue their hobby horses via the media to gain personal publicity, rather than direct with BR.

Delays & Cancellations

Passengers cause delay, by boarding moving trains. Trains accelerate rapidly, and a slip leads to amputation if lucky and death if not. Often the offender gets aboard before his stupidity is observed, leaving the door open, so the train is stopped by signals to close the door safely, hopefully before someone falls out. If it has been damaged by another train, there is not only delay to hundreds of passengers in that, and other trains following it, but also coaches out of service for repairs, giving rise to more complaints about lack of seats. Of many such incidents which came to my notice, the most incredible was on 13th August 1990, at Reading, when I witnessed a man, a woman and two small children boarding a moving Inter City train, the man got in first! Staff trying to stop him received a mouthful of abuse - a not unusual reaction. The train was stopped by the guard, causing four minutes delay. Doubtless, he would blame BR if a member of his family had been killed. The worst offenders in boarding moving trains are commuters, a practice only curtailed by closing barrier gates - which some managers wished to remove as part of a new 'Open' image. If obstructed, some push through, with a curse. They are saving minutes by not waiting for the next train but may delay a full train, giving them an opportunity to complain about the lack of seats ignoring that they could have got a seat in the next train in perfect safety. In 1979, one of 40 recommendations I made in my Report for improving punctuality was to close terminal station barrier gates 45-60 seconds before departure of main line and commuter trains.

An unusual incident which caused widespread delay occured on Anglesey in 1975. The line was blocked at a level crossing and its approaches by about 200 cars in protest at the import of Irish cattle, which were carried by rail. The senior Police Officer at the site told me by telephone that police had attempted to move the cars, but had been prevented from doing so. As it was my duty to clear obstructed lines, I ordered the Chester breakdown Vans to clear the line. When the crane arrived, owners moved vehicles at once, as I knew they would - none would risk cars being craned clear on a rusty chain sling. But their publicity campaign had succeeded by spreading delay to London, Birmingham, Manchester and the East Midlands, and causing annoyance to passengers who could not comprehend how one such remote incident could have such widespread effect. Later BR ended the conveyance of livestock, when it became unprofitable, but this created more criticism.

Despite reminders from guards (sometimes prompting sarcastic comment from some passengers), passengers still leave articles in trains, and rush back demanding the train be stopped, causing delay which is invariably put down to BR incompetence. In a typical case, at Watford, my train didn't depart as promptly as usual. Looking out I saw the guard with a passenger - boarding the train. Presently the passenger disembarked and the train left. Although retired, I asked the guard what had happened - the passenger had left a mobile phone behind, but couldn't remember in which coach. They had searched for it, at a cost of five minutes delay. On my suggestion, the Guard, in making his announcement as the train approached Euston, laid the delay at that passenger's door. It should be standard practice.

Passengers who become hysterical about trains being a few minutes late are philosophical about delays and lack of information for air and road travel. At Airports I have observed two-thirds of inbound flights late, with no explanation or word of protest. After planes have landed, anyone meeting a passenger may wait without information for them to emerge. One may travel to an airport to meet a plane which is diverted elsewhere. Booking in at an airport two hours before scheduled departure is accepted even when flights are badly delayed by hours or days, waiting a few minutes to buy a rail ticket is not. Motorists sit for hours on blocked roads without knowing how long they will wait, often as a result of idiocy by another road user. You will receive no apology or compensation from other motorists or the haulier whose lorry shed its load, burst its tyres, jacknifed or broke down. Government should recover compensation from offenders and use it to compensate delayed motorists. The Public accept package tour conditions which would have them reaching for 'pen and acid' if BR were involved. A change in booked departures of Package Tours of under 12 hours does not apparently entitle a customer to redress. A customer requesting a change of destination for good reasons, can forfeit a sizeable sum. Package Tour companies are said to be 'self regulated', unlike BR whose more modest disruptions are subject to independent "watchdogs" and a Citizens Charter.

An extreme example of Public participation in cancellation and delay is the "Final Solution". Since North Sea gas replaced coal gas, the preferred method seems to be to put his/her head on the track. How we wished they would use other means. Road traffic can be easily diverted. When the police arrived, all trains were stopped for some time, and they often demanded that the innocent train which hit the lately departed be held for examination. Whom they called on with the expertise to examine a train and test its brakes was not disclosed. Each incident delayed scores of trains, affecting thousands of passengers, and the delayed trains caused others to be cancelled, inconveniencing thousands more over a very wide area. So serious was the problem that when we were planning trains to the first Birmingham Motor Show in October 1978, I directed that if a body was found, the signalman should say that he couldn't stop trains without Divisional Control authority and they must say they had to ask my Regional Control at Crewe, giving time to set up diversions - this was not standard procedure. Trains would run at reduced speed and police given a lookoutman, which should be standard practice. The problem didn't arise but the prospect of the first Motor Show being cocked up was too horrendous to ignore.

Vandalism, Misconduct and Crime
No review of the Public's participation in delay and cancellation would be complete without a reference to vandals, whether travelling or not, who cause derailments or damage signalling equipment, locomotives or coaches. **BRB 1974 Report**, page 5: 15,900 cases of vandalism occurred; there were 2435 prosecutions. Recently, BR stated that vandalism was costing £45m pa in delays, cancellations, repairs and lost fares. These cancellations and delays were unfairly attributed to BR's Operating Department. Among some of the more reprehensible vandals were those who climbed onto the outside or top of trains. The problem of vandalism is not new: **CTCC 1958 Report**, Para 61: "a number of football excursion trains in the North West were subject to serious and wanton damage by passengers. The Report also referred to trains in the Aldershot area vandalised by soldiers returning from leave. This development of mob violence is expensive and difficult to prevent and often causes delay and inconvenience to other users whose trains are held up while damaged coaches are taken out of service".

Some trains are damaged by children throwing stones. On one occasion which I witnessed, the offenders looked about five years old - they hit a window which, luckily, was not broken. Other culprits used air guns, a location on the Trent Valley line was a recurring problem. Coaches with broken windows had to be taken out of service - more delay - fewer seats - more complaints.

Serious delays arise when lorry drivers who do not know the height of their vehicles collide with bridges. Pending an examination by an engineer, trains are diverted, stopped or delayed. Repairs require diversions or speed restrictions, reaction is often widespread. A regular casualty was the clearly signed Glebe Road bridge, Stoke on Trent.

Another example of misbehaviour involves those who use a BR line as a Civic Amenity tip. Recently, I noted that BR could be prosecuted for not removing litter from the lineside. Rubbish on linesides is thrown there by some of those whose homes back onto the railway or others who go to the location to dump refuse. It is not a new problem. When I moved to the Rugby District in 1960, I learned that what BR designated the Coventry Avoiding Line - from Three Spires Jcn to Humber Road Jcn - was known by staff, as the "Cat and Dog line", a reference to the dead animals thrown over the fence. In fact, I found that it could also have been called the "mattress and perambulator line" or any other combination of domestic rubbish which would be costly to remove. I found other lines with similar reputations. Some "litter" caused delays and cancellations, when trains collided into large items or when overhead wires were damaged. In 1984, I replied to criticism by local authorities on litter strewn linesides by saying that the answer was not for BR to be running costly weekend rubbish clearance trains, but for local authorities to provide waste skips nearer to houses than our lines, so that it was easier for them to dump rubbish in skips rather than on our lines.

As if these many actions by some of the Public were not enough, trains were delayed, and stations cleared due to bomb warnings which we had to presume were genuine, until experts had arrived and proved otherwise. Clearly all hoaxers ought to be jailed and made to pay heavy compensation. I noted that a tougher line was being taken in June 1991 - it was long overdue.

The media and public do not seem to comprehend the knock on effect all these problems have to hundreds of trains, often over a wide area. I found when I moved to Regional HQ that it was the practice to categorise all these delays as 'Operating'. I recommended that we should publicly attribute such delays and cancellation to the public, but it was not a change which BRHQ adopted.

Standing Passengers
In 1970, an officer of HM Forces, travelling from St.Pancras to Leicester complained that she had to stand. I explained that it was impossible to ensure that enough seats were available on every train for every passenger without limit, and asked if she had considered reserving or travelling on the next train (30 minutes later), but she wanted to be on the first train, and said a seat should have been available. Such unforecast demands could not be met in the absence of an elasticated train.

Some passengers are selfish and unhelpful in seat occupation, creating false shortages. An example occurred at Nuneaton in March 1986 when the line to London was blocked by a derailment. En route to London, I found that trains were being diverted, requiring diesels to replace electric locomotives. As BR could not afford £1m diesel locos hanging around for this eventuality, there was a resource problem. To minimise requirements, passengers were transferred into fewer trains in accordance with Contingency Plans. Those boarding one train said that there were no seats. Before the diesel loco arrived, I went through from end to end, questioning every passenger seated next to a seat on which coats or luggage were placed and seated over 70. That this was necessary was an indictment of public behaviour. There was a well known saying in the Services which summed it up - "Pull the ladder up Jack, I'm alright". All staff, including some who were working out redundancy notices, worked with a will in very bad weather conditions.

At Birmingham, in May, 1986, I joined a train in which three ladies occupied unreserved seats in a compartment, whilst on three reserved seats there was luggage, which they admitted was theirs. The practice of reserving seats and occupying adjacent unreserved seats is not uncommon. After a train departs, passengers will often notice, that adjacent or opposite to unoccupied reserved seats, there are passengers occupying unreserved seats. Invariably, the unoccupied reserved seats can be safely taken, but one may notice a fleeting glance of displeasure from the other passenger(s) indicating that their selfish plan has been thwarted. Some reserved seats are unoccupied because passengers missed the train. Others reserve on two or more trains to safeguard against late running meetings - a not uncommon practice among businessmen. All create artificial shortages. (CTCC 1966 Report: "some means should be devised to minimise the practice of users making multiple reservations without the intention of using them". CTCC 1986/87 Report: "Passengers are reserving seats on more than one train"). Many passengers must have written to complain that there were no seats when other passengers had created artificial shortages.

In late 1992, travelling from Chester to Crewe, I noticed that a boy in an aisle seat had, alongside him, an unoccupied window seat. I pointed this out to a lady standing next to me and suggested that she ask the boy if the seat was taken. She did so - it was free, but his occupation of the aisle seat was clearly intended to dissuade someone from taking the spare seat. When the train arrived at Crewe, he walked off with a couple who appeared to be his parents and had been seated behind him. Years ago, parents told a child to stand up for an adult, had he not already demonstrated his upbringing by doing so. That taught one respect for one's elders. Parents who do not subscribe to this practice will be the first to complain of being badly treated by the younger generation. (See also Page 106).

In 1969, the CTCC told the NBPI that "some standing could be avoided if the passengers spread themselves more evenly through the train". On commuter trains this masochistic practice arises from an obsession to be nearest to the station exit on arrival. I have told standing passengers on Inter City trains that there were seats further along the train, but they have not moved. No one compels anyone to stand on trains, any more than they are compelled to stand in buses or to queue in banks, building societies or supermarkets. They make a choice to do so. Standing passengers interviewed on TV were not asked if they had considered reserving or travelling later.

Peak Demand
Every commuter expects a seat, but is unable to comprehend the quart in the pint pot syndrome which they and their employers have created. None give instant service in their own peak. Their customers wait, and should they have the temerity to complain, will be told that they are unreasonable. Standing in the bank or building society queue at lunch time - the time many customers can get there, and cashiers are thin on the ground, customers should time their wait and complain with the same sarcasm usually reserved for BR, coupled with frequent gestures at a wrist watch. Similar treatment should be meted out to retailers who are out of stock and tell one to come back for something needed now, in three weeks - not in minutes as for the next train. The sharp edge of the tongue should be used on those who failed to fulfil a promised delivery two months ago, "due to heavy demand".

CTCC 1954 Report: MoT has requested that CTCC consider and recommend, as soon as possible, the best methods of securing a staggering of hours of working to reduce congestion during the peak hours on travelling by LT & BR. The CTCC decided to refer the remit to the TUCC for London. CTCC 1955 Report states that the TUCC for London need more time. I found no further reference to this remit in annual CTCC Reports. In 1958, the MoT appointed Committee for Staggering of Working Hours in Central London, reported on the results of its first year's efforts. Their report, "Crush Hour Travel in Central London" recorded that approaches to employers had resulted in a 3.6% **increase** in staff signing on at times between 08.00 and 09.00 hours, and 0.6% **increase** in those signing on between 08.00 and 09.30 hours! Within the period 08.00-09.30, the number of employees, which had ranged from 11,200 - 157,200 per quarter hour changed to a range of 11,200 - 149,700, leaving the lightest period at one fifth of the average, and the heaviest period at over twice the average - in effect a non event in public transport terms.

BTC 1957 Report, Paras 182-184: "Improvements in the speed or frequency of peak services attract more passengers, and worsen conditions for all. The majority of peak passengers were season ticket holders who were paying about a half of the standard rate"; **BTC 1958 Report**, page 61: SR peak arrivals, (which were pushing costs through the ceiling), had risen alarmingly: taking 1958 to 47% above 1938; **BTC 1960 Report**: "Government stated that people must be prepared to pay more for rail travel. Increases are needed not only to offset changes in the value of money but to compensate for costly trends in problems of transport", (e.g., the further growth in peak travel which in the Southern Region morning peak was 56% above 1938, the evening peak was 60% higher than 1938. At Waterloo 12,000 travelled in the peak hour, compared to an average of less than 1000 per hour during off peak hours).

CTCC Memo included in the **NBPI Report 1969**, Para 17: "As no effective staggering of hours seems likely it is difficult to see an end to overcrowding. The peak has grown sharper in recent years as manual employment in Central London has fallen and been replaced by office workers". Appendix G: showed fewer passengers on the SR before 08.00 and after 09.15 comparing 1968 with 1951, but a marked rise between those hours. Thousands of passengers per Quarter hour period starting at the time shown:

TIME	0745	0800	0815	0830	0845	0900	0915	0930
1951	22	17.5	26.25	42	46.25	39	26.5	18
1968	11	28.75	43.75	55.25	52.25	40.5	25	13.75
%Change	−50	+64	+66	+31.5	+13	+4	−6	−24

MoT "Transport Policy", 1976, Para 2.1.2 : "the peak has been a factor in keeping unit costs high"; (this is the understatement of the post war period); Para 3.6: "It is the higher income groups who use railways the most regularly for travel to work and business journeys, while those on lower incomes travel by rail much more sporadically."

CTCC 1985/86 Report: hopes that "a commercial organisation with Government support and encouragement would be able to respond to demand by providing more rolling stock rather than discourage demand by increased fares or imposing greater restrictions". The Government has shown that it will not give to BR, whose activities it controls, the infinite funds required to overcome peak standing. It is, therefore, inconceivable that they would give those same funds, plus a profit element to a private company.

CTCC 1988/89 Report said that "the key [to overcrowding] is availability of rolling stock which are reliable and sufficient to cater for demand". (Peak travel problems are insoluble, except at a cost which most commuters are not prepared to pay. Privatised railways will make commuters pay and level peaks by pricing. The discounted alternative to pricing, is to stagger hours. Industry responds to peak demand by extending delivery dates).

CTCC 1991 Annual Report: "It will cause no surprise that overcrowding remains the commuters curse". (It is commuters' demands which have literally been a curse on railways since the war. With shorter working hours, an increasing number have packed themselves into a contracting peak, whilst expecting to pay an ever declining percentage of their own escalating earnings. There was a time when the CTCC saw that the only solution was a staggering of hours. If the commuter services fall into private sector hands, they will solve the problem by pricing up, and will not spend billions of shareholders money in a fruitless pursuit of the unattainable to further worsen the utilisation of costly assets - see page 114).

Cleanliness

It is remarkable that, in a country notorious for litter louting, BR should be criticised for dirty and untidy trains and stations. Managers who studied Dutch carriage cleaning practice reported minimal litter in long distance trains. On journeys in mainland Europe, I noted the absence of litter in trains and streets, whilst here, it is a fact of life. Compared to a few newspapers left in their trains, our staff picked up litter by the sackful. This was not due to inadequate litter receptacles, although this is true of our streets. The public will not carry litter 100 yards to a street litter bin. In Inter City trains the furthest bin is barely 10 paces away. I have never had difficulty in placing my litter in bins provided. I have checked trains at the start of their journey, finding them well cleaned before passengers boarded. Litter louting starts before a train departs. Chewing gum on seats and floors is a common problem and graffiti is a national pastime. It must be most disheartening for staff to tackle, day after day, the task of removing these "calling cards" again, to restore the standard achieved yesterday. Passengers dropped litter one pace away from very large station litter bins. Some must think that it is less untidy to throw litter onto the track. It is worse, taking longer to clear, and can only be done safely with a lookoutman to give warning of trains. Anyone who thinks that is an unnecessary use of manpower has not been to an inquest into the death of a railwayman killed on the track because he worked without a lookoutman. One man wrote to a newspaper complaining that BR did not have enough staff on stations sweeping up passengers' litter, by inference, as soon as it was dropped. He seemed to be trying to solve the UK unemployment problem at a stroke. (CTCC 1966 Report: "The CTCC believe the public could do more to co-operate in proper disposal of litter than they do").

Some complaints of "dirty trains" refer to soiled seats. Presumably, complainants do not place feet on seats, realising the effect on other passengers' clothing, but cannot fail to notice offenders, especially when looking for a seat. It happens daily. I first spoke to a passenger in 1947, and have remonstrated with others ever since, including many in the first class. Mostly they removed their feet without comment, as I pointedly inform all, that that is why BR is criticised for dirty seats. Only one argued saying his shoes were not dirty. "Have you walked from home to train on a red carpet?" I asked. It is without excuse and the most irresponsible and anti-social behaviour. To prevent this malpractice, resolve confusion over reservations, and create more seats per coach I advocated in a letter to the three Passenger Sector Directors on 17th June 1986 that BR should ignore opposition and break from the stage coach seating layout, (face to face), going for face-to-back, as in aircraft or buses. Some complain of dirty windows, accepting that car windows become dirty in traffic, but not trains under the same sky. As most think that BR alone should have no problem moving in snow, they must assume some supernatural power should be shielding trains from the elements. Others criticise BR for the condition of toilets, lack of toilet paper or soap. Toilets are left in appalling condition by some users, who must be unfamiliar with WC's, be lacking in basic hygiene and common decencies, or unable to afford basic purchases.

Politicians believe that contracting out all carriage cleaning would reduce costs and improve quality. I have the advantage of having carried out a detailed investigation. BR had used contractors so there was hard evidence. Depot records showed some vehicles returned by BR for further cleaning. BR was still held as culpable for any faults. My experience of contract office cleaning, which is much easier than carriage cleaning, was that it was not all of a good standard. Dirty crockery, cutlery and glassware provided in private sector establishments confirm that the private sector is not perfect in a location in which supervision should be easy and thorough. Waiting in bank queues, I have given ledges the finger test, finding dust thereon - so much for private sector standards. Contracting out quality tasks as opposed to quantity tasks, creates problems of control. It is easy to check whether enough 'widgets' of the right size are supplied, but to ensure coaches are properly cleaned, requires BR to inspect before contractors leave the premises. To improve quality, costs will go up, including replacing ageing coaches (not replaced due to Government policies) which look dirty after cleaning. I did recommend using contractors in a few isolated situations.

It is incomprehensible that the Public can see vandalised or unkempt unstaffed stations as 'obscenities' without acknowledging that their own "have their cake and eat it" attitude, took away the patronage which was the first step down the slippery slope. No one, especially those who do not use trains, should expect BR to spend money tending gardens on branch line stations or clearing up litter the instant it is dropped. Do they criticise the late owners of shops, which ceased trading, when a similarly minded clientele took their business elsewhere so that empty shops became magnets for vandalism, flyposting and graffiti? The same people expect well tended streets, but object to paying for the service. They should be less myopic and accept that local misconduct is the root of the problem on stations as it is in towns. However, there is scant prospect of that, since such people seem to be of the "Don't confuse me with facts, my mind is made up" brigade.

Folklore
Many members of the public have a tendency to jump to the wrong conclusion on a subject of which they are clearly ignorant, thus adding to the volume of folklore. "Why don't they put on more trains ?" "Because, Sir," I said to a man at Doncaster in Christmas 1958, "every single coach is in service to provide the 400 extra trains publicised in the press. If they are not used now, they would be scrapped as there is no time of greater use". It is difficult to understand why adults could not perceive this. Why does the public accept as meekly as lambs, that if they haven't reserved by air or coach they will be unable to travel? No word of criticism appears in the media that the private sector didn't provide enough seats, because the overflow go to the station and complain that their unforecast journey should have been anticipated and a seat provided. Why does the public accept that the purchase of a bus or air ticket only entitles one to travel by a particular service or flight, because one has specified a departure time? Public and media go into hysterics because BR say that the purchase of a ticket doesn't guarantee a seat on an unspecified train. The passenger may

136

be travelling three weeks after Michaelmas, and then again, he may not. A ticket is available for hundreds or thousands of trains. It is unrealistic to expect that a ticket entitles an infinite number of passengers to a seat on an unspecified train. Anyone running a business which held instantly perishable stock (which is what a train seat is), for a customer who may not require it on a given day, would be bankrupt. BR experienced unforecast traffic diverted by the train load when fog shut airports down. BR could guarantee a seat by specifying that a ticket is for a particular seat on one particular train. Miss the train and you will get a partial refund or no refund as usually applies with a theatre, hotel or package tour. Obviously, that is not what the public or media have in mind. That will not be allowed on BR, but privatised railways will not be constrained! The facility to join any train at short notice will become a distant memory.

In 1959, en route to Sunderland, I was working on my papers, when a lady opposite to me in a First Class compartment, spoke, gesturing contemptuously at some men standing at the lineside, "there's no wonder BR are losing money". "Why is that?" I asked. "All those men leaning on shovels". "It's a good thing they are", I replied "otherwise they would be dead", explaining that the men were working on our track "between trains". Incredulous at finding the wrong ear to bend, she asked how I knew that. I showed her a booklet - the 'Engineering Notice' - which I carried on my travels, pointing out the entry concerned. I have encountered many who became affable and understanding having found a professional willing to answer back.

People skilled in their own business, quickly jump to conclusions on anything as simple as managing BR which they see as a bigger version of the model railway of their childhood - in some cases adulthood. In 1966, a Sheffield businessman asked why we didn't run twice as many trains from the Hope Valley where his daughter lived. I explained that the potential business from this rural area wouldn't finance extra trains. "Well, double the peak service for commuters". I explained that would double the costs. "Can't you use them somewhere else during the day?" I replied, "No, the whole of the UK has the same peak hours, and we have thousands of coaches used for 3-4 hours per day." I quoted examples of the adverse effect of the peaks on utilisation of stock and manpower. He was graceful in admitting "that he hadn't realised that". Him and several million others.

Travelling from Crewe to Euston I overheard a man in the First Class, saying that drivers were under instruction to increase speed when the train was running alongside the M1. He was unaware that trains were timed to travel at maximum line or train speed (whichever is the lower), throughout their route, slowing for permanent and temporary speed restrictions. To increase speed when passing the M1 drivers would have to exceed maximum authorised speeds. Any manager who told a driver to do so, when drivers knew that anyone exceeding speed limits was disciplined, would himself be disciplined when an inevitable justifiable complaint was made by the Unions. I had not heard anything so totally uninformed and utterly absurd in my whole life. Conversely, passengers who proclaim that drivers are not driving as fast as they could, because they slow down en route, are unaware of permanent or temporary speed restrictions. Perhaps they expect BR drivers to behave like motorists - until all end up in hospital, when a witch hunt would begin.

A common criticism is that "everyone knows of BR's inability to run trains when it snows". Those making most noise usually travel by car, deciding at the first hint of snow not to risk their precious toy. Regulars who complain may be forgiven unfair comparisons if they have not experienced immovable road traffic jams, even in good weather. In February 1969, within half an hour of the onset of lightly falling snow, we had a virtual blizzard. Anyone who has experienced snow blowing back to the space just cleared, over and over again, will know what hard work is. Towards the end of a fourteen hour day I was constantly on the move and keeping in touch with my large Area. In a Supervisor's office on Leicester station a passenger was berating the supervisor in sarcastic terms for delay and demanding to know when his train would be leaving as he had a flight to catch. It hadn't crossed his mind that the airport was probably snowbound and he didn't take up my suggestion to phone them at our expense, foreseeing probable embarrassment. I said that we were moving, unlike road traffic, for whilst at the station front, I had noticed that vehicles in a jam there had hardly moved since my previous visit an hour earlier. I offered an immediate full refund since he was dissatisfied with our service. Having apparently revelled in playing to a gallery of passengers, he calmed down, admitting he hadn't realised how bad things were. Well he wouldn't, being nicely sheltered indoors. What motivates people to criticise BR for delay when other transport is virtually immobile? Not one person to whom I spoke, during this period had paused to consider that our staff had to get to work on snow bound roads congested with traffic. Even those who rate themselves above average intelligence are not immune. If those in industry had been as motivated as BR staff in getting to work in such conditions, there would be no balance of payments problem. In very bad weather, fewer trains will run, especially when staff are delayed en route to work, but BR is beseiged by "bad weather travellers" who will not risk their precious car, and others using BR because "it is safer". Instead of a word of thanks to staff who have really "taken the strain", we were treated to the childish spectacle of passengers making silly gestures with a wrist watch because - in appalling conditions BR had not kept to schedule - a word without meaning to motorists even in good weather.

The onset of winter has its effect on road and air travel. Aside from an almost passing reference by the media, it is accepted as a fact of life. When snowstorms close roads and airports, and trains are delayed with some consequential cancellations, the media will criticise BR for being unable to run like model railways when its competitors have thrown in the towel. BR is expected to cope with the bad weather and the motorists who leave their precious pride and joy in its igloo and trudge in unaccustomed wellies past several bus stops to the station, where they grumble about the inability of BR to cope with the problem which brought them there. Do they perhaps imagine that a Supernatural power shields BR tracks from the snow which blocks their own drive ? With years of model railway expertise, they will speak knowingly of the need for more point heaters, something they wouldn't recognise if they fell over one. They are blissfully unaware that point heaters are not designed to remove snowdrifts or cope with blizzards. It does not occur to them that the private sector has failed to come up with any appliance which will prevent snow blocking open tracks. Since most have not had to tackle wind blown snow, sweating inside thick clothing, and done nothing more arduous than switch on an extra heater in the office that is hardly surprising. The average passenger does not seem to appreciate that the drivers, signalmen and others whose presence is essential to operate the railways, have to clear their own drives and struggle over snow bound lanes and roads, often while passengers are sound asleep and, perhaps, dreaming of an excuse to avoid going to work. Doubtless they assume that all BR staff still live in rows of terraced houses behind the engine sheds and can walk to work in minutes. It will not occur to them that one reason for private sector railways "coping better with snow" was that the labour force was much bigger and many staff lived close to the line on which they worked. Not unreasonably, they wanted a piece of the good life and moved to desirable residential neighbourhoods.

This incomprehensible illogical public attitude is an extension of other unreasonable expectations - that train catering services shall operate 24 hours a day compared to doors closed at 2.0pm sharp in the typical private sector establishment, that BR shall never run out of food as if the term "that's off the menu" had never been uttered in the private sector. They accept the shop's "out of stock" or the hotel's "we're fully booked", but not the BR's "no seats". They suffer a 30% increase in insurance, 280% in Leisure Club fees, 1119% for an electrical part (see Page 111), but not a 15% increase in fares. It is the same tunnel vision which causes them to become hysterical at a 30 second wait when telephoning BR compared with three minutes experienced with so many private sector companies, whilst they try to find Joe Bloggs only to tell you he is not back from "a late lunch" at 3.0pm, when you had just missed him at noon.

I am convinced that many commuters who are late for work due to their own tardiness, conveniently blame BR. In 1984, I read a letter in the Liverpool Echo from someone claiming that people could lose their jobs because trains were late. I replied inviting employers to write to me with details of each case for investigation and received not a single letter, and there were no further letters in the paper. I was not saying that no trains were late, but on average, about 75% arrived right on time and over 90% within 5 minutes. Few people, if any, would have a train which, if on time would give them exactly the number of minutes required to walk to their place of employment, arriving there on the stroke of signing on time. Most would have an unavoidable margin. If the rail delay was less than that margin, BR did not cause them to be late for work. Doubtless, some rising too late in the morning would use poor old BR as the scapegoat. Those who commute by car cannot blame "busy roads, heavy traffic and road accidents" too often - an employer would tell them to set off earlier. As BR rarely answer back the excuse is almost 24 carat, at least to the complacent employer.

It was an open secret that many staff in industry and commerce travelled as a group in one car, whilst each claimed for the rail fare. Clearly such people would have to invent anecdotes about rail journeys, and it would be the prudent course to adopt common perceptions picked up from the media or elsewhere. They could hardly claim rail fares and say they had been held up on the motorway! These people, and others who claim rail fares whilst hitching lifts, are only too pleased to see higher rail fares because it increases their "expenses".

BR is attacked for risks to children when crossing the line. I replied to a letter in the Cambrian News which criticised BR for modernising a level crossing which was near a children's playground, stating that if children were too young to cross the railway safely they were too young to walk along the road to get to the railway crossing and the playground beyond it. I also pointed out that there was no public footpath on the playground side of the road, to which more significant danger there had been no complaint. Whatever happened to parental responsibility? Can none comprehend that the frequency of motor vehicles, which leave you just as dead, is many times greater than the frequency of trains ? CTCC 1963 Report: "bus stops are more dangerous than unstaffed rail halts". (By the same token, crossing at unstaffed road crossings is far more dangerous than crossing at unstaffed railway level crossings - where traffic levels are invariably less).

Financial Aspects
The Public's contribution to delay and to dirty trains and stations, costs good money to redress. If the British public were half as tidy as those in mainland Europe, BR's costs would be much less. Money spent on cleaning up their "calling cards", repairing damaged trains and equipment, paying overtime to staff working delayed trains and on refunds to those affected or delayed by the unsocial behaviour of others, could have been put to better use. Few realise that these actions push up fares. But there is one group

who can have no doubt of the effect of their actions – those who defraud BR.
BRB 1963 Report, Para 43: "to curb fraudulent travel, the validity of an
ordinary single or outward half of a return ticket in and around London has
been limited, as from October 1963, to the day of issue only, return halves
must be used on the same or next day ....". **CTCC 1974 Report**: BR and LT
were losing £10m pa through fraud.

Travelling on out-of-date, used or forged tickets, or without a ticket with
intent not to pay, loses revenue which would fund improved services. In the
1980's, BR estimated that fraudulent travel was costing £20m pa. In 1991,
£35m was the estimate of fraud for the South East, and £50m for BR as a
whole, and it is the taxpayer and other passengers who lose. Loss of
revenue occurs in situations which may not appear to be fraud. A frequent
situation is someone in the First Class with a standard ticket – vainly
trying to focus on a place without a "First Class" label – saying "Oh is
this first class?" Some bought a standard class ticket, but said that they
would pay the difference 'if the ticket collector comes round'. Those who
urged BR staff a few years ago not to collect fares as part of 'a political
protest', were doing so for selfish motives. There is not the slightest
prospect that they will carry their 'principles' to the limit by allowing
you to walk out of their employers' premises without paying as part of a
protest. That would lead to an appearance in court for them and you.

Anyone on retail premises with goods but no receipt, may be arrested and
charged with theft. If you claim against an insurance policy, your word may
not be accepted. A newspaper report in June 1991 said that "Car insurance
is set to rise 25% due to false claims", (BR is expected to prevent fraud).
An Insurance spokesperson was reported as saying that "A lot of people think
their word will not be questioned". If a customer on a train, without proof
of purchase, claims to have paid, there is an automatic public belief in
that person's honesty. Media reports seem to imply that an ability to pay
should be accepted as proof of innocence by BR, whilst in a retail case, it
is usually discounted. This is illogical. Those who charge others with
theft of retail goods or fraud would be the first to express indignation
that their word is disbelieved by BR should they say they have lost their
rail ticket. It is accepted that a private sector company will use a debt
collection agency, but when BR do so, there is an outcry! (see Page 155).

NIMBY
The media and the public are quick to comment on the consequences of the
NIMBY (Not in my backyard) attitude. Not one has acknowledged that BR's
inability to match French train speeds arises from the NIMBY philosophy
towards railways, from the very birth of railways. Hence we have lines
which make their circuitous way around towns which didn't want railways in
1850, but are now critical of a dependence on connections or slower
services. Today's generation are continuing the attitude towards the
Channel Tunnel link line. The blindness of those who blame BR for the delay
in planning a high speed link when faced with so much opposition, not to
mention Government decisions, is incomprehensible.

Analogy
When a branch of the British Institute of Management visited my Crewe office
on 14th March 1979, I explained that my job as Regional Operations Officer
was similar to a works Production Manager. My roofless 'factory' was 2500
miles long, with customers constantly on the 'factory floor' wanting our
'product' the instant that it was produced. We had no margin from their
gaze for quality inspections to put things right before the (next) customer
uses it, as the Private Sector has, but despite which, they still sell
defective goods. They grasped the analogy admitting that the unique nature
of our task had not occurred to them. Them, and several million others.

Professional Studies

Dr.Joy, Chief Economist with BR 1968-72, wrote in his book: 'The Train that ran away' that "Massive Staff economies under Beeching, proved that the BTC had not been running a very efficient railway". We had economy cuts from 1948 - staff called them the 'Razor Gangs', and my own earnings were reduced thereby. Thereafter came the Unremunerative Facility economies, the Branch line review teams, Modernisation and then Work & Method Study. He said that Beeching's efficiency measures "were mainly based on branch line closures". In fact, by 1963 - the year of Beeching's Plan - 13.5% of route had closed with more in the pipeline, despite vociferous opposition, not least from politicians. Those who believe Beeching did it all overlook several facts:-

* Pre 1963, Governments did not act effectively on closures.
* Beeching's predecessor said in 1956 that retention of loss making lines was wrong and that no one was listening - he could only be referring to the Government, since all under him would have to listen.
* Beeching listed all lines which were not paying - a change of tactic from the BTC policy of submitting a scheme when it had established the facts. That system had progressed closures faster than the TUCC's and MoT could finalise them. The preparation of a "Master Plan" for closures was counter productive, alarming industry unnecessarily and causing premature revenue losses. Some of Beeching's proposed closures were blocked by the MoT.
* TUCC's were averaging 9-10 months to progress a closure scheme before it reached the MoT for a decision, (some took up to three years), despite BTC pressures from 1956 to speed the process. It was eventually speeded up to 8-10 weeks, following a further approach to the MoT by the BTC in 1958. Thus Beeching benefitted from this improvement and from the 1962 Act, by which TUCC's had only to consider hardship - reducing the task of preparing massive memoranda - enabling BR to prepare schemes more quickly.
* The rapid growth in ownership of cars, 'C' licence vans and lorries abstracted rail traffic. As BR were prevented from closing lines actually making losses, they could not have made closures in anticipation of losses arising from the expected growth of motor vehicles, hence Beeching was bound to find new loss making lines. (This continuing expansion of road traffic explains why the list of lines for closure in the 1963 Reshaping Report was less extensive than that in the list of 1969 submitted for grant aid - upon which Dr.Joy remarked). Moreover, improvements in costing technique and the provision of new office equipment assisted the task on both occasions.
* Beeching Plans included 435 stations "already under consideration, of which 235 have already been closed" (these inflated his plan). Included in the Plan, were some which had been put forward by the BTC and rejected by the TUCC and MoT; and one branch line which BR was directed to reopen ten years earlier, after the track had been severed by sea storms, (see Page 43)
* New methods of operation were devised and implemented by career managers before and during the Beeching era.

I must take issue with Dr.Joy who said that the statutory freight rates imposed on railways was not damaging, claiming that for this to be so, BR would have had to show that it would have been better off without low rated traffic. On the contrary, what BR needed to show was that they would be better off if all traffic was conveyed at common rates or rates determined by BR, which were not open to inspection by competitors. He said that the pricing of unprofitable traffic off rail had always been available and that the 1953 Act "implied the freedom of railways to accept traffic only at rates which ensured its profitability". Acts should not imply. This one enacted that a new Charges Scheme be prepared, which provided for maximum rates. Until 1962, maximum rates were controlled by the Tribunal, which prevented BR from unilaterally increasing rates for such traffic, BR's proposals to increase rates on the very unprofitable smalls and returned empties were reduced by the Tribunal and the MoT, (see Pages 84 & 86). The 1953 Act did not, as he said, remove BR's "common carrier obligation", which was set out in the "Reasonable facilities" clause of the 1854 Act, which was not repealed until 1962. Neither was it simply a matter of closing branches on the premise that unprofitable traffic was confined to them. Rates control ensured that every line had some good and bad paying traffic.

He said that "Commercial Managers could ignore pressures from ..... the Transport Tribunal". The Tribunal did not exercise "pressures" - but exercised total control of passenger and freight charges, until 1968 and 1962 respectively. To ignore them was to flout a Court of Law - in 40 years I met no one who had ever contemplated that action. The Government would have stepped in had they done so.

He also said that commercial freedom under the 1953 Act was "subject only to a maximum rate". This unique type of freedom did not apply to any other industry. It was akin to telling a prisoner that he was free, provided he didn't leave the jail. A maximum rate precluded "pricing unprofitable traffic off". The Tribunal reduced BR's proposed maximum rates in the 1957 Scheme, which was heralded by Government in 1952 as BR's shortly forthcoming freedom. Some new maxima were below rates which BR were already charging.

Dr.Joy interpreted the fall in freight rates from 1939 to 1956 as proof that price control was irrelevant to the attraction or retention of traffic. This overlooks the wide disparity of rates from the lower to the higher classes, (see Page 59), the latter being well above average, were undercut by road haulage. Rates below average were mainly for bulk traffics, which were not as susceptible to competition - a lower rate could not attract traffic when BR were carrying virtually all of it, hence speedier price increases would improve BR finances. Replacing the archaic classification structure by a freedom to price at the average would have attracted or retained higher value commodities without losing lower valued bulk raw materials. Likewise I dispute his argument that price control was irrelevant because falling fares were not accompanied by rising travel. Had fares been freed from statutory control, sub standard fares would have been sharply increased, captive business priced up, that subject to competition priced selectively, and business which could not be held in the light of car mania would have been unaffected. As it was BR was left with the worst of all worlds. Nothing BR could then have done would prevented those who tried to "keep up with the Joneses" from diving into debt to purchase that new symbol of affluence. Competition with cars today over longer distances has been made possible by acceleration of trains which was achieved following the closure of intermediate stations and removal of junctions, which were held back for many years due to Government policy and the protracted procedures which BR had to pursue. It is also significant that from 1983, with fares outpacing the RPI, recession apart, many trains are crowded.

He said that had [passenger] subsidies been made for loss making lines from 1948, instead of 1968, that it would not have solved BR's problems. That is obvious - making up losses on loss making lines does not create a profit for reserves. It does not create profits for investment and reserves for lines which were not making losses, nor provide funds for interest payments and the redemption of capital. Nor would it have affected freight traffic, whose viability was blocked by rates control and legal restraints.

He argued that if a Track Authority owned BR infrastructure, it would not be doing its job properly if it did not reduce capacity to a level more closely aligned to BR's requirements. As Highway Authorities do not close roads to reflect changing levels of utilisation arising from increased construction or recession, it is illogical to say that a comparable Highway Authority should single out BR's highway for rationalisation to meet a situation which may not be long term, (see my calculations at the end of this Chapter on the underutilisation of roads). His reference to motor vans still carrying drivers' mates, 'presumably to hold the reins of long deposed horses' was a picture I did not recognise. When I worked at Rotherham in the late 1940's we had horse drawn vehicles, none of which had anyone in addition to the driver. At the many depots at which I worked, the only motor vehicles, with drivers' mates, were either towing four wheeled trailers, (for which Road Transport Law required a second man) or delivering 'Vulnerable' goods - wine, spirits and tobacco. These commodities were not merely 'vulnerable' to theft, but were subject to extensive theft before the introduction of vanguards. In my research, I found a media report in July 1963, which records that a van driver and woman vanguard were kidnapped in Hyde Park, London - their vehicle 'loaded with tobacco' - was later found abandoned. Some items being delivered required two people to unload them. In the 1951 wage negotiations, BR did call for the "discontinuance of the unnecessary use of vanguards in London" confirming there were some who did not fall into these categories - but that they were in London, not throughout BR. Perhaps in London, thieves were less selective and would take anything from the back of a vehicle hence more vanguards may have been necessary. Very few UK industries could claim to have rid themselves of unproductive staff even 10-20 years later, or there would still be a UK manufacturing base.

Dr.Joy states that between 1948 and 1968 branch line coaches were replaced twice. Generally, branch lines were allocated fully depreciated cast-off coaches from main lines to replace fully depreciated much older coaches. With the introduction of DMU's after 1955, most branch lines received new vehicles for the first time since before the war. BR began in 1948 with a total fleet of 40,000 coaches, and in the next 20 years built 24,000, scrapping 45,000 leaving them with a total of 19,000. To say that they had been replaced twice conveyed to me an impression that they were replaced twice with new coaches. These statistics show that was not possible.

He referred to the BTC "defying the expressed wishes of the Government to break even". On the contrary, it was the Government itself which took the momentous and conscious decision to undermine the principle of "breaking even", and Cabinet minutes and other Papers show that they did not accept the BTC should recover all its costs from revenue (see Pages 20, 22, 68, 74)

Dr Joy suggests that BR staff reductions did not arise from improved productivity because staff 'were not working any harder'. Productivity gains in any industry mainly arise from :-
* More capital investment and Research & Development expenditure.
* Elimination of unproductive time, including "tea breaks" which UK industry tried vainly for so many years to end.
* Improved product design - to reduce the labour element in production and maintenance.
* Introduction of work study, which was more readily accepted on BR than it was in other UK industry where a stop watch was a signal to stop work.
* Introduction of method study - which in private and public sectors was based on staff working at a '75%' standard, and other management techniques.
* Ending demarcation - the private sector was notoriously ineffective; BR took action long before many companies.
* Training and improved Health and Safety conditions.

The incidence of staff actually "working harder", in any industry is rarely of significance in improving productivity - it is immeasurable, and, hence, valueless in determining rewards. Those who claim to be working harder, cannot factually substantiate such a claim. Perhaps some could "work faster" or longer hours, but with risks to safety if operating machines or driving (which is of particular concern on BR). BR managers were certainly active in exploiting the productive and measurable avenues. My own first efforts to improve productivity, which increased in pace over the following years, predate Beeching by 12 years. Most BR managers acted likewise.

Consultants
The cost of Consultants required more ventilation. Some managers were keen for BR to be seen using external "expertise" to demonstrate a willingness to "listen". In 1986, a company which wished to show us how they could train BR staff more effectively, required £1100 per day for each instructor and £800 per day for an advisor! What they had to offer was unimpressive - we did not use them. During a presentation one of them made an error, to which I drew his attention. With a forced laugh, he said that that was his one mistake for today! I knew that the Private Sector made mistakes, but not that everyone made one per day. If all BR staff made a daily error that would cause 51 million complaints pa instead of 63,000 we had in 1983.

The impressions I gained from one Consultant's Report sent to me, was, I told BRHQ, "almost entirely unfavourable". It was couched in generalised terms, contained little or no data to back up criticisms and did not identify unsatisfactory locations, providing no information to take remedial action. It caused me to comment: "A costly independent survey would carry more impact if some of the more emotive adjectives had been replaced by statistics"; that it was "excessively repetitive", and had duplications been eliminated, could have been contained in one volume instead of three. I added: "This Report is not a confessional in which researchers' findings are to be kept to themselves". It would have been compiled more effectively and at less cost had a BR manager been detached for the study.

Academic Suggestions
In April 1978, when I was Divisional Operating Superintendent at Stoke, I was asked to consider a plan submitted to BRHQ by a University lecturer to improve Cambrian line services. It was not costed and had no forecast of revenue, but envisaged "doubling the service", (his train mileage was a 50% increase), and "doubling passenger journeys", (there was no evidence to back this up). 19 trains were to be "retimed beyond Shrewsbury or Wolverhampton" - BR timed main lines before branch lines. I had his detailed 24 page plan costed. £9.2m was the cost of signal boxes, new rolling stock, locos and turntables (for steam locos) to run additional trains. A further £4.8m, bringing the total to £14m, was needed to replace existing DMU's to improve reliability. These excluded costs of track upgrading for new locomotives, coaching stock and higher speeds. £14m investment needed revenue to rise by £3.5m - seven times prevailing levels. He did not propose fare increases, but criticised BR policy of "continually increasing fares" (which lagged behind the RPI for the 30th consecutive year - see page 34). Operating costs would rise by £0.95m pa requiring revenue to increase by £4.45 pa (£3.5m + £0.95m) - to hold losses at current levels. He proposed a two year experiment, requiring capital and extra labour costs, (i.e. £15.9m), to be recovered in two years, and that his scheme (requiring new assets), could be implemented "without much investment" in two months which would "demonstrate [or disprove] its' potential viability". Usually, those making suggestions are 100% confident, believing only that BR intransigence in refusing to fund their ideas stand in the way of their ultimate glory. The plan required 85 extra staff, whose redeployment would be difficult and costly, if the experiment failed - which, in view of the costs, was beyond doubt. He would use "Students at a low wage" - a non runner - no comparable industry would entertain such an idea. He said that better stock and assets would not alone run trains punctually - it required "benevolent heavenly protection", (not least, I thought, from tides which flooded the line, and other external

factors). Unlike most others, he submitted his plan direct to BR rather than via the media. We heard no more of his plan.

Amateur Opinions
No activity has more self professed experts than Railways. Their ill conceived ideas take up management and staff time which could be employed pursuing real improvements rather than considering proposals to convince outsiders that BR are not rejecting ideas due to bloody mindedness. I am sure that no other industry (including privatised railways) would spend a fraction of the time on such matters, but then they have no fear of claims that they are "not prepared to listen to practical suggestions and ideas".

Via the Media
A letter from a member of the Cambrian Coast Line Action Group (CCLAG), in the Cambrian News, in November 1983, was entitled "What the Cambrian Coast Railway Really Needs". My published response commenced with the words "What the Cambrian Railway Needs Most of All is a respite from a barrage of uninformed comment, unqualified advice and unfounded rumour. All these misguide local people, rupture good relationships with local authorities and put at risk grants I am obtaining from outside sources to improve the line. Over the past 10 years or so, I have seen papers submitted by various authors - all including this one, have had one thing in common, they lacked an assessment of costs or additional revenue. Now, if the proposals were in respect of new road construction, that would be of little importance. Railways, however, have to justify, by demonstrating a return on any capital investment and must avoid increasing Government support on loss making lines. Social benefit - the sole reason for road improvements - is totally discounted for Railways". Points made in his letter were as follows (my responses being shown in brackets):-
* "CCLAG had invested £2000 in the Cambrian"; (He confused investment and income: they paid to run trains, any 'profit' reduces losses, but provides no money for investment; I invited them to invest but none was forthcoming)
* "BR **claimed** to have spent £8-900,000 on Barmouth Viaduct" -to counteract burrowing by the Teredo sea worm in the timber piles. (The money had been paid out to suppliers, contractors and staff).
* "BR should hold a locomotive at Machynlleth on Summer Saturdays to cover possible failures"; (Even ignoring the heavy cost to the loss making line, we had none spare to deploy in this way anywhere - see Page 132).
* "BR hadn't tried to get funds"; (A presposterous allegation for which he advanced no evidence. I had obtained new money from Industry, Welsh Tourist Board, Development Board for Rural Wales and Local Authorities).
* "The line lacked publicity"; (Councils had agreed from early in 1982 to issue BR brochures in their offices - some issued joint publicity. BR provided free training in 1982 for Wales Tourist Board staff and organised a competition for the best display of BR publicity in Tourist Offices).
* "Bus services to be provided for Pwhelli-Porthmadog-Bangor and Wrexham-Barmouth"; (I said that these may benefit some but would reduce revenue on the line, and was totally incompatible with the title of his letter).
* "A lack of excursions was due to shortage of locos"; (It was not, I invited him to charter trains, and pocket the profits, he did not do so).
* "BR should offer cheap Ranger tickets on Saturdays in July and August". (This was when trains were full. Professionals knew that this was the road to reduced income and increased complaints).
* "There should be a manager for an independent Cambrian line"; (Practical only with no trains beyond Shrewsbury: the last thing passengers wanted).
* "Running the line remotely was ineffective", (Disproved by revenue increases achieved by our actions, including 'My Civic Round' - Page 115).
* "BR had cash which could be unlocked by pressure from the local community" - (An incredibly naive statement as BR Accounts clearly showed).
* He referred to "reducing the deficit", (But his ideas were not costed)

The most pointless remark was to urge us to introduce Radio Signalling as if he had invented it and we knew nothing of it. Few professionals and NO amateurs understood it in 1983. It was developed by BR at Derby, where I had gone, as LM Region Operations Officer, TWO YEARS before I knew he even existed, to examine it and, if suitable, select the line to be used in my Region (almost a quarter of BR's route mileage). Its potential was evident to me, as were its initial limitations - requiring trains to be fitted with equipment which effectively tied trains to the section of line concerned. Having considered several locations on the Region, I personally decided that, if the system was approved by the MoT, we would try it on the Cambrian line, subject to developing easily transferable equipment to avoid trains being tied to that line, since we ran through trains beyond Shrewsbury. He implied a lack of funds was holding it up, when we expected it to be self financing. I had already informed local authorities of our plans adding that one control centre for the whole line would improve the service and may facilitate excursions by reducing signalling costs, and had mentioned it in a letter to the Cambrian News - two months prior to his letter.

My response wound up: "In conclusion, I would sum up by saying that the article is neither constructive nor helpful. It merely serves to underline a lack of appreciation of the real issue, which is to improve the finances of the line. The article contains no financial appraisal to justify a single one of the proposals. These are the principles which we, in management, need to consider, the very worst thing we could do now, would be take the plunge he suggests - spending millions of pounds for an unknown, but clearly inadequate return. It would certainly be the road to ruin and closure. In contrast, we are pursuing a steady, well planned course to improve the finances of the line. A number of researched ideas are being implemented between now and next summer to attract revenue on the line. I cannot help reflecting when I digress and respond to, presumably, well meaning, but impractical advice, how much new revenue I could have generated, in the same time, by developing properly evaluated proposals put foward by professionals. I was relieved to learn that the purpose was 'not to knock BR' otherwise I might have gained the wrong impression".

There was no immediate reply to my letter - no offers of investment, no offers to subsidise or charter trains. But four months later, in March 1984, he wrote to the Cambrian News urging local people to use trains "then BR can have no reason for not completing the full repair of the [Barmouth] viaduct". It was a preposterous remark. I replied to the newspaper: "I was astonished to read that he is still pursuing his phantom crusade in respect of the Barmouth Viaduct despite my quite unambiguous statement in your issue of 11th November 1983, where I wrote 'We have clearly stated our intention to continue with repairs'. Anyone who has made a journey by train over the viaduct last summer, or does so this summer will see clear evidence of work in progress. Our fares are very attractive. These unjustified insinuations of lack of integrity only serve to sow unwarranted seeds of distrust between BR management, staff, the community and their elected representatives. Such actions are not analogous with a professed friendship to railways".

In 1982, as Divisional Manager at Stoke on Trent, I presided, in my first month, at a ceremony at Aberystwyth. BR's only narrow gauge steam railway, the Vale of Rheidol (VoRR), was bringing its oldest steam loco back into service after being painted in its original colours to mark its 80th birthday. The work had been carried out by BR staff during the winter of 1981/82 when my predecessor, Hugh Jenkins was in office, and had been funded jointly by Davies & Metcalfe Ltd (builders of the loco) and VoRRSA (the Supporters' Association) at a cost of £500. Had it been funded by the Supporters alone, I would have been grateful but not euphoric since their objective ought to be fund raising. It occurred to me that if one private sector company was prepared to fund improvements of BR's tourist railway, maybe others would do so. On the spot, I initiated a project to secure outside funds for re-painting VoRR coaches in GWR colours (which looked more attractive), to repaint another locomotive, and to have 'First Class' and an Observation car. During the ceremony, I asked a guest - from the Development Board for Rural Wales if they would assist - within days they phoned to pay for my proposed observation car. Knowing that the Wales Tourist Board had helped to fund a Festiniog Railway extension and the Blaneau Festiniog new station, I contacted Harold Naylor, Chief Executive of that Board to ask for similar help on the VoRR, which I pointed out was a tourist attraction. He agreed to match £1 for £1 anything subscribed by the Private Sector. I contacted Westinghouse Brake & Signal Co., Shell Oil, and Permaglaze Paints - all of whom funded parts of the plan, whilst from the Tourist Board I obtained £11,000 to match these funds. Dyfed County and Ceredigion District Councils gave financial and other support - the latter funding our conference to publicise the project. Within a year, the work was done and I wrote an article on it for "Railway World" in September 1983.

Having initiated this, whilst tackling major issues, covering operational improvements, revenue generation, station facelifts and industrial relations in my large Division, I was annoyed, after my retirement, to have my attention drawn to an inaccurate sentence in a book on the VoRR which claimed that this work had been done after much "prompting by the Supporters Association". I received no letters and had no meetings with them at which "much prompting" could take place. Moreover, having set the plan in action within four weeks of my appointment, there was no time for "much prompting". I wrote to the Cambrian News refuting this petty claim, pointing out that if the Supporters had been half as innovative as was now claimed, they would have contacted the Wales Tourist Board to match the donations of Davies & Metcalfe and themselves for painting one locomotive, but they lacked that vision - an opportunity missed. Months later, not having current access to the Cambrian News as I had had in my working life, I learned that they had published a reply from a member of the Supporters Association - not refuting my letter - but again claiming credit for the Radio Signalling!

Recently, my attention was drawn to a book which criticised BR for "neglect of the Cambrian line". Even an industry which has not been placed in the financial situation by external influences as BR have, will invest its capital where it can secure the best return. The Cambrian with its negative cash flow is at the very bottom of that league. Those who talk of neglect clearly know absolutely nothing of the framework in which BR and other business must invest. Had BR been in private ownership from 1948, the Cambrian would have closed long ago, and without a public hearing. That author praised the Supporters Association for sponsorship of the VoRR. The complete refurbishment of the VoRR arose because I went out and secured £30,000 from external sources in a few weeks which puts the Supporters' modest contribution in the shade, especially since I was also making many other improvements and pursuing other projects in my large Division.

At Meetings
As Divisional Manager at Stoke, I was asked to meet the Wrexham - Birkenhead Rail Users Association, on 21st September, 1982, convened by that Association, I didn't hesitate to point out, in a hotel miles from the nearest station, causing everyone to arrive by car. So much for Rail Users! In introducing me, the Chairman urged me to reduce fares and electrify the line. I began by replying to these unexpected comments. "When I started working on the LMSR in 1946, the price of a return ticket to London from Rotherham was about £2. As a Junior my salary was £2.50 per week. The same ticket now costs 13 times as much, whilst the wage has gone up 25 times. Taking a bar of chocolate from my pocket, I said that this had gone up 34

times - the newspaper I bought had gone up 42 times. Fare increases since the War will stand comparison with anything you care to name". They didn't name any. From experience in electricification, I said that the capital costs required traffic volumes far in excess of potential on or near this route, [costing £3 to operate for every £1 of revenue]. No unprofitable line was a candidate for electric traction. My talk proceeded as planned, explaining timetable changes. They had set up a project for a consultant to submit ideas to improve the line. He referred to potential "operating economies from electrification" (which were nil), "and social benefits" (a formula not used by Governments for BR investment. The MoT has carried out **one** rail Cost/Benefit Analysis, i.e. on **Retention** of the Cambrian Coast line - totally different to its application to roads, which is for **new** roads, not for determining whether existing roads shall be retained. The rail study had envisaged cost reductions, postulated by the MoT. It was not used to determine whether an **improved** railway would have had social benefits).

Railways into Roads

The most misinformed critics claim that railways could be converted into good roads. In 1955, the Institution of Civil Engineers debated Brigadier Lloyd's paper. Obvious weaknesses included converting Waterloo railway station into a bus station, with a bus departing every 4 seconds to move the evening peak. If one driver turned his ignition key twice, the peak would be a complete shambles. 12,000 commuters finding their way to the correct bus would be a sight to behold. One ticketless passenger lacking change to pay the driver would cause a lynching by impatient season ticket holders. One driver attending the calls of nature would create a riot. In addition to coaches, the number of which he calculated, there would be countless motorists demanding the right to use this and other new routes out of London - and they wouldn't wait until the peak ended. Negotiating flat junctions in and around London against conflicting flows would demand skills far in excess of prevailing standards, keeping garages and hospitals busy. Delays would be horrendous. The idea was preposterous. An examination of the DoT publication, "Requirements for Passenger Lines and Recommendations for Goods Lines" would have shown him that track widths were too narrow for good roads and many routes were below standard for historical reasons. Bus company conditions of service suggest they would have difficulty complying with his high standards, typically reserving "the right to alter, cancel or withdraw services without notice, and not liable for loss, as a result of delay to services. Running times are approximate and the company does not undertake that services will start or arrive at the time specified in the timetable". He envisaged "a reserved toll road on the converted railways, which would have no dangerous bends, having single carriageways which were safer than dual carriageways because drivers would have to remain alert. Use would be restricted to vehicles which passed regular road worthiness tests and drivers who passed stringent driving tests". He said that "traffic would travel at 60mph, at 100 yard intervals, users achieving that voluntarily over the entire system, round the clock and over the four seasons". (They would all have to accelerate to 60mph and brake to a standstill at precisely the same rate). "Prompt sanding and snow clearance would be arranged and radar fitted to vehicles to operate safely in fog. There would be new traffic rules: keep strictly in lane, except at clearly marked places of transfer to adjacent lanes; no overtaking at all on two lane stretches of roadway; no dawdling; special driving licences would be forfeited for breaking the rules. Buses would have one or two trailers, which could be discarded in the non rush hours (probably at the wrong end) and could also be used as 'slip coaches'"; (picture 60mph buses slipping trailers without stopping on a single carriageway). He said that there would be no problem with the rush hour for "at Waterloo station the gross daily passengers are no more than 200,000 - requiring 60 seater bus-trailer combinations from each of the 21 platforms at the rate of one every 1½ minutes". He claimed that the rush hour flow of 840 vehicles (one every 4.2 seconds), would not amount to full capacity of one single lane and mentioned the multiplicity of lanes at Clapham Jcn (overlooking that they are on one level). His proposal was totally demolished by road experts.

Dr.Glanville, Director of Road Research, DSIR (later renamed Transport Research Laboratory): "Could not see how buses could run, fully loaded for 8 hours a day, 6 days a week, and if this did not happen, the financial basis for conversion was affected most seriously. The MoT had stated that traffic lanes on motorways would be 12 foot wide, further affecting the proposals which were based on 10 foot lanes". Dr.Glanville did not accept that "higher standards of professional driving would be sufficient to overcome the dangers of high speed traffic on the same carriageway".

Major Aldington, Technical Adviser, British Road Federation: "knew no one who believed that a single 22ft or 24ft carriageway was adequate for heavy volumes of traffic and said that it was quite preposterous". He "viewed with alarm the prospect of travelling at 60 mph on single carriageways against opposing traffic, particularly at night with glaring headlights. Driving from London to Birmingham, [in 1955], at night was quite terrifying". He said that "it was impossible to get a 20ft carriageway through an ordinary double line rail tunnel".

Mr.Burnell, LTE Buses: "it was totally impracticable to ask staff to drive on a road 22-24ft wide at such speeds. They would quite rightly refuse". He postulated a driver handing over to a relief driver saying: "Engine pulling well, there is ice and snow and fog, but the radar is alright."

Mr.Osborne, Resident Engineer, Wilson & Mason: said that "highway width must be 88-93ft with dual 22ft carriageways and 15ft verges; Double track rail formation is 39ft reduced to 19-22 ft in tunnels and deep cuttings with retaining walls; quadruple track was only 55ft wide (and these had the heaviest flows). Railway gradients are a serious problem; less than 1 in 200 (which is commonplace) is inadequate for water drainage on roads, hence a completely new drainage system would be necessary". He contradicted Brigadier Lloyd who had said there were "no dangerous bends", pointing out that "BR had curves of 660-1320ft radius [often on viaducts, bridges or through tunnels and stations], against a motorway standard of 2865ft and said conversion had no potential and was economically impossible".

Other objections included: Most railway junctions are on the flat and would have to be replaced with flyovers or clover leaf junctions to allow traffic to keep moving; the enormous number of bridges and tunnels (over 63,000 and 1050 respectively) would represent major engineering obstacles; 30,000 under bridges would require new floors because rails were laid on longtitudinal girders which could not carry a roadway; and as much of the railway was built on embankments or in cuttings, enormous road works would be required.

In 1984, the British Road Federation held a series of meetings around the UK to pursue a campaign for improved roads. In Manchester, BR were invited to send a representative and I was asked to represent BR. I was not impressed.
* the presentation included a list of road schemes around Manchester, some of which others at the meeting said had been withdrawn.
* the speaker referred to the "surplus £7000m of road tax revenue".
* he suggested converting under utilised or unused railways into roads. I said that only 60 out of 7000 miles of track closed in the past 20 years had been converted into roads and before they set their sights on lines which **they thought** were under utilised, they should get cracking on the 6940 miles of closed routes begging to be used.
* on the technicalities of conversion others present had no facts. I had!

I said that independent surveys of conversion showed that only one of ten recently closed lines had any prospect of conversion. Even that line had less width than the minimum 7.3 metres the DoT required for carriageways; being 6.9 down to 5.9 metres in places. Typical routes had formation widths of 5.3 - 5.9 metres which would rule out HGV's and double deck buses.
* I took considerable pleasure in pointing out that the cover of their glossy brochure showed a High Speed Train on a single line passing under a hump backed single arch bridge of low clearance, remarking that this showed up the problem of conversion very clearly.
* The Manchester University representative challenged the '£7000m road tax surplus', "which disregarded the debit to the NHS". Others said this was "academic nonsense". It isn't "academic nonsense" when forecast reductions in accident costs are used to justify road improvements. Road users get a refund - from savings they make by using new roads - the "social benefit".
* The Chairman of the meeting said that my revelations on the 6940 miles of closed railway and the narrow widths "would doubtless open many eyes".

In "The Conversion of Railways into Roads in the UK", the Railway Conversion League, said a 39 mile section of single track railway had been used as the route for a dual carriageway motorway with hard shoulders. Even those with the most basic and rudimentary railway knowledge will realise that a single track railway is inadequate for an ordinary road, much less a motorway.

The Railway Conversion Campaign advertised in July 1989, that 'The railway system is only working at 3% of its potential', and regurgitated Brigadier Lloyd's discredited theory. I wrote to the Daily Telegraph that road utilisation was worse than BR's, there being 22 times as much road mileage, and about 80-100 times as much acreage, for nine times as much traffic. If the League is concerned about 'our precious green land' (their phrase), then close 60% of roads to bring road utilisation up to BR's level. Lines most underutilised are in rural areas, which BR tried to close, but Government kept open. One couldn't get a fraction of the volume through the network by road on London commuter lines. I repeated the data set out above regarding the unused 6940 miles of closed railway and the inadequacy of rail track widths for single carriageway roads, which with limited rail bridge heights would be usable only by cars. Converted railways would not provide space for existing road traffic due to the poor utilisation which road traffic achieves. In addition to converting 11,000 miles of railway, it would be necessary to build 16,000 miles of new roads to cope with traffic displaced from railways! Roads are built on the basis of social benefit, an **ingenuous** formula based on the time road users **may** save by using new roads. BR in contrast, has to justify investment in money terms. Anyone believing that rail utilisation is only 3%, need only sit on a main line for 58 minutes in an hour to be proved fatally wrong! The League said that a Department with such poor utilisation ought to be sacked. I would have sacked anyone who produced misaimed statistics such as theirs. Despite the appalling under utilisation of roads, users create most horrendous problems for themselves.

In July 1993, a Sunday Times item of eight lines reported a 100 mile queue on the M5, but did not assess the total hours of delay. Expressed in car loads, it affected 212,000 people! Improved signposting, timely removal of roadworks signs, lights and cones, and no speed related accidents are a cheaper option than new roads. In view of the poor utilisation of roads, a better option, is to convert some roads into railways! Observations on the M6 revealed 620 juggernauts per hour in one direction - less than two trains per hour, which would not tax one converted lane of the M6. Huge financial benefits would accrue. Cars would have higher average speeds, producing "social benefits", HGV fuel consumption and manpower would fall and fewer HGV's would be imported, leading to an improved balance of payments. Road repairs would cost less and fewer accidents would reduce NHS costs.

I have a theory on attitudes to prices by companies or individuals - the Theory of Tunnel Vision, each saying purchases are expensive, everything they sell is cheap. Many claim that fares reductions would solve BR's problems. A 25% reduction needs 33% more volume to produce the same gross revenue. That requires more coaches, trains, fuel and staff where trains are loaded to more than 75% capacity. This demands still more volume to cover these costs, and maintain losses at the initial level. Yet a further increase in volume is necessary to reduce losses, which theorists expect to follow fare reductions. Logical minds will perceive that volume increases of 40-50% are essential on a 25% fare reduction. The logical business mind must address the down side scenario - who picks up the tab if the experiment fails? I do not share this simplistic pricing theory but would be happy to see reduced prices of every commodity I buy. For some items, I would buy the same quantity, but pay less, for some I would spend less but consume more, but for no single commodity would I spend more. What I saved would be spent on items which hitherto, I was unable to afford and that I believe applies generally, and especially to those who advocate lower rail fares.

When I was Area Manager at Leicester, I was in conversation with a passenger who suggested that we should reduce first class fares so that his wife could accompany him to London when he travelled on business. I pointed out that we would need more people to produce the same revenue and first class already being in high demand from Leicester, what would happen when with his business paid ticket he couldn't find a seat ? I explained it was money which paid the bills not bums on seats. I asked the nature of his business, and he said he was a Director of a Mail Order company. I enquired what was important with them - net profits or units sold? He acknowledged my point.

Hearsay
En route from Chester to Crewe in January 1979, in a cold First Class coach, I asked how long the heat had been off, a lady replied "from Holyhead". Ascertaining that she had not been told of an unresolved heating defect, in accordance with BR policy and that the train could not be further delayed, giving details of the next train, some 15 minutes later, I made a note to take action. She was charming and understanding of human failings. The other passenger, similarly courteous, said: "Fares are too high", but didn't know the cost of his ticket, when I asked! "Someone gets my tickets for me", he lamely explained. "Hearsay" is not a sound basis for criticism, but typical among many who couldn't recall the year of their last rail journey. An examination of his ticket revealed that he was travelling - first class - at under 4p per mile, about a sixth the cost of motoring at that time. Giving this comparison, I pointed out by train, he could work, eat, sleep and stretch his legs. In response to my question as to the nature of his business, as a prelude to my usual remarks on pricing analogy, revealed that he was a barrister (they say "Objection, my Lord," if witnesses give evidence based on Hearsay). I said that legal costs were outrageously high, quoting my experience of fees for preparing standard documentation for house transactions. He stoutly defended the legal profession and changed the subject, saying that there should be less freight on the roads. I delivered my 'pocket lecture' - on Government regulation of railway rates from the birth of railways until 1962, leading directly to unfettered road haulage creaming off railway freight. That was not an apology for BR. Any company compelled by Government to overprice some products and underprice others, whilst competitors had total freedom would soon go out of business. Other than complain to an unlistening Government, they would be helpless.

Road to Ruin
I refer on Page 106 to an amateur's ruinous advice. "Rail Fan's" letter to

the "Crewe Chronicle" in February 1984, referred to recent excursions run at fares of £5 to London - about 60% below our cheap Savers. This promotion was aimed at persuading those who may not have travelled for some time to travel by rail and was conducted selectively at times when spare rolling stock is freely available or after a dispute. He wrote that the solution to our problems was easy and didn't need a University degree to see that reduced fares would fill some trains. I finished full time education at 15 but had had 35 years professional experience. It was possible that ultra low fares may fill trains, but what I knew which obviously he didn't was that it wouldn't pay the bills, (see Page 66). I suggested that whilst he may benefit personally from such dramatic reductions could we have **equivalent** reductions to benefit everyone else - a new car for £800, petrol at 36p per gallon, and commensurate price reductions in holidays, food, clothing and newspapers - they were less than ½p **after** the War. All could produce increased sales. He couldn't resist another letter, but still concealed his identity and employers, which I challenged him to reveal so that I could urge his bankruptcy inducing theories on them. There was no response, not even from the businesses I mentioned. A perspective of rail fares can be gleaned from a comparison with newspaper prices. Rail fares are now 14 times 1948 levels, newspapers are up to 80 times 1948 levels. See also my unpublished letters to the media on pricing (Page 110).

Private Sector Pricing
In June 1986, "Which" magazine published a report on BR fares, showing how users pay different fares. The principle applies almost universally. We do not all pay the same for every product - motoring and air travel are two examples, but some secure reduced prices of almost anything. Many are offered products for less than others have paid. A friend wishing to fly to Amsterdam found that prices for the same journey and same period varied by 100% - "the cheap tickets had all been sold". The objective of pricing - by any company - is to maximise profit or minimise losses - equality is ignored. Among examples "WHICH" identified was a baby in arms travelling free, children at reduced fares and a dog at a special rate. Imagine the reaction if BR charged every user, including these, the same standard fare.

What BR can learn about pricing from the Private Sector :
* Do not advertise price increases, publicise only bargain offers.
* Charge more for items in short supply or during peaks - hotels charge more in the peak. They also increased prices for the one day rail strike on 28th June 1989 due to "a shortage of accommodation", not because of increased costs. In 1980, when Friday evening trains from Euston to the North were subject to a demand in excess of supply, I urged sales colleagues to charge a higher fare or restrict cheap tickets - a practice later adopted.
* Increase carpark fees to match those at Airports and private sector parks.
* Use psychological pricing - £19.99 - because the "public believes it's getting a bargain". Buyers are not expected to notice these are 1p short of the next pound. When we paid one old penny below a pound, one could buy a newspaper with the change. Now it needs 1p (equivalent to 2.4 old pence), from up to 60 "bargains" to buy a paper.
* Use a non existent coin - the decipenny as used for petrol, needing eight tanks full before one can use the savings to buy a newspaper. Fractions are rounded up.
* Quote the base price, and then mention "add-ons"; e.g., for a car, a charge for delivery (from the factory) and number plates. Many firms casually mention VAT as if it were an optional extra.
* Offer "Free Fitting or Free Delivery" - These cannot be free unless staff work without pay, but are fully covered in the price. BR could offer "free food and drinks", included in the price - after increasing fares.
* Charge for some telephone Enquiries, like BT and Gatwick Airport.
* Impose surcharges upon all tickets purchased in advance, including season

tickets, when unforeseen increases in costs occur.
* Advise passengers to insure against delay, as some air companies do.
* Offer gift vouchers. Closing dates often pass before I have collected enough for a gift. Products can be seen with labels offering free gifts when the closing date has already passed. I am in dispute with an oil company which abruptly ended an offer, without advising me, so that I was unable to secure a gift. They expressed regret for my disappointment, and suggested I take advantage of their next offer!
* Increase prices by, say 35%, for 28 days, then reduce them to, say, 25% above the original price - this qualifies as a BARGAIN SALE.
* charge £5 for local calls made on behalf of customers - as Banks do - and charge for copies of invoices or receipts as credit card companies do.
* Issue indecipherable receipts, and fail to clear the till computer for a previous transaction.
* Increase prices by thrice the rate of inflation to pull the business "back from the verge of bankruptcy" as one newspaper told me when I complained.
* Demonstrate 'seasonal goodwill' in December by increasing prices.
* Ignore the rate of inflation like the insurance company which increased my premium 100% above the 1991 level - 25 times the inflation rate - when I had neither increased my insurable assets nor made a claim. They did not improve their quality of service.

An impression of the attitude of the Private Sector to prices will be gleaned from notices exhibited in their premises. A not uncommon one reads: "There is hardly anything in the world that some one cannot make a little worse and sell a little cheaper. The people who consider price only, are that man's lawful prey".

Inflation Linked
During a training session on TV Studio techniques for BR managers, I was asked by Richard Linley [of BBC Panorama], in an unscripted mock interview, if BR would guarantee not to raise fares above the rate of inflation. I replied "when the Private Sector guarantees to do so". BR Public Relations staff should take this line. There is a phobia among the media and public - including those responsible for raising private sector prices - that BR alone should not increase prices above the rate of inflation, despite the evidence that some BR suppliers and other industry, raised prices above the rate of inflation (see Chapter 1 - Part II). It fits neatly with the common hysteria that BR alone should be without defects or delays, not run out of stock, and have no complaints. I guarantee BR will be the second industry to reach this epitome of perfection, since there will never be a first.

Where, from 1948, onwards were all those who now want BR to keep prices at the rate of inflation? Why did they not pursue this philosophy then, instead of campaigning to hold BR prices so far below the then inflation rate that they fell below pre war levels? Had they applied today's theories then, this generation would not be complaining about rail standards. I have calculated that, at today's prices, the effect of holding BR passenger fares below the rate of inflation represents a loss, at 1991 prices, of £7.8 billions, (see Page 34). Had prices followed private sector practice and exceeded the inflation rate, BR earnings would have been vastly greater. That is for passenger fares alone - losses due to interference in freight pricing and blocked closures of loss making lines were over and above that. I recall no front page protests that BR were not keeping to the rate of inflation from 1948 to 1982. To be fair to BR, the whole Private Sector should keep prices below the rate of inflation for a similar period - about 34 years, whilst BR price above the inflation rate. The current view that BR should not price up unless quality is improved should be applied to all industry and commerce. Most are increasing prices on goods whose quality has not changed. Government would then solve inflation at a stroke.

Official Reports

BTC and BRB Annual Reports & Accounts (see Chapter 1, Part II), demonstrate that fares and freight charges were held below the RPI, Wholesale Price Index and National Earnings levels from 1948 into the 1980's. Year after year the BTC revealed in their Annual Reports that fares and charges were below prewar levels and drew attention to ever rising costs. In the BTC 1961 Report, the newly appointed BR Chairman [Dr.Beeching, recruited from the private sector] stated "During the first 15 years of the inflation which began with the Second World War, passenger fares rose much less than would have been necessary to compensate for the fall in the value of money. Even with the rise in the past ten years the average level of fares on all the Commission's services remains at or below the pre war level, though it is widely accepted that the prices of services in a modern economy must be expected to rise faster than the prices of manufactured goods".

A sound way of demonstrating the scale of change in the cost of rail travel is to relate it to average earnings. BR did this in 1957, [BTC 1957 Annual Report, para 181 refers], (see Page 25). I have made recent comparisons. In 1988, after 40 years of nationalisation, average industrial earnings were £4.98 per hour [8.3p per minute], whilst the average BR fare per mile was 8.3p per mile, requiring 20 minutes of work for 20 miles of rail travel - the yardstick used in 1957. These compare with 28 minutes of work required in 1957, 45 minutes in 1949 and 52 minutes in 1938.

The Price Commission, 1978: Para 18: "It is clear to us from the wide ranging studies made by both the [British Rail] Board and outside bodies that there is no prospect that general reductions in fares as distinct from the Boards practice of making selective reductions might increase revenue"; Para 19: "They [BR] have successfully developed marketing techniques for this purpose" [referring to the filling of spare seats in off peak periods]. On price increases they stated: Para 15: - "Past experience of resistance to price increases is usually temporary"; Para 16: "Over the past decade fares have been market oriented. BRB estimate it produces 6-10% more revenue".

When comparing motoring costs with rail fares, many motorists think only of the cost of the petrol, which is but a fraction of the costs. A car left in a garage for 12 months, not having driven a mile, will fall in value. A car used for above average mileages, has a lower resale value. The CTCC Memorandum - Appendix 'H' in the 1969 NBPI Report compared costs by train and car :
* "BR Season fares per mile were: 1.8p, 1.45p, 1.25p, 1.08p respectively for 10, 20, 30 and 40 miles".
* "Motoring costs per mile; 'Full Costs': under 1000cc: 7.47p; 1-1½litre: 8.56p; 'Costs excluding depreciation': 3.12p or 3.79p respectively". (As age and mileage are major factors in car value which translate into running costs, the separate figure is irrelevant, but is often used to minimise the disparity. These costs would have been higher if Government had compelled manufacturers to bring cars up to BR's safety levels. Rail passengers have walked away from 100mph collisions - lower speed collisions on roads produce horrendous casualties and incur heavy expenditure by the emergency services - a cost picked up by all taxpayers, including non-motorists. Designed safety will increase motoring costs. All cars should have been made thief proof long ago, reducing deaths of the innocent and the guilty, and thus reducing State expenditure. Some motorists do not hold vehicle licences or pay insurance - a problem which Government ought to have resolved long ago. Anyone who does not pay vehicle tax does not require an MoT certificate. All motorists owe other road users, including pedestrians, a duty to keep a car in a roadworthy condition, but the evidence of cars seen on roads and in car parks shows that this is not happening. The requirement for a more comprehensive MoT test should commence when a vehicle's guarantee expires).

CTCC 1951 Report: "would not support a claim for cheap weekend fares for workers working away all the week, as the concession would cost revenue and be subject to abuse.

CTCC's Passenger Charges Scheme Report, 1952 , para 55: "in the national interest BR should pay its way and must increase charges to meet this objective; BTC has a duty under the Act and therefore must increase charges; Para 56: It is a fair scheme to the public. CTCC are opposed to staging increases for those facing the biggest increases to bring them [sub standard fares] into line" [with standard fares]. Government rejected their advice.

CTCC 1991 Report:
* The LT&S pilot scheme for a penalty fares scheme "has reduced the incidence of ticketless travel; there has been some public opposition", (One would expect those who, hitherto, travelled without paying to object, but those who always paid their fares would not object. Neither would taxpayers who were subsidising commuters' fares).
* "Fare rises should be broadly in line with inflation". (This is not a Private Sector policy. Increasing fares on services which receive taxpayers support reduces the cost to taxpayers, many of whom do not use rail. There is no Quango looking after the interests of the 90% of the travelling public who do not use BR but pay to subsidise the travel of those who do).
* "Fare increases should bear some relation to improvements". (Why? The 38% - seven times the rate of inflation - increase in car insurance demanded from me offered nothing more. My previous complaint against car insurance concerned an increase of 23%, over three times the inflation rate, and their quality was worse because they didn't reply to complaints).
* "Fares on routes where quality is poor should not be increased anything like as fast as inflation". (Reducing the fare the passenger pays in real terms - but increasing the sum paid by the taxpayer).
* "Disapprove of Inter City raising season fares much faster than the rate of inflation". (Seasons are priced below ordinary fares, so passengers will buy them. Must it wait for privatisation to be free to raise prices when it wishes to do so? The taxpayer should have the benefit now. Bus companies, which may be franchisees, have no restraint on their power to raise fares).
* "Object to BR telling passengers in their first letter" that if an unpaid fare is not paid within seven days it might be referred to a debt collection agency. They suggest it should not be mentioned in the first letter. (This implies that a debtor should have two or more letters written in order to recover a debt which ought not to have arisen in the first place. The majority who pay in advance - or the taxpayer - will then be picking up the tab for increased administration and postage costs. As debtors should have paid in advance, they have had free time already. What would be my position if I didn't pay my car insurance, but took advantage of the cover note. Would they write two or three letters to me before taking legal action? The invariable rule with motoring, coach or air travel, unless you have an account, is cash up front. Such debtors are enjoying interest free credit. Far from allowing extra time, BR should add an element to cover the interest paid to Banks for the overdraft. Privatised railways will waste no time in pursuing debts, for cash flow reasons).

Misguided Policies
Those who reduced the Exchequer's burden on roads expenditure - building turnpikes, navigable rivers, canals and railways at their own expense - were told how little to charge users. Those who used public roads, drastically increasing repair and maintenance costs were able to charge users as much as they wished and for many years did not pay the State a penny to use roads, enabling them to build reserves to fund expansion. Despite past promises of freedom, Government continues to interfere in BR pricing decisions, but then distances itself from the inevitable and predictable consequences.

Managers made errors and some were less competent than others, faults shared by the Private Sector, or there would be no balance of payments problem. Some experts claim that ineffective private sector managers pay a penalty by losing their jobs.   In fact, some leave with golden handshakes, others put their firms into bankruptcy, leaving shareholders with nothing.   BR managers' biggest errors were: not opposing Government interference in charges without control of suppliers' prices; not threatening to close large sections of track requiring renewal after heavy wartime use when essential materials were withheld; and not publicising the failings of suppliers.   By 1963, despite interference in prices and wages, and Government inertia on closures and availability of materials, BR managers had contained annual deficits before interest to a total of £174m (see BTC Annual Accounts).   In contrast, BR was compelled to forgo £643.6m in revenue (Passenger: £502.3m; Freight: £141.3m - see pages 34 and 25 respectively) by prices held below the inflation rate, plus millions more from delayed or rejected closures, and bus subsidies.   Deficits created by Government and Tribunal action were then horrendously escalated by interest on loans, and on BTC stock, so that BR was debitted with a total debt of £1,560m, by 1963.   BR managers were guilty   of   not   outguessing   Government,   Industry   and   other   experts   by forecasting industrial decline which decimated BR business :-
* that engineering, shipbuilding and machine tools would almost vanish,
* the replacement of coal gas by natural gas,
* the recession in steel and coal around 1958 and 1963
* replacement of coal in the generation of electricity,
* the virtual abandonment of the motor cycle, and some other industries.

BR managers failed to succeed where the private sector also failed - in ensuring a 100% turnout of staff (see page 114).   BR's failings are apparent at once in the form of cancelled or unpunctual trains, but private sector's failings which must affect vast numbers of consumers rarely become public knowledge.   Thousands of motor vehicle recalls and advertisements recalling defective goods rarely reveal how many are inconvenienced.   It is noticeable that media reports on other transport failings are often brief whilst BR's are magnified.   Sometimes managers responded to external influences.   In 1952, the Tribunal authorised the BTC to abandon Traders Season Tickets in a Scheme which the CTCC said was fair, and approved by Government which overrode parts of the Tribunal's Decision, (see Pages 67-71).   The BTC reintroduced the tickets, in response to a CTCC approach (CTCC 1954 Report); dropping them when they remained unremunerative.

Investment
The 1955 Modernisation Plan was dictated, not by a return on capital but by the state of obsolescence into which BR had drifted due to external control of charges, Government interference in wages and inequitable control of raw materials which prevented speedy replacement of war worn assets.   [White Paper - Cmnd 813, July 1959: ".... aims to put right the accumulated effects of the starvation of capital investment"].   The option - to let BR run down until it closed, was political suicide, which would explain why Government accepted the Plan, without a scheme by scheme justification.   A return on capital required charges to be freed to permit increases which a modernised system would warrant, but Government policy had forced real charges down! The case for electrification was not as strong as commonly believed.   In 1963-5, I was on the BRHQ Team remitted to check the LMR/Scottish Region scheme to extend electricification from Crewe to Scotland - then mainly steam hauled.   I obtained financial data which applied to the scheme, showed that economies from electric compared to diesel traction didn't justify proposed expenditure on fixed equipment.   Previously, electric traction had only been compared to steam.   The scheme could only be justified against

diesels by increased revenue, the prospect of which was subject to differing opinion, in view of external control of fares. Suburban electrification had increased revenue, but there was little main line evidence, and there would be none, if no main line electrification was progressed. The scheme was modified to increase the return. A comparison between electric and steam traction in the 1955 Plan was justifiable because UK industry did not have the capacity to produce diesels quickly enough. With electrification from 1960, benefits would arise earlier than waiting until sufficient reliable diesels were available. SAG papers (closed from 1961 to 1991), stated that the return on the Euston to Manchester & Liverpool electrification was less than could be obtained from diesels. This took insufficient account of delivery times, which would have put back modernisation by several critical years. Government accepted the whole Plan on the basis of creating the best possible railway (see Pages 15 & 38). Experience has shown that electric traction has many commercial benefits and does attract increased business.

Arising from my investigation into performance in 1979 (see page 120), I pointed out that improving reliability of train services needs investment on infrastructure, communications and rolling stock which is not transmitted into moving the goalposts. Manpower pared to a level adequate for 100% reliability faces problems when the unforeseen arises: vandals, adverse weather, public delays and when equipment is not 100% reliable. Many opinion formers do not understand the implications for privatisation.

For 100 years, Railways tried to obtain Government authority for a Chunnel, so as to create the distances essential for rail freight competitiveness. Had it been constructed, even 30 years ago, BR's freight business would have expanded. The concept was held back, in 1881 because the military couldn't protect a land frontier the width of a tunnel, in 1930 by Parliament, and since the war by the road lobby and short sighted Governments. Now it is imminent, the pay off will be to franchisees, who may have been objectors. Originally, cash would have come from private railways; after 1948, it should have come from money Government gained from wartime railways.

Performance Standards
Unlike the Private Sector, BR's management has been too willing to debate standards, and has acceded to pressure for statistics to "measure" quality;-
* "A passenger should not wait more than 3 minutes, off peak or 5 minutes, peak, to buy a ticket". These standards did not derive from the Private Sector, if Supermarkets, Building Societies and Banks are any guide, where over 5 minutes in a Bank or Building Society and 10 minutes in a Supermarket will be found. I have been unable to obtain their target queueing times. CTCC 1991 Report: "BR seems no closer to formulating a realistic means of measuring queueing times at ticket office windows. Complaints continue to be received from customers who have been forced to miss their chosen train or risk being penalised for travelling without a valid ticket". Perhaps BR will copy the Private Sector, when they introduce targets and methods of measurement. The public accept that when the wait in a Supermarket is too long, one cannot take the goods now and pay later or they will certainly be penalised! They will not be allowed to take the plane without paying. When the same people travel by BR, attitudes change - they demand rights with BR which they do not enjoy elsewhere.
* "Not more than 5% of those ringing Telephone Enquiry Bureaux (TEB's) should receive an engaged signal". From whence did BR copy this? If every company had standards remotely approaching these, I would be impressed. This data could not be obtained from new computers purchased by BR to monitor standards. No means of measurement was devised, until I decided to investigate TEB's and found it could only be obtained by asking BT to monitor our lines, which they would do, on an occasional basis.
* "Not more than 10% of calls to TEB's should ring out for over 30 seconds".

Instead of this concept, the Private Sector seem to prefer "entertaining" callers with unsolicited music, rarely to one's taste, and not worth the extra time or costs. Using a stop watch to monitor calls I suspect that three minutes not 30 seconds, is a target in parts of the Private Sector.

Having such statistics for internal use is invaluable, but with no private sector precedent, they should not be published. Carriage cleaning statistics supplied were wholly without value, even for internal use, (see Page 100).

Media and Management
The image, which is a consequence of Government policies, and fostered by rumour, folklore, industrial anecdote, and the media, was compounded by some within BR who accepted that our failings were not mirrored in the private sector. BR complaints had not been related to the total of customers (see Page 89). The Private Sector published no data, but personal experience shows that they dispense inferior products and poor service. I could not convert colleagues to this view, when reporting on my original research, nor persuade them that price should be excluded from complaints statistics, because the customer has the same option not to buy, as in the Private Sector and that fully loaded trains proved that prices were not high.

BR's public relations staff did not seem to be contesting BR's image. BR was no worse than industry and commerce at large. My unsuccessful attempts, since retirement, to persuade the media to publish contradictions suggests that PR staff may have had an uphill task. What is seen as criteria of success in other industries, when applied to BR is regarded by critics as evidence of failure. In any other industry, a demand in excess of supply equals success, whilst a supply in excess of demand equals bankruptcy. Perversely, with BR, overfull trains are regarded as failure. A hotel asked for a room in the peak at a weeks notice will produce a patronising response, which will be accepted. BR's apology for an inability to provide a seat in the peak with five seconds notice creates hysteria. Industry avoids excess stock because it costs money. Those who practice these principles cannot see the BR analogy, where excess stock is a permanent irretrievable loss, whilst in the private sector it is merely a delayed profit. Contrary to popular opinion, an infinite number of coaches or trains will not eliminate standing nor reduce losses. Passengers break into a cardiac inducing gallop to catch a departing train, rather than wait minutes for the next, and criticise BR because the train is not elasticated.

One area which BR managers have not clearly publicised is that the main reason for drivers slowing down is safety not incompetence because Drivers obey speed restrictions, which is incomprehensible to a typical motorist.

BR's media image on Flexible Rostering in 1982 was poor. An agreement on shorter hours specified that it would not increase costs - no formula was put forward by unions which would achieve this. It was said on TV that a Scottish depot already had flexible rostering because some drivers signed on for eight hour shifts at progressively earlier times through the week. This created a long weekend, but was of no value to BR, since it could lead to a driver being too late back from a days work to leave the minimum rest period before a next turn of duty, requiring a relief driver, and increasing driver complements. On "Any Questions" someone spoke of creating unsocial shifts by altering **signing on** times. The concept enabled BR to reduce unproductive time at the end of shifts by altering **signing off** times. The incidence of unsocial signing on times would remain largely unaltered. Only those with no railway experience could be surprised by the scale of traincrew signing on at unsocial hours which are an unavoidable factor of 24 hour operation.

A Sunday Times article in August 1993 said that privatisation would sweep away inefficient working practices and ingrained demarcation lines that BR executives never managed to break, but did not identify any. BR managers successfully pursued such issues more than the private sector seems to have done, or they could not have lost a world lead in so many fields. This book is not the place to catalogue the many changes made by BR, suffice it to mention the widespread use of management techniques, (some unused or unknown in parts of the private sector, others unadopted or abandoned in the private sector because they caused strikes), the series of job mergers in the 1960's under P & E, included tackling craft demarcation by merging mechanical and electrical fitters, and internal reorganisations. Modern equipment which displaced staff was not resisted with the violence which welcomed overdue changes in the media, or other industries. In 1982, BR introduced Flexible Rostering, ending the fixed 8 hour day forced on railways by Government. When I explained to private sector managers that one benefit was to cut overtime payments, they said that they would not risk doing so. Failing to eliminate or even reduce the incidence of craft demarcation was at the root of manufacturing decline. BR managers have been continually tackling measures to reduce costs - the private sector only wakes up during a recession, promising to emerge "leaner and fitter" - without explaining how they became fat and unfit since the previous recession.

It is unfortunate that BR's first generation of managers did not publicise that 19th century railways were the first industry to **need** the concept of depreciation, and that BR followed prewar practice. Rail lengths have unequal lives, even in the same mile, so they treated track as maintenance as it was continually "rejuvenated". Legislation did not alter that. The practice continued as audited Accounts show: "Expenditure on **replacements** is charged to revenue account"; "**new routes** are amortised over 40 years".

Commercial Freedom Lost Again
BR has been told not to increase fares to a level they consider essential to balance the books (standard Private Sector practice). This cannot be justified unless the MoT makes up the difference - as he would have to do if he held down, say, the price of continually rising car insurance, affecting far more. How he can do this in the light of history is incomprehensible:-
* In 1952, Winston Churchill envisaged BR's pricing freedom, (see page 49).
* The 1962 Act was intended to give BR commercial freedom, albeit, it didn't become even theoretically "effective" for another six years.
* In December 1983, a Minister told the House of Commons: "it is for BR to determine fares", (see page 96).
* A major part of the PSO is given to alleviate South East road congestion (see page 14), for which Network SouthEast this year receives £218m, which would not buy very much road nor provide one bridge over the Thames.
* In 1956, the Attorney General said (see page 74), that the MoT had powers to issue a Direction on fares if increased costs could be met by economies. If that is still valid in 1993, the MoT should say precisely where new economies will fall. He could make a selection from the following:-
* reduce track inspections - affects safety and reliability.
* take away all station staff - creates political fall-out.
* fewer drivers - run less trains - creates political fall-out.
* fewer conductor guards - reduces revenue and information.
* fewer signalling staff - affects safety and reliability.
* fewer clerical staff - delays answering inquiries, buying tickets, etc.
* take out managers - MoT to deal direct with Unions, staff and complaints.
* remove rolling stock maintenance staff - affects safety and reliability.
* cease to clean coaches - increases complaints staff.
He could cease to direct BR to improve safety, until other transport, which avoids expenditure by pleading the law of diminishing returns, has been compelled to catch up on BR's standards. Many of us made improvements to safety which were far more cost effective than changes enforced on BR.

BR staff and unions made errors of judgement, including opposing 'open' freightliner terminals, which lost business and cost them jobs. In this, they had much in common with staff in other UK industries.

Media and the Staff

The image which those, who did not travel by rail, gained of BR staff, was from the media, whose industrial relations record was uninspiring. The misconduct of a few BR staff are more likely to be publicised than the helpful conduct of the majority, especially to the disabled or elderly. There is no publicity for the majority who regularly get to work on time, at all hours and in all weather, signing on at unearthly hours to prepare trains. Commuters, whose sleep is disturbed by storms, may seek an excuse for not going to work. BR staff are already at work removing graffiti and chewing gum yesterday's passengers left behind, repairing upholstery or vehicles damaged by passengers and non travelling vandals, and bringing trains to stations for those who can so readily see the mote in your eyes, but find endless excuses for the beam which is in theirs.

In April 1993, a Sunday Times article criticised BR and the Unions :-
* **"Staff complain representatives give themselves the best shifts".** As elections are by secret ballot (since 1919), offenders are easily ousted.
* **"Union officials vet shift plans".** Staff representatives discuss rosters with managers, and may change them by producing less costly rosters !
* **"Union officials are given time off".** Union officials are not employed by BR and hence cannot be given time off. Staff representatives have time off for meetings with management. Some attend only one meeting per year. It was so unrewarding, at some depots, no one would take on the unpaid job.
* **"Drivers & signalmen get extra pay for walking time".** This applies to Relief Signalmen but not Signalmen - if working away from a home station. Private Sector staff working away, get tax free payments which make BR's taxable amounts look like a widow's mite. Walking time for a Driver occurs, for example, after arrival with a train at, say, Crewe and he is required to work a train from say Basford Hall. Obviously "walking time" is unavoidable. Without "Beam me up Scotty", even the Private Sector couldn't avoid that.
* **"Staff queued for up to an hour to collect pay".** In 40 years, which included paying out duties, I never encountered that. Many had pay taken to them because they couldn't be released from duties for five minutes.
* Finally, they likened BR practice to Peter Sellers' film, overlooking that the film involved a factory strike precipitated by a stop watch. In my experience, stop watches for Work Study on BR did not create disputes.

A letter to the Cambrian News in 1982, by a Civil Engineer's inspector said that BR was losing revenue because passengers were joining trains at Barmouth without calling at the ticket office. I replied that many passengers had return or Ranger tickets which do not require them to call at the ticket office. This form of media contact is counter productive. A prudent way to criticise managers was used in 1967, at a meeting to reduce traincrew complements, by a Driver who alleged that my economy scheme of weekend closure of BR's Deepcar sidings caused the Stocksbridge Steel Co to send 50,000 tons of stainless steel by road during a recent weekend. Having total authority for all freight working, I had invited their transport manager to phone me, at my office or home, if he required BR sidings open at a weekend. He had not done so. As it was a two day meeting, I investigated the facts and told them on the second day: "Their stainless steel production is 50,000 tons pa, the order was 1500 tons and because the stainless steel mill only holds two wagons - they asked us to move it on BR road vehicles to Sheffield Freight Terminal and tranship it onto rail wagons to go to

Liverpool for Canada. BR carried out the customers requirements and got the whole of the revenue". Had that rumour gone via the media, we may have been unable to contradict it.

Industrial Disputes

On those occasions when Staff were slow to accept change, it would hit the headlines, but there were countless cases of rationalisation, staff economy, and introduction of new techniques which proceeded unknown outside BR. Had industry been as effective, UK would not be a net importer. Staff accepted change if management demonstrated that proposals would work. Many of us implemented scores of schemes for significant economies through Joint Consultation, in which management set out in writing, proposed changes to working arrangements and manpower levels, facilitating a smooth introduction of change. Thereby BR secured substantial economies without disruption. It was equally unknown, outside BR, that from time immemorial, key railway staff — such as supervisors, signalmen and some technicians, had arrived early for duty, by 10-20 minutes, to ensure a safe and smooth handover from the person being relieved. Staff were not paid for this time.

Disputes, however infrequent, had more adverse effect on BR than any other **internal** aspect. The 1955 strike was costly, but its effects could have been reduced, even reversed, had BR been free of rigid statutory control of freight rates, and able to quote flexibly, rates and conditions to attract traffic back to rail. Customers did not accept that disputes were in their long term interests, being concerned about today, as staff must be — without today's business, there is no tomorrow. No doubt, Unions and staff became exasperated by Government treatment of BR, but industrial action was not the way to respond. Action to support other industries disputes by blacking traffic was not reciprocated. I heard of no case of traffic forced back on rail, after their own or a rail dispute ended, when it was in the power of those who load lorries to refuse to do so. There were reports of employees in industry who threatened to take such action, but who changed their minds.

Some disputes were welcomed by passengers, but harmful to the industry. In the 1970's, some Guards opposed a National Agreement signed by their union, which ended commission for collecting fares, the value being included in new pay scales. Some staff tried to reverse the agreement by not collecting fares. Machynlleth Guards threatened to do so. I decided that we might as well cancel all trains — the line was losing £5 for each £1 in fares — seeing no point in running trains for nothing. I asked the Area Manager to send an Assistant to the depot for start of work, to ask each Guard whether he was going to carry out all of his duties. The first man, said he would not collect fares, and told he could not sign on, said that the trains would not run, which the Assistant Manager confirmed. After a little thought, that man, and all others signed on to carry out full duties. In my view, it was a nonsense for people to receive full pay for performing part of their agreed duties. If they wished to sacrifice their own pay in support of an issue, that was one thing, but "work to rule" protests where part of the duties were performed for full pay were an entirely different matter. Managers could not break agreements by paying less than agreed pay rates. Circumstances have changed and commission payments have been reintroduced.

Unofficial disputes caused problems, but managers could minimise the effect. Warrington signalling centre staff demanded that their claim over grading and manning be dealt with immediately. Their own Sectional Council staff representatives would not take the case out of turn, in preference to cases in the pipeline which had progressed through agreed machinery. The staff banned overtime, including Sunday duty. I devised Special Instructions to implement on the first day, enabling trains to run safely through the area, under automatic colour light signals when the centre was unmanned. This had never been tried - had it failed or a mishap occurred which could be laid at my door, my head would have been on the block. Had there been the slightest risk of a mishap, I would not have had those instructions issued. It did not fail. After a period of Special Working, staff resumed normal duties.

National overtime bans in 1968 and 1974 left key jobs uncovered, but staff co-operated when some of us decided on our own initiative to introduce special measures - exploiting Rules and Regulations, the basis of safe train working, not red tape as outsiders think. These were totally safe measures, despite several consecutive signalboxes, not equipped with "switching-out" facilities being unmanned for the first time since 1926. HQ said that "signalmen's rosters must not be changed", but I rerostered **relief** signalmen to some very peculiar starting times (such as one minute after midnight), to keep open as many routes as possible. They carried on. Staff would respond to reasoned argument, as I found when an express passenger train was held up at Brightside Jcn., near Sheffield, which was, for a short time, without a signalman. The Station Master went to operate the box, as he was qualified to do, (and would do in any other emergency), but the box ahead refused to accept the train. I telephoned that signalman and pointed out that when their "dispute was over, we would all want these passengers back". Listeners in the Control Room thought it was a forlorn hope, because I had a reputation for making staff economies, but the train proceeded. These examples show that BR staff do co-operate, where in analogous situations, private sector staff do not. Those who think they will get more from BR staff in a Privatised company will need to show they know something about running railways, and have a sound knowledge of operations and safety.

In August 1939, ASLEF called a strike over a pay claim, but following an appeal by the Minister of Labour that "we may need you to get the children away" [from cities which may be bombed if war broke out], they responded by calling off their strike. This was in direct contrast to staff in some essential industries who went on strike during the war! Such examples of public service by railway staff were forgotten by the media after the war.

Delays
Some staff delay trains for passengers rushing up as a train is about to depart. They may be thanked by those who overslept or allowed too little time to get to the station, but those passengers will chorus "Hear, hear" when criticising delays, despite their own contribution. Managers and Staff even say that punctual trains are late! When changing trains at one station I witnessed an unhappy scene involving some young people who travelled daily, and had been told to keep together. I asked a member of staff what was amiss and he said that one had arrived late so all had to miss the train. The late arrival was being harangued by the others and all were distressed, doubtless without cause, at their possible treatment for being late for work. I told him to phone their employers and say their train was an hour late, and tell the passengers of our white lie. This created yet another anecdote of delays, but was a small price to pay to end such misery.

Which Perfect Industry?
Examples set out in this book show that public opinion can be changed by speaking up for BR. When a farmer criticised BR's "subsidy", I pointed out it was less than that to agriculture, and we hadn't asked for ours, which was to benefit the customer not the producer. He changed the subject quicker than one could say "Common Agricultural Policy". Staff must take care, if defending BR and personal pride because the self righteous and self opinionated will find a ready ear from those outside BR who can make life difficult. Off duty, staff can speak freely, and should stand up for their industry, answering any critic with my favourite question - "Which perfect bloody industry do you work for?" and laugh at the answer - if there is one!

Since BR's problems stem from those "Blueprints" which were Government Acts and acts, beginning long before the War - there is but one logical solution. Firstly, MoT should cease to interfere in BR's business decisions, and have powers only to hire and fire the Board and define its objective. Secondly, Government should fund rail infrastructure as it does that of road, charging BR for its' use on a similar basis (see page 53), which is probably how franchisees will pay for use of Railtrack. Thirdly, assets required to avoid road congestion should be overtly funded. Fourthly, competitive forms of transport, notably road, should be subject to legislation compelling them to improve safety, whatever the cost, until it approaches BR standards.

Government's Solution
MoT powers to interfere in business decisions must end with Privatisation, otherwise no company will bid. To prove that Privatisation can succeed where BR could not, requires them to be subjected to the same interference, and to have the same social burdens as BR have had. Comparisons between the performance of private sector and existing BR operators will be invalid, if the former pays for track use, since BR is debitted with full infrastructure costs. The Private Sector should be required to buy the infrastructure and assets it needs. No franchisee should receive subsidies if they pay only for track use (see page 53). With privatisation, passengers may expect:-
* To avoid standing there will be compulsory "free" reservation - the cost covered by higher fares. Seats may be guaranteed - not necessarily on the service for which a booking was made - as applies with some airline bookings. Those missing a train will need another ticket to replace the invalid original. Anyone without reservations or unable to find a seat will travel by other means or go on the next train - options currently available.
* Punctuality will improve - by breaking connections with trains operated by other companies and pruning services. Passengers will be unable to delay trains - automatic doors will lock a minute or so before departure. It will not be possible to abuse station staff - there will not be any, but passengers may swear at the machinery to their heart's content.
* Trains cancelled and delayed will not be "due to incompetence", but "circumstances beyond our control" - private sector's exclusive excuse.
* Responsibility for delays due to leaves on the line will be attributed to lineside residents and local authorities who developed green phobia 15-20 years ago and planted little acorns, forgetting the old adage.
* Snow will cause delay when it is found that costly snow machines are not justified for 5 days in 365, even if companies could agree on priority of use. If a Track Authority provides machines, users will have to foot the bill, unless Government funds them for the first time as a national asset.
* Profits will come from higher fares, fewer trains, off charging of joint facilities to other companies and withdrawing from less lucrative (not necessarily loss making) routes. Companies will demand compensation for losses incurred pending authority to close - or be subsidised at prices specified by the railway company concerned - not, as now, by the Government.
* Refunds will be replaced by "sincere apologies". Debtors will be pursued promptly, notwithstanding Watchdog opinions. Travelling without tickets, for whatever reason, will be deterred by private sector notices similar to "shoplifting is theft" or "we always prosecute and humiliate shoplifters".
* Cyclists who criticise BR for not providing free or ultra cheap facilities for cycles on trains will be disappointed when franchisees realise that even modest provision will displace 20 seats per train and eat into profits.
* New owners will not accept price restraint, notably of peak fares, which prevents them earning an honest profit. The MoT has said that the Franchise Director will prevent unreasonable fare increases. If he prevents increases which franchisees believe are reasonable and essential, Privatisation will collapse. Fares must give a return on assets and provide profits.

Directors of Privatised Railways will demand many legislative changes :-
* Track costs to be funded on the same basis as road, (see page 53), and linesides fenced at the expense of adjoining owners, as applies on roads.
* State to fund replacement of level crossings by bridges, diversion of footpaths which cross lines, and the preservation of historic buildings.
* As safety standards are well above other transport modes, particularly road, the Exchequer must meet external calls for more expenditure, as being in the National Interest, or dividends will vanish - £10m was the cost for one station. In any event, railways must not be subject to shorter notice to effect safety changes than seems to apply to other forms of transport.
* An unambiguous guarantee that Government will not sequestrate railways for next to nothing as they did in two World Wars, nor require them to use loco, carriage and wagon works to build tanks, landing craft or planes so that rail assets cannot be replaced. If war looms, subsidies to be given for new rolling stock on the same basis as road transport had before World War I.
* Total freedom in planning improvements on stations and no restraint on Private Siding development to prevent Councils blocking or delaying lucrative development of BR sites as they have done in the past.
* Investment to shorten commuter journey times and improve punctuality should be funded, as applies to road investment, with a "return" accruing to the State from "social benefit gains".
* Performance targets and Citizens' Charters to apply, overtly, throughout industry and commerce, with no external dissemination of financial data.
* The role of the CTCC and TUCC's to be replaced by self regulatory bodies as applies generally in the private sector. Failing this, their role to be extended to cover all transport - air, sea, road, travel agents, etc.

Shareholders should be warned that when railways were privately owned, Governments were not noted for sympathy to railway problems or profits. They should be under no illusion, as some are, that all that is needed for profitability is to "break the power of the unions" which ended a long time ago. If the private sector had been able to achieve as much change with their unions as BR did, there would still be engineering and shipbuilding industries, a bigger car industry and no balance of payments problem. Nor will punctuality improve, except at the expense of safety, by urging drivers to drive faster as some believe. Legislative and other measures which are essential for privatisation to succeed are exactly those which would enable a State owned system to succeed. State owned BR should be given the benefit of changes, which Privatised owners will successfully demand. If BR fail, having been given an even break, and an end to perpetual interference, for the first time - that is the time to consider Privatisation. Profits which would accrue to Shareholders, would go to the State, if BR were given the same conditions and freedom as the Private Sector will be granted.

Theorists who believe that competitors can efficiently run trains on the same tracks have not considered the prospect of a train not being ready to depart on time. If they doubt that will happen, they must believe that we are about to see the first 100% reliable piece of equipment in transport or industry. No company will allow a schedule to be held up for a competitor's late departure, hence delays will be prolonged. A worsenment in service will arise from each company having its own Enquiry Bureaux, as none will break new ground by advertising competitors, and all will be reluctant to give schedules of "connecting" services operated by other companies, lest they are delayed, in strictly private sector parlance, by "circumstances beyond their control". Disputes over 'paths', use of platforms, accident recovery costs, apportionment of through fares, compensation, shared costs and facilities will ensure a rewarding future for railway accountants and lawyers. If the same tracks are not shared, then there will be no competition. Companies supplying a product to a different clientele in a different area cannot possibly be deemed to be in competition, no matter how much window dressing takes place. If a passenger wishes to travel from A to B, it will benefit him, not a jot, that another company offers a lower fare from C to D which are equidistant.

With privatised freight and passenger using the same track, an independent Track Authority will have problems in deciding on conflicting demands and may find their company sued for causing delay to one company in preference to another. Twenty-five passenger franchisees and freight companies bidding for track space will create problems. Several will bid for "paths" as BR refer to track space. Selling an immovable object to the highest bidder presents no problem, even if a Quality override is applied as with TV. Here the analogy ends. Complications arise from selling paths on a rail network:
* A path relates to a train of a particular speed, making calls at specified stations and may be broken into parts for comparable trains using sequential parts of the path. It ceases to be a path, if parts are used by trains at higher or lower speeds, or at the same speed but making different calls.
* Each bid will be for at least two paths – out and return, most will be for several pairs. Where competition applies on a route, some bids will be for the same outward path (or variations thereof), but with different balances.
* Bids for conflicting and overlapping paths magnify the balancing problem.
* Bidding will prolong the already long period for planning a timetable. The range, interaction and comparison of bids will be daunting.
* Selling plum paths to highest bidders, will leave a mess of uneconomic paths for BR's residual services creating higher costs and worse quality.

Unless franchisees do not have to cover all track costs, or receive larger subsidies, those who expect Privatisation to reduce fares will be in for a rude awakening. Chapter 1 – Part II shows how fares lagged behind the RPI. A comparison of earnings and fares on page 154 shows that fares are less costly now than in 1938, so those looking for fare reductions must be aiming at taking them back even further – perhaps before the First World War to 1913 levels. They may care to look at fares charged by private railways in this country. In 1992, ten privately owned standard gauge railways charged adults an average of 31p per mile – compared to BR's average fare of 10.5p per mile, (BR 1991/92 Acounts). Whilst the latter includes reduced fares, privately owned railways have staff who work for nothing – one advertises that 50% of work is done by volunteers. They do not maintain track for 125 mph trains, 3000 ton train loads or junction occupation of one commuter train every 30 seconds. It is said that Private Sector operators will have more staff on trains. At the same time, they are expected to reduce fares by having fewer staff. They should identify which staff will be displaced, to reassure the public that safety will not be affected.

Privatisation plans suggest that fragmentation will be the basis and there are fears that Safety may be the victim. A media report stated that the MoT had referred to railway staff operating away from the "constraints of the national rule book". This book is the cornerstone of safety, and contains not one word which smacks of demarcation or the like. Napoleon's jibe: "a Nation of shopkeepers" is brought out in the Plan for new station shops. If tenants are found, most selling foreign goods, more shops will close in town centres. In view of external demands for rail safety to continue to rise well above levels of other transport serving the Public, it is imprudent to put safety in the hands of those without expertise.

Most of the private sector publishes neither complaints statistics nor performance targets. Many use buyers in a "Quality control" capacity replacing a defective item when a buyer makes a special journey, although as I found recently, they may refuse to do so if one does not drop everything and drive down immediately. It is to be hoped that future owners of railways will not be drawn from companies such as these.

To improve services, privatised railways require a new deal from Government and improved public behaviour - new trains and new staff will not be enough. Buyers of a Track Owning company require improved behaviour of those who use the lineside as a refuse dump. In time, railway companies will "rediscover the wheel", finding, as early pioneers did, that too many cooks spoil the broth. They will remedy this in the same way, by mergers and takeovers, and will not shrink from closures, none of which will be a political liability.

BR is to be responsible for safe operations of competitors. It is akin to taking flight slots from British Airways and making them responsible for the safe operations of the intruder. If BR says an operator is unsafe and shuts it down, the cries of "Foul" will be deafening. We will be hearing next that BR will have to replace, at short notice, a Private Sector train which breaks down, even if that inconveniences BR passengers. Privatisation is being promoted by a series of unquantified generalisations and pious hopes:-
* "There are too many staff", (without specifying where or on which tasks, whilst the Government creates highly paid Railtrack and Franchise jobs).
* "To end Restrictive Practices", (without naming one).
* "To improve reliability", (all industry and transport have breakdowns).
* "To reduce fares", (without promising redress when it doesn't happen).
* "To eliminate complaints", (no industry is free of complaints).
* "Government doesn't know where the money is going" (overlooking that the their own Act of 1974 ended the practice of paying support on the route by route basis under the 1968 Act). They claim to have invested "A lot of money" (but do not say how much was from BR revenue, how much from other BR sources, how little for loss making lines kept open by Government, how little for London commuter services for which Government holds down fares, or how little to avoid horrendous road building costs in and around London).
* "To reduce the 'subsidy'" - companies are expected to so increase profits that they will voluntarily cease to receive so called "subsidies". (In fact subsidies may increase if losses are focussed onto sub groups of services).
* "Past privatisation proves the case for privatising BR" - (invalid as they did not require premises to be shared by 25 companies).

Alternative Options
There is an alternative to privatising BR which has not been ventilated. Despite a Tory MoT saying, in 1956, (see page 22), that the BTC did not have, and never had had, a monopoly, an illusion has been created that BR is one, and can only be broken by joint use of BR tracks. This is absolute nonsense. Any company could build a railway to compete with BR. It would have none of the structural restraints inherent in routes built 150 years ago, which restrict gauge and speed. They could follow the French TGV example with straighter routes and no level crossings. Its high speed would attract traffic. It would have to pay for its own infrastructure instead of sharing with BR - but that has benefits. It has disbenefits too, because when their trains are delayed or lines blocked, they will be denied the excuse of blaming someone else. It will be very embarrassing for them when their 21st Century technology proved to be less than 100% reliable. They would be unable to keep prices artificially low as they would if charged only for track use on BR lines, so another assumption would bite the dust. Government could have sold the 6940 miles of closed track, which included some main lines, to the Private Sector - to end BR's theoretical "monopoly". If thinking was applied to the wider issue of transport, and of escalating costs of road transport provision by the State, instead of new or wider motorways and privatised BR there should be a thorough review to establish how little new railway is needed to make a substantial reduction in the volume of heavy freight on roads, beginning with dangerous goods - in view of recent adverse roadside safety checks. With business levels well below their peak, and in the light of the appalling under-utilisation of roads (see page 150), there can be no justification for more road space.